RELIGION
AND
SOCIAL TRANSFORMATION
IN
SOUTHERN AFRICA

RELIGION

AND

SOCIAL TRANSFORMATION

IN

SOUTHERN AFRICA

Editors
Thomas G. Walsh
Frank Kaufmann

PARAGON HOUSE
St. Paul, Minnesota

First Edition, 1999
Published in the United States by

Paragon House
2700 University Ave. W.
St. Paul, Minnesota 55114

Cover design: Larry Orman

Library of Congress Cataloging-in-Publication Data

Religion and social transformation in southern Africa / co-editors,
Thomas G. Walsh and Frank Kaufmann.
       p. 266 cm.
    ISBN 1-55778-776-X (cloth). -- ISBN 1-55778-777-8 (pbk. : alk.
paper).
    1. Africa, Southern--Religion Congresses.   2. Religion and
sociology--Africa, Southern Congresses. 3. Progress--Religious
aspects Congresses.   I. Walsh, Thomas G.   II. Kaufmann, Frank,
1952-
BL2463.R445   1999
291.1'7'0968--dc21   99-37666
                                                          CIP

Manufactured in the United States of America

Contents

Preface

The essays in this volume offer perspectives on the role of religion in southern Africa, a region of the world which has attracted great attention in recent years. The reason for this is related both to the plight of its people who suffered under the apartheid system and to their indomitable spirit which has given rise to dramatic social transformations and renewed hope for Africa. Here religion has been neither a passive social phenomenon nor a regressive social force. Rather, it has proven to be a vital and powerful force for positive change.

This volume was first envisioned at a conference of the Inter-Religious Federation for World Peace (IRFWP) on "Religion and Social Change in Southern Africa," convened at the University of Witwatersrand, Johannesburg, South Africa, on January 9-12, 1997. The conference was chaired by Professor Gerhardus Oosthuizen, University of Durban-Westville, and Dr. Albert Venter, Distinguished Professor of Political Science at Rand Afrikaans University. Through their able leadership the conference attracted a diverse group of distinguished participants who produced these excellent papers.

We wish to acknowledge the generous support of the Inter-Religious Federation for World Peace which made the conference possible. Gratitude is due to Paragon House Publishers for their encouragement and guidance in producing this publication. Also special thanks to Louise Perlowitz for doing the layout for the book. Articles which appeared earlier in draft form in *Dialogue & Alliance* are published here with permission.

We are honored to have an introduction by Professor Jacob Olupona, Director of the African American and the African Studies Division at the University of California, Davis, and a long-time advisor to the IRFWP.

It is our hope that religion can flourish as an agent for true and lasting social progress and human good. The experience of religion's role in southern Africa offers hope that this ideal for religion can become a reality.

The Editors

Introduction

Jacob Olupona

African American and African Studies Program
University of California at Davis, USA

Insightful and illuminating, this present work underscores the significant role religion has played in the new social and political dispensation in the region beginning in 1980, with Zimbabwe's independence from apartheid rule, and continuing through to the current post-apartheid reconstruction and rehabilitation in South Africa.

I am pleased to write this introduction because of my commitment to international scholarly discourse on religion in any part of the world, especially in Africa, and because of my several years of friendship and scholarly collaboration with, and indebtedness to the volume's editors, Frank Kaufmann and Thomas Walsh.

At a time when few outsiders cared to listen to African voices, even on purely African subject matters that related solely to Africans themselves, and when others spoke only about the marginalization of African scholarship in the world of learning (a cliche that aroused little or no practical response), the editors of this volume opened a vista that made it possible for African scholars from countries of considerable diversity to engage in timely, thoughtful and scholarly discourse on core African themes and concerns.

These essays make clear the genuine desire of southern African scholars to speak for themselves without inhibitions about the new social and political order. South African scholars, in the post-apartheid period, are ready to be active participants in scholarly debates and discussions that affect South Africa and Africa in general.

A second reason why this volume deserves our attention is that soon there will be several international conferences on religion taking place in South Africa. Among them are the XIX Congress of the International Association for the History of Religions, the Parliament of World Religions, and the international meeting of the Society for Biblical Literature. Thus, for scholars of religion and lay people visiting Southern Africa for the first time, this book will prove invaluable. From all over the world, all roads will lead to South Africa.

The theme, "Religion and Social Transformation," emerges from the realization that religion, especially Afrikaner civil religion, played a large role in the ideology of apartheid that once upheld the iron curtain of color prejudice, and which for centuries kept millions of Africans from dignity and a humane existence. On the other hand, religion, especially Black liberation theology, contributed greatly to liberating oppressed Black people. This gives hope that religion can play a positive role in the transformation of South Africa in the post-apartheid era.

South Africa, it is often said, is a rainbow nation, a multi-religious, multi-racial, multi-ethnic society unparalleled in any other part of the continent. Success in a new, reconciled nation will augur well for the rest of the continent, and indeed for the whole world. Witness, for example, Archbishop Desmond Tutu's continued admonition that, on the question of race relations, Americans have much to learn from the South African experience.

In 1993 I visited South Africa at the invitation of the newly inaugurated South African Academy of Religion. During this visit, I was impressed to see scholars of various persuasions and religious traditions—Jews, Muslims, Christians, Hindus and African Traditionalists—gathering together as a community of intellectuals so as to discuss the role of religion in post-apartheid South African civil society. At that very challenging moment, a common language to address the problems at hand had yet to appear.

As we end one millennium and begin a new one, scholars and other persons who appreciate the social significance of religion,

especially those visiting southern Africa for the first time, will benefit richly from this book. It contains unique and up-to-date information on the current status and role of religion in the region. As
a religious road map, this volume will help its readers understand
their experiences as they encounter the region for the first time.
This volume represents an interreligious, scholarly response to the
reality of the social transformation in southern Africa. The essays
are informative and provide detailed illustrations of the religious
and socio-political situation of the region.

The transitional period in South Africa is filled with uncertainty
and nostalgia. Transition entails not only political change, and the
passing of the leadership baton from a white to a Black leader, but
a more profound change: namely, transformation at physical, economic, cultural and spiritual levels. Several contributors, such as
Cornel Du Toit, Thillayvel Naidoo, Obed Ndeya Kealotswe and
Christina Landman, have examined the implications this current
transformation has for nation-building agendas and the search for
an authentic African identity. Precisely what constitutes an African
identity in South Africa is highly contested and contextual. Ultimately, there is considerable diversity in Africa. In the end, African
identity may be defined as multi-cultural and pluralistic.

Several of the essays in this volume present South Africa as a
nation riddled with real conflicts, sharply divided along ethnic,
class, racial and religious lines. In response, the authors offer
modest proposals for the achievement of a peaceful and enduring
democratic rule. These diagnoses of the rifts and the potential
areas of conflict will be most useful to those seeking to understand
South Africa's potentially volatile situation.

At the core of the debate about social transformation are
questions about the democratic process in South Africa. This, of
course, is related to the re-democratization agenda throughout
Africa following a time when its young independence in the 1960s
was hijacked by military dictatorships through a series of coups
d'etat. Often debate about the democratization of civil society
focuses on what form of western democracy should be adopted, but
the essays in this volume introduce concepts of self-rule arising
from Africa's own indigenous religions, traditional values and
political culture. This is an especially worthwhile aspect of this
particular collection.

Briefly now to the essays in this volume. Cornel Du Toit remarks that religion has the potential to foster unity. For Africa, where religion is a major source of social values and cultural expression, it has a greater potential to define identity. The marginalization of African religion, as we will also learn from other essays in this volume, is a cause for concern given the fact that African cosmology remains the strongest element in African identity construction. The situation calls for serious reflection. Transition from apartheid society to an independent state portends both good and bad for South African citizens, depending on where in the social strata individuals are located. For some, independence from oppression is feasible, but for others privileges may diminish. In assessing the overall effect of this transition, it is often the unforeseen consequences that are most problematic. Du Toit, along with several contributors, calls our attention to the rising crime rate, unemployment, and what he calls the influx of cultural immigrants from other African countries. I am surprised that he did not mention non-African immigrants.

In addition, Du Toit provides a phenomenological and practical analysis as to what transition implies in the South African situation today, and how other African countries stand to benefit. As is cited in several places, the South African post-apartheid government has great potential to move the continent toward cultural and economic prosperity. South Africa, says Du Toit, may contribute to "the generation of cultural and material wealth for the continent." He also warns against the danger of reducing transformation to technological advancement. Western society clearly shows that the latter does not guarantee peace.

Another central aspect of Du Toit's essay concerns the nature of African identity. He notes that transitions for South Africa have led to the search for what was once lost, especially for Black people. This is understandable given that those who were marginalized under apartheid society, and portrayed in the mass media as barbaric and unglamorous, are beginning to deconstruct such social images through a process of restoring tradition. At the same time, South Africa has not witnessed a full-blown Afro-centrism like the Blacks in the USA. There remains the daunting challenge in the new South Africa to find a national, unified identity.

In the second essay in this volume, Albert Jan Venter addresses the success so far of post-apartheid South African experimentation, which could be said to be the leadership provided by Nelson Mandela. Undoubtedly, Mandela possesses many African leadership traits. The image of a benevolent African ruler, whose kindness, spirit of forgiveness, humane compassion and understanding remind us of *ubuntu* ethos, represents a model of leadership developed in the truly traditional African democratic spirit.

Venter provides a comprehensive view of the deep-seated historical problems in South Africa as well as the prospects for a lasting peace. In spite of the rhetoric of South Africa's rainbow nation, Venter insists it is "a deeply divided society." Venter outlines some of the political and social problems that have exacerbated the situation since the end of apartheid government, especially the rising crime rate and ethnic xenophobia. He argues that ultimately economic justice will determine whether South Africa survives or not. Uncontrolled capitalism and free market economic policies are potential sources of racial conflict in the near future. Venter also examines the role of the church in fostering racial harmony, which to him seems blurred as some of the churches, especially the Afrikaner Church, are unrepentant about their unholy alliance with the apartheid regime. Afrikaner civil religion, as I mentioned earlier, contributed in no small measure to fostering racial inequality. This is certainly a problem.

L. D. Jafta's essay, "Religion and Democracy in South Africa," offers reflections on the relationship between religion and the formation of democratic institutions. Jafta argues that there are a variety of models of democracy and that the Western model need not be the one best suited for Africa. Rather, he suggests, an African democracy should emerge from the core values of the African context. Given that the traditional African worldview is religious, Jafta maintains that religion cannot be removed entirely from the political process.

Abdulkader Tayob, in "The Role of Islam in the South African Political Process: Defining a Community in a Nation," discusses the "positive role" that the Muslims have played in the transformation of South Africa. Tayob identifies a remarkable moment in the recognition of the Muslim community's pivotal role in the anti-apartheid struggle as occurring when Nelson Mandela made a visit in 1977 to the Shaykh Matura on Robben Island, honoring the Muslim community's opposition to oppression and colonialism. The essay defines the identity of the South African *ummah* and shows how through the print media, South African Muslims continue to influence their society and build a vital community of believers. Tayob points out that varying groups of Muslims in South Africa are developing political coalitions.

Pratap Kumar's essay, "The Role of Hinduism in Addressing Human Rights Issues in South Africa," examines precisely the place of Hinduism in the new nation. The challenge facing modern South Africa, according to Kumar, is how to utilize the resources of her religious minorities for the transformation of the nation. While Hinduism does not represent a majority religion in South Africa, its spiritual resources and values have made a significant contribution to the development of the new democracy. A central area of concern for Kumar is human rights. He argues that contemporary and classical Hindu thought professes a concern for human rights and for the positive transformation of human society. Generations of Hindu nationalists, intellectuals and human rights activists have anchored their struggle in these ideas. A perfect example is Mahatma Gandhi, whose fate, paradoxically, was tied up with the civil rights struggle of the indentured Indians in South Africa. Today, as Kumar claims, the Hindu struggle for justice and change centers on issues internal to their own community. It is the liberation from various forms of oppression that Hindu men place upon Hindu women which constitutes the most pressing matter. The struggles against domestic violence, and for property inheritance, from which Hindu women are excluded, deserve urgent national attention.

Human rights abuses are the focus of Christo Lombard's essay, "The Role of Religion in the Transforming of Namibian Society: The Churches and Human Rights." Lombard puts into perspective both the response of the churches to the struggles of Namibians against South African hegemony in the apartheid era, and the abuses of SWAPO, the Namibian Liberation Organization in exile. While the church has received praise for its strong stand against South African apartheid rule in the post-apartheid era, it has received reprimands rather than praise for its silence and lack of criticism of the state's abysmal human rights record. Lombard

borrows from the vocabulary of South Africa's Truth and Reconciliation Commission to confront the continued abuses committed
by SWAPO leadership against Namibian detainees in exile. This
essay brings to our attention a larger issue that is even more crucial
for South Africa in the post-apartheid era. It asks, how can the
church continue to be a witness to truth now that most African
nations have become independent?

H. Christina Steyn, in "The Role of Multi-Religious Education
in the Transformation of South African Society," engages the
subject from a different perspective. Steyn informs us that the role
of religious education in the new South Africa is beginning to
generate a heated debate. South Africa is caught between those
who favor placing religious education in the private domain and
those who favor giving religious education a public face. The secular mind-set that propels policy-makers in several African states
may be gaining an upper hand in the emerging nations of
southern Africa. The false tendency, especially borrowed from the
West, to equate religious education with indoctrination and more
recently with religious fundamentalism and anti-progress may be
propelling the anti-religion forces in public education. Hopefully,
South Africa will weigh its options and formulate a policy that
favors multi-faith education in the schools.

At a time when African scholars are asking for a rethinking of
the status of African traditional religion in contemporary life, an
up-and-coming South African scholar and a representative of
indigenous traditions explores the role of indigenous religions in
the new South Africa in a very illuminating way. In "From Racial
Oppression to Religious Oppression: African Religion in the New
South Africa," Nokuzola Mndende highlights some of the agonies
adherents of African indigenous religion in South Africa face as
they define their identity in a society already overtaken by various
forms of non-African Christian traditions and colonial heritage.
Colonialism encourages conversion from indigenous identity, and
the substitution of another tradition from outside without the opportunity to choose between the old and the new or to accept both.
Mndende tries to raise a vexing problem that few other scholars
dare consider, namely, the lack of official recognition for the
continent's indigenous traditions.

In my view, the more fundamental issues are the practical and ontological implications of the marginalization of these traditions for the continent. Ontological, in the sense that this marginalization strikes at the very core of the soul of the continent and pertains to the identity of the millions of people who have been the objects of conversion to Christianity and Islam in Africa. One practical response to the current identity crises is to explore the way in which African religious symbols, beliefs and socio-ethical tenets might influence the life of the people and the identity of the continent in our contemporary society. For example, I have always wondered why, in spite of the enormous conversion to Islam and Christianity, Africans scarcely take seriously the ethical ideals of these two traditions as compared to the ideals of their own indigenous tradition, which remains in their unconscious minds despite the fact that they have converted to the world religions.

Consider, for example, that African nations are often governed by corrupt leaders whose main purpose for governing is to line their pockets with kickbacks from the bribes collected from multinational corporations. These leaders would lie under an oath taken with the Bible or the Qur'an, symbols of two world religious traditions, but they hesitate to take a similar oath with the symbol of any of the deities in the African pantheon. This is because the judgment of the African gods is considered to be swift and precise, and salvation in African thought is here and now and primarily this-worldly. On the contrary, Islam and Christianity suspend judgment, with the punishment of the sinner reserved till the afterlife. What does this practical example tell us about African society today, about its way of religions and cultures? Nokuzola Mndende is one of several young scholars who believes that to restore the dignity of the African people, a return to indigenous traditions is imperative for South Africa. The continued advocacy of the National Committee on African Traditional Religion together with the government's commitment to the freedom of religion will be steps in the right direction, Mndende argues.

The role of African Independent Churches (AIC) in South Africa is what the essay by the doyen of AIC scholarship in southern Africa, Gerhardus Oosthuizen, takes up. The essay, entitled "The Future of the Church in South Africa Closely Related to Indigenous Christianity," provides a masterful clarification of this religious tradition. The historical relationship Oosthuizen establishes between indigenous traditions and the African Independent Churches, the two most creative religious movements on the continent, illuminates this subject in Christian history. The historical and social context for their emergence, especially in South Africa, is clearly stated. AICs in other parts of Africa arose in reaction to the white leadership of the mission churches, and in South Africa they were among the first anti-apartheid, nationalist movements in the region.

AICs allow oppressed Blacks to demand self-respect, and a change from an inferior status in lands where they form a majority. Paradoxically the indigenous churches were the first to break the color bar by throwing open the membership of their churches to people of all races. The AICs also produced some of the most creative minds of the twentieth century, such as Prophet Isaiah Shembe, the founder of the Nazarite Baptist Church. Shembe's teachings and innovations are comparable to the teachings of other African prophetic luminaries such as Prophet William Wade Harris of the Ivory Coast and Liberia, and Pastor Bileou Oshoffa of West Africa's Celestial Church of Christ. The success of the AICs, as Oosthuizen clearly demonstrates, lies in their pragmatism and the relevance of their theology to African daily living and their promotion of a theology that encompasses the whole of Africa's being. On this note, the essay ends with a summary of the positive impact of the AICs on African society, such as their holistic approach to life crises, the emphasis on human relationships rather than western individualism, faith healing, and the accent on reconciliation and harmonious living. The AICs have enjoyed phenomenal membership growth in southern Africa.

In "The Role of Religion in the Transformation of Southern African Societies: A South African Jewish Perspective," Jocelyn Louise Hellig clearly speaks against the isolationist tendency among the small Jewish community of South Africa. Against the background of very vital, though scary economic and demographic statistics, which Hellig provides, she underscores the Herculean task facing the new South Africa as it embarks on its reconstruction and rehabilitation. A stagnant economy, rising crime rate, increasing gaps between the rich Whites and the poor Blacks—even when in principle Black majority rule is in place—high unemployment rates, and increasing demands for education, housing and health care may rightly derail the new democratic freedom. President Nelson Mandela's direct invitation and mandate to the Jewish community was to use its skills, experience and knowledge to assist in uplifting "those who have been denied fair opportunities" during the apartheid era. The essay argues that the Jewish community must be fully engaged in rebuilding the new South Africa. But beyond the provision of material resources for the welfare of the people, it is in the transformation of South Africa's sense of identity and "the habits of the heart" that Judaism and other religions can play the most vital role.

Thillayvel Naidoo, in "A Hindu Perspective on the Transformation of Southern African Society," provides a general reflection on the way forward in the new South Africa. Although the essay claims to be mainly from a Hindu perspective, several of the issues raised would apply to other South African religious traditions as well. He presents a strong argument for a relationship between religious traditions and socio-ethical ideals.

"Issues in Shona Religion: A Metaphysical Statement and Dialogical Analysis," by Jameson Kurasha, provides an insightful overview on the place of the ancestor in Shona cosmology. The essay focuses on the Supreme Being and the deities, and the meaning of salvation and revelation in the Shona context. In this tradition, ancestor beliefs, the recognition and propitiation of the spirits of deceased clan members, provide the social network through which relationships and unity are built across generations, clans and marriages. The essay also provides fresh insights of historical and linguistic significance to correct some of the errors in the conceptualization of God found in previous scholarship on African religion. The contrast Kurasha outlines between Shona religion and Judeo-Christian religion provides helpful insights into a complex problem.

Hebron L. Ndlovu looks at traditional religion in "Swazi Royal Ceremonies and Religious Tolerance in the Kingdom of Swaziland," and illustrates the centrality of the ideology and rituals of Swazi royal kingship in unifying the people of Swaziland and in promoting values of Swazi nationhood. *Incwala* kingship ceremony, the focus of this essay, once celebrated as a harvest festival, now provides a rallying point for the Swazi nation to express its unity and cohesion in relationship to their divine king. *Incwala* also provides a forum for the king to display his royal symbol, communicate with his ancestors, and demonstrate the efficacy of his authority and sacred power among Swazi citizens. As a form of civil religion, *Incwala* demonstrates the enduring role of sacred kingship in African society and cultures, though it has been radically transformed as a result of the coming of Christianity, colonialism and more recently, the rise of the indigenous African churches. Ndlovu points out how the "Good Friday Ceremony," another national event, illustrates the way in which an indigenous African society has responded to modernity and social change. It is ironic that the members of the indigenous African churches are the sponsors of this national ceremony which in principle brings about the unity and integration of Swaziland, while the mission churches, which the Swazi royal family welcomed and to whom it gave red carpet treatment when they first came knocking on the king's door at the end of the 19th century, had a lukewarm attitude towards this royal ceremony.

In his essay, "The Role of Religion in the Transformation of Southern African Societies: The Botswana Case," the Rev. Obed Ndeya Kealotswe presents a historical overview of the severe impact that Western tradition has had on Botswana's religion and values. Upon contact with Western culture, elements of indigenous religions, such as ancestor veneration and puberty initiation ceremonies of young men and women, went through significant changes. The emergence of the African Independent Churches hastened the indigenization of Christianity in the country. Today, religion has a major impact on society. With the increase in new religious movements, a wide range of diverse creeds, religious cultures and sects have attracted close to 60 percent of the nation's total population.

The final essay in the volume, "Eco-Stories and Transformation," by Christina Landman, reinterprets Venda folk stories as a resource for constructing a feminist theology of nature. A major concern of the women's movement is empowerment. Women's appeal to and invocation of eco-stories as a resource for their own uplifting and empowerment may be the basis of a dialogue between African Traditional Religion and Christianity.

Religion and Social Transformation in Southern Africa provides welcome insight into the religious landscape of South Africa and the region. This book brings together a wide variety of essays that inform us about the nature and tenor of southern African religious pluralism. Its deep and thoughtful reflection on the role of religion in social transformation will enrich several disciplines devoted to African scholarship.

The Quest for African Identity and the Concept of *Nation-Building* as Motives in the Reconstruction of South African Society

Cornel Du Toit

Research Institute for Theology and Religion
University of South Africa
Pretoria, South Africa

1. Introduction

Nobody can deny that South Africa is a rainbow nation. What one can differ about is whether this rainbow is a sign of harmonious co-existence or whether it is an indication of co-existence in a thundering storm. The transitional process in South Africa has just begun. Political transformation has been relatively successful because of various factors.[1] Transition can take place at many levels and political transition, for many people, may not be the most important level of transition, although it inevitably affects all spheres of life. For many the transitional process is the long-awaited outcome of years of struggle—for others it is the end of the road. Many poor people find that little has changed for them and they

1

are looking for some meaningful form of economic transition. Others consider that acceptable levels of transformation have been transgressed and they emigrate—either physically, or spiritually into an inner world of their own. There are also those indifferent to the transition process, a different government, or the new constitution, because they succeed in maintaining the lifestyle they were accustomed to before the transition process began. It is, however, impossible to imagine that, in a context of radical change, any person will remain unaffected or will not have to undergo radical mind shifts.

Transition processes are characteristic of most societies today, although they take on different forms. Although the transformation process in South Africa has been peaceful, it can be typified as revolutionary and not evolutionary. The implication is that customs, attitudes, mindsets and so on had to be changed over a relatively short period of time. This does not exclude the fact that social evolutionary changes are also taking place rapidly. Although evolution always engenders change, the different and new forms of life (life-styles) it engenders may be different but not necessarily progressive. A new society may be so totally different from a previous one that it does not really make sense to compare the one to the other.

Transition cannot be constructed exclusively from the top. Real transition is not a top-down, but a bottom-up process. This comes through a natural evolutionary process of interaction and critique, experience and learning. There is also the right an individual has not to change, not to transform. This concerns especially religious, moral and cultural values. In an insecure context people may tend to over-emphasize these cultural values. The less threatened people are, the easier and more spontaneous the change. Threaten a language and you stimulate passionate patriots to construct all kinds of organizations.

In South Africa, most people are distressed by the side effects of the transition process. Issues like crime, the influx[2] of millions of people from African countries, the lowering of standards, the inefficiency in medical and other services, the weakening of the rand, unemployment, uncertainty about reform in education, and many other factors which accompany this process of change are alarming to most people. Unfortunately, the side effects of the transition process are often mistaken for the new order itself. The question is whether these unforseen side effects will be overcome or will become part of South African life. These side effects must be taken seriously as they are important symptoms of more deeply rooted problems like poverty and unemployment, illiteracy, a lack of community life and value systems, and a lack of both identity and a feeling of belonging.

Transitional models, prescriptive ideas and suggested systems usually abound in a situation of transformation—all having their covert power strategies. The twentieth century abounds with such examples—of which apartheid is still fresh in our memories. Authentic transition, on the other hand, is primarily a movement from below—from those who experience the taxing effects of systems imposed upon them.

There are some very positive side effects of the transition process. Apart from having a more just and democratic society, many people may for the first time experience personhood, self-respect, identity and belonging. One can also expect that cultural transformation will affect most cultures, issuing in a re-interpretation of cultural identities. The transformation process stimulates a radical recontextualization of all cultures in the new environment.

This paper wants to deal with the issues of identity, roots, nation-building and transition, to ascertain their importance and contribution in the transition process.

2. The Politics of Transition: From What to Where?

The idea of transition implies a discontent with one's present situation and the will to move away from an undesirable status quo to a better society. In South African terms it implies moving from poverty, exploitation, underdevelopment and uncertain identities to the contrary. It means, for many, replacing the black under-privileged situation with the privileges whites enjoy. The ideal for a new South Africa would be to reconcile the desires of the most advantaged individuals and groups with the needs of the most disadvantaged individuals and groups.[3] To replace one order of things with another implies that you know what you want and how to proceed. Constructivist blueprints do not always succeed in practice. It need not, for example, be only positive factors that transform society—negative factors can do so as well. Positive motives do not necessarily transform society for the good, and negative motives are not necessarily a negative transformative force. The predominant factors driving present-day transformation in South Africa vary from positive aspects like the new constitution to predominantly negative ones like crime and violence. The latter have the indirect benefit of bringing together different people who would not otherwise have met. This galvanizes people into action, stimulates job creation and, ironically, stimulates the security and vehicle enterprises.

One can expect that in the initial stage of the transition process, with the new government and constitution in place, material issues like schools, houses, medicine, jobs, and equal opportunities will receive more attention. It would be a mistake to think that the transition process concerns only the material. Material needs are only prerequisites for deeper issues such as those concerning African identity, which includes African worldview, religion, and value systems. On a material and technological level it is relatively easy to reach consensus on diverging issues. The nearer one gets to spiritual concerns like values, lifestyles, religion, custom and so on, the more complex and irreconcilable issues seem to be. Changes on the religious or cultural sphere are not always considered to be of the same decisive importance.[4] This may prove to be a severe mistake in judgment. The division between the cultural and economic and technological areas must be seen as a Western dualism, not appropriate for Africa. The importance of the cultural and religious spheres for success in the economic and technological spheres cannot be emphasized enough. It is exactly on these levels that Africa has an important contribution to make to a one-sided Western approach.

2.1. Multilateral Transition

Transition is always seen unilaterally, in binary terms, as transition from one single entity to another single entity. We move, for example, from an apartheid to a post-apartheid society; from exclusivist white minority rule to a democratic, inclusive way of government; from a race-based to a class-based society; from a Western-oriented mindset and value system to an African-oriented mindset and value system, and so on. Although unilateral explanations provide us with metaphors for explaining what is happening, it remains reductionistic, ignoring the complicated and multi-dimensional nature of the process. Transition is multilateral. Binary opposites should be broadened out to include different perspectives, and fixed terms should be appended by other terms indicating the complexity of the process. There are different levels, phases, and aspects of transition. It is not simply a movement from a fixed A to a fixed B, but from a multiplicity of affairs (say A, B and C) to a variety of other things (D, E and F), and so on.

The reductionistic aspect of binary opposites implies that these opposites capture the whole problem and, if dealt with, can settle the issue. The terms used (like free market, democracy, meritocracy, and so on) imply that they have a specific and fixed meaning. These terms are often developed from one specific culture and may have different emotional values in other cultures. The term "meritocracy" serves as an example. This term is Western, and refers to a competitive environment where individual merit and input determine success. But who determines what merit is—and whose values are represented by these merits, and how objective are they? Terms like meritocracy have been coined by those whose mentality, political strategy and customs they suit. Although this term ostensibly distinguishes non-racially between people it obviously concerns races, since most blacks are disadvantaged because of the past. If one would accurately apply the term in a white, privileged context, a different picture—not so highly moral—may evolve. Within a capitalist environment merit is not always an indication of excellence, competence and diligence. It is often a case of acquiring the best output with the least input, and without deviousness being discovered. We are all aware of the cunning of white-collar crime in a competitive context. Africa needs survival skills and not competition on white levels of merit.

2.2. *Transition as Metaphor of Hope and Desperation*

Transition in South Africa must be seen against the background of the African continent. For many, Africa remains an enigma. Questions pertaining to Africa's identity frequently surface: "What is Africa?"; "Does the Africa that you refer to exist at all?"[5] Africa appears as a puzzle made up of fifty-five countries, thousands of ethnic groups, and arbitrary boundaries inherited from the colonial period. The continent still reflects neo-colonialism which, through technical assistance and forms of cooperation and the present debt system, has made the African people dependent on the industrialized powers. More than 25 years after the colonial times most African countries have recovered neither their language, history and art, nor their spiritual heritage.[6]

Against this background the new South Africa stands out as a beacon of hope for many. Hope that it will become a generator of cultural and material wealth for the continent. Hope that it will succeed as an African country. The relatively strong economic and technological position of South Africa provides the structural background against which pan-African ideals can be promoted. This includes the ongoing process of regaining and redefining African identity; determining the relationship between Africa and the West; dealing with ethnic multiplicity and competing interests; finding overarching and uniting symbols; dealing with the past and its feelings of guilt and victimization; restoring the underprivileged, and so on.

What counts as hope for one may be experienced as desperation by another. Hope has different meanings for different groups. For many whites hope lies in maintaining past privileges, Western standards, a free market economy, law and order, and so on. The differences between dominant white and black perspectives on transition symbolize past inequalities.

The ideal of pan-Africanism, however, may be seen as somewhat utopian and outdated. African life is paradoxical. This can be attributed to its ethnic diversity and the multiplicity of worldviews.

3. The Continued Search for African Identity as Motive in the Transition Process

The post-apartheid era introduced an unforseen search for African identity. This includes issues like a common culture and a shared history and language.[7] The quest for identity is in a sense the focal point of the very complex process of cultural re-interpretation. The quest for identity in South Africa is per se highly politicized and cannot be completed without dealing with the past.

In African culture one normally finds group identity (inherent in collective and communal participation) taking precedence over individual identity.[8] Although this has been attenuated by the urbanization process, group identity is still of vital importance. The question is how to accommodate a multiplicity of group identities in the process of nation building and in the development of national unity.

Identity has always been an issue in Africa. This must be seen against the background of colonialism and continued economic dependence on the West. After liberation a new surge in the quest for African identity makes sense. There is, however, no consolidated effort made or any fixed method followed in this reconstruction process. Perhaps the infinite number of uncoordinated efforts suits the process best.

Anger has always been a result of the denial of identity. Africa has reason, in this regard, to be angry. Violence is seen as a way to freedom, as part of the struggle for a changed self-image, which takes place both among the subjugated and against the dominator.[9] The history of liberation struggles testifies to this.

From a Western perspective the search for African identity may be experienced as inconvenient as it inhibits the process of development. This is because the promotion of African culture is wrongly perceived as preventing the development of a technological society. The lack of technological advancement must rather be ascribed to the general underprivileged background of black communities and the absence of proper education from the pre-school level onwards.

There is a strong recognition that Africa needs development and this seems to be impossible in isolation from Western aid, ideas and involvement. Apart from this the question must be answered as to whether development—which is unimaginable without science, technology and industry—can be purely African. If a so-called Afro-centrism (there are many African identities) is to be promoted, this cannot be done by isolating Africa.

3.1. Backward Transition: The Search for Our Roots

Transition functions as a metaphor for many aspects and levels of change. The tenure of the transition metaphor implies that one is changing for the better. Transition thus implies progress, advancement, development, improvement, growth and the like, which are, as we have seen, not always what transition brings. The linkage of transition to development is modernistic and even utopian. Transition need not be development to be progress. It need not be forward to be good. Transition need not always be forward, it may be backwards too—like searching and rediscovering one's roots. The searching and finding of one's roots may be determined by what one is looking for and how one appropriates what one finds. Although the past can never be restored, it remains important for understanding ourselves in the present. "Root thinking" can give direction to the present. There may be recognition, insight and identification when encountering one's past. Root thinking can be stimulated, but should not artificially be enforced upon communities. To a large extent Africa need not excavate too deep to find its roots. It can simply affirm and appropriate these roots.

It is not clear how and to what extent African identity must be changed, recovered or reformulated. The process of recovering one's identity affects the African worldview, mindset, religion and the whole of African culture. It seems that the strongest rationale behind the wish to recover African identity is the urge to rid Africa of its negative self-image, its mindset of dependency, and its poverty and underdevelopment. Poverty has become a very macabre part of African identity.[10] Uprooting poverty is an important aspect of the transition process and a prerequisite for its success. As Cheryl Carolus said: "The only way that we will finally bury apartheid is by the development of our people."[11] People who are systematically handicapped by poverty are relegated to second-class status, necessitating remedial action through equalization.[12]

The process of transition has marked a resurgence of the search for Africa's roots. The African worldview is oriented more towards the glorious, perfect, primordial state of the past and less to an unknown, uncertain future. The world of the ancestors is always the best, closer to the perfect origin, and it therefore has more potency than the present or the future. The best in life lies in the past, the world of the ancestors and the origin. Anything passed down from the ancestors—like culture, religion and technology—must be maintained and protected and passed on to the next generation. The moral obligation to conform to traditions and conventions overrides the desire for change.[13]

If identity is never static but always historically, geographically and sociologically conditioned,[14] and therefore contingent, what is the sense of trying to find and identify with some roots from the past? Questions abound when one starts the process of excavating and of restoring one's identity. Is it possible to regain this former identity; can it be verified, and if so, can it be forced upon a community? Is it possible to know exactly what African identity was before colonialism? Do the majority of people want to restore this former identity? Root-searching and root-thinking do not impress everyone. Kristeva[15] sees the cult of origins as a hate reaction: hatred of those others who do not share my origins and who affront me personally, economically, and culturally. I then move back among "my own," I stick to an archaic, primitive, "common denominator."[16] This is a real danger in root-thinking. Over against this stands the idea of the cosmopolitan, the person saying in the words of the Greek dramatist, Menander, "I am a man, and nothing human is foreign to me." In biblical language, the Pauline ecclesia, where there is neither Greek nor Jew, but only the new creature, identifying with the death and resurrection of Christ, is another example.[17]

3.2. The Open-Endedness of Western Identity and Africa's Struggle to Regain Its Lost Identity

While the West seems to have outgrown its quest for identity, to some extent, Africa is in the process of trying to restore its lost identity. The quest for an African identity symbolizes the harm done to Africa during the colonial era, its struggle with poverty and illiteracy, and Africa's relative unimportance in world events. Western identity is an open identity. This excludes the idea of a fixed and stable identity and replaces it with the notion of a continuous and dynamic process of re-identification. The Western notion of identity must be linked to mentality or attitude, which indicates the volatile nature of Western identity. This does not mean that the West has no identity or that it is not interested in identity. The very process of continuous re-identification and relating to a multiplicity of identities emphasizes the importance of it. What can, however, be said is that the quest for nationalism or group consciousness belongs, for the West, to a foregone period of development. For Africa these issues are of vital concern.

It is thus not only blacks who are involved in a process of re-identification. The process concerns all races, although on different levels. In South Africa, white identity is challenged by the transition process. Many whites have outgrown the very presumptuous and modernistic claims of science, technology and the different epistemologies. There is a new appreciation for the contextual, pluralistic and contingent nature of truth claims, values, styles of living, worldviews and so on. The transition process adds to this by challenging the old and fixed white mindsets, perceptions and attitudes, as well as the associated unwillingness to identify with and open up to Africa. This challenge implies exposure and commitment to this continent in a way that differs from how it was done before. On a different level, the colored and Indian groups are also involved in a process of repositioning, reformulating their identity by new ways of interaction with other groups, and contributing to the South African story in their own very specific way.

This complicates the quest for African identity, especially in the light of its ethnic and cultural nature. African identity is local and contextual, bound to issues occupying a community's mind and influencing its worldview. African identity differs not only from community to community but is quite different north and south of the Sahara.[18]

There have been several efforts to indicate the past importance of Africa. The oldest palaeontological finds were made here—elevating Africa to the cradle of humankind, and Egypt as part of this continent—making the history of the West via the Greek culture dependent on Africa. It must be said, however, that many of these ideas originate within Afro-American circles and may not be typical of African thinking. While these issues are of tremendous symbolic importance to some Africans, Westerners may, apart from contesting the historical validity of the claims, simply shrug and say these claims change nothing, and make no difference to the fate of Africa. To a large extent the quest for identity is a battle to recover from negative aspects of African identity. The quest for identity is, as we have seen, the effort to escape the association of Africa with poverty, underdevelopment, suffering and a striving for empowerment. Are there not better and more realistic ways to restore the African's intrinsic sense of value and self-esteem than by following the identity route? Africa does have identity. There is no need to identify African culture with ancient Egyptian culture, as Africa has more than enough to offer and to identify with. African identity is, however, also a plural identity—incorporating a multiplicity of languages and religions, lifestyles and customs, stories and rites. This cultural wealth, with its spiritual strength and moral vigor, simply needs to be promoted and propagated.

3.3. Characteristics of African Identity: The Importance of Religion

Pobee sees the quest for identity as universal and not typical of Africa alone.[19] The new identity is about developing a new anthropology because the old Greek, biblical and African anthropologies have collapsed. He sees Africa as searching for a new identity alongside other continents. To Pobee this does not mean that Africa's identity is to be found solely in Africa. The search for African identity is not wholesale acceptance of either African or European culture; it is an acceptance of what is good, presumably for the dignity and well-being of homo africanus.[20]

There is not one African identity. There is no going back to some supposedly pristine African.[21] This does not mean that Africa has to cope without identity. He finds Africa's identity in present characteristics. African identities are tied into the question of who people, persons, human beings are, and these questions are directly linked to their relationship with God.[22] This relationship has been inhibited by colonial attitudes. For the growth of a genuine African identity, Africa must be exorcized not only of the spirit of colonialism but also of a missionary paternalism. Africa must develop authentic African theologies.[23]

Africa must find its identity in the religion typical of Africa. The development of authentic African theologies is a necessary undergirding of African identities.[24] Pobee identifies some characteristics typical of homo africanus[25]: The view of the sacred and secular as one; a communitarian epistemology and ontology; a distinguished sense of finitude, bound up with Africa's vulnerability and high mortality rate; the experience of reality through song, dance and ritual; and the culture of poverty.[26]

Africa must reject all factors that render African spiritual resources impotent. This means that to a large extent Western rationalistic theologies and ecclesial initiatives must be rejected, for the difference between the spiritualities of the African Indigenous Churches (AIC's) and black mainline churches is conspicuous.

3.4. Identity through Dealing with the Past: The Re-interpretation of Black Identity as Determined by Apartheid History

It cannot be denied that the very fiber of the identity of black South Africans has been colored by the history of apartheid. One can accept that apartheid will function as a negative reference point, against which black identity will be explained. This history determined black self-consciousness, black self-esteem, and black identity. Dealing with this will be a lifelong struggle as one cannot simply change perceptions formed over many years. The Truth and Reconciliation Commission (TRC) plays an important part in helping all people to deal with the guilt, suffering and legacy of the past.

Identity is closely linked to memory. My past memories determine my present identity. The past, however, is not always appealing. It often takes courage to deal with the past, especially if that past is filled with feelings of either guilt and shame or of suffering, horror, anxiety and fear. It is thus understandable that we often lack the courage to face the past and prefer bygones to be bygones. We do not wish to remember if this is a form of self-torture. Dealing with our past is, however, proof of our courage for the future. We want to deal with the past in order to understand and change the present and so face the future. We cannot wipe out the past and start with a new slate, as if nothing has happened to us. But we should also not get stuck in the past. We will always bear the scars of the past, but we must, as far as possible, overcome the pain from the wounds inflicted upon us.

Memory is a prerequisite for identity. It is not only what we remember, but also how we remember, and how we interact with memory that co-determines our identity. We must excavate the past—not to our detriment, but to our benefit. For some, memories can overwhelm and depress; for others, less afraid perhaps, it becomes addictive. History cannot be reduced to memory, nor can identity be specified in terms of history or memory alone. Identity and memory are open entities that can be colored and interpreted in specific ways with different emphases.[27]

3.5. The Celebration of Identity

It is still a long way before an overarching South African identity can be celebrated. The acceptance of a new constitution, the person of president Mandela, the victory of our sport teams, the success of the TRC as an instrument of reconciliation, and other facts can contribute to such an overarching identity. This process, however, is frail and can easily be derailed. It is uncertain what the value of such an identity really is. The idea of an overarching identity is only possible if it is complemented by the plurality of local identities. It is impossible, however, to evade a clash of identities, or to always harmonize conflicting identities. The replacement of statues, the renaming of streets and buildings, and so on are examples of the establishing of new identity to the disadvantage of another.

4. A Unified South African Identity: Is a South African Nation Possible?

Nationalism spread to most parts of the world after the Second World War. Virtually the whole world now consists of independent nation-states. After the collapse of the Soviet Union, the re-emergence of strong nationalisms from its ruins became evident. Smart believes that through cultural contact, new intermediate social forms will be produced and that contact between great religions will give rise to new varieties.[28]

However, when nation-building is at stake, questions abound: is nation-building possible in Africa, with its plenitude of ethnic groups, languages and cultures; is race or skin color sufficient to create the idea of a nation; is nation-building a prerequisite for economic development; is a transcendent South African nation at all possible?

The advancement of national unity normally presupposes commonalities. Are these present in Africa? There is not one Africa but many. In spite of many images of Africa, it will always be possible to find commonalities to bind people together. These need not be linked to race or ethnicity, since shared suffering, religious interests, economic interdependence and so on can fulfill this common purpose. Ironically, most of the factors binding blacks together are negative elements like poverty, suffering, discrimination, illiteracy, the fact of being black (seen as negative by some), and so on.

The work of Johan Degenaar on nation-building is informative in this respect.[29] He rejects the possibility of forming a South African nation, simply because the idea of nation-building cannot accommodate all the interested groups. Stalin's definition of *nation* explains the exclusivist concept of nation. It reads as follows: "A nation is an historically evolved, stable community arising on the basis of common language, territory, economic life and psychological make-up manifested in a community of culture."[30] This fixed and exclusivist view is termed by Degenaar "Nation One."

Nation One entails the congruence of culture and power, people and state.[31] Nationalism is linked here to ethnicity, one language, a common culture. There are several variations possible under the *nation one* heading. In the past, these variations concerned isolating and grouping different race groups or ethnic groups in several combinations, mainly to the benefit of white political expediency. Predominant was the idea of protecting the white race and Afrikaner *volk*. Afrikaner nation-building was always a high priority. Self determination and autonomy play an important role in nation one, as does the common history, language, values, land and so on. This model was forced to fit the South African scene for many years.

Nation Two, on the other hand, refers to *nation* in a multi-cultural situation in which "nation" is constituted by a common loyalty to a transcendent factor. This transcendent factor establishes a core which binds the different cultures together. This common loyalty forms a transcendent nation. The following possibilities come to the fore in this category:

- A *common culture* in which a plurality of cultures are accommodated in a multicultural context through their mutual commitment to transcendent values. These may be a common constitution, economic interdependence, shared religious beliefs and ethical values, a common consumer culture, and so on.
- A *culture of modernization,* in which modernization is the uniting force seen to transcend ethnic divisions and to converge life-styles. Examples of such forces are science and technology which are seen as neutral, overarching realities incorporated by the worldview of most cultures.

- In the *socialist culture* a nation is constituted by overcoming the class antagonisms of capitalist society and by acquiring the loyalty of a classless society.

- The *democratic culture* is based on competition between rival political parties. The will of the people is expressed through a single party. Values like citizenship, government by consent, the rule of law, a bill of rights, and checks and balances are determinative for this view.

Degenaar opts for a situation in which nationalism abdicates in favor of constitutionalism and in which the concept of nation makes way for the concept of civic society.[32] The ideal for him is a constitutional pluralist democracy based on a sense of common citizenship with mutual respect for different cultural traditions. Although this ideal has to a large extent been realized by the acceptance of the new constitution, it may still not satisfy many underprivileged people who do not experience a change in their fate. Common citizenship and mutual respect also imply equal circumstances for subjects.

There are many difficulties in trying to establish an overarching transcendent culture. One problem is that the dominant group (and there may be several dominant groups) may still decide (to a greater or lesser extent) on behalf of other groups what the common culture is, and use state (or other) powers to impose it.[33] The most sensible approach may be to allow opposing ideas to be expressed publicly in an open and democratic climate; to experience the interaction between theoretical ideas from the top, meeting practical realities from below. It will be unrealistic not to allow for a process of change, in which time is allowed for overlapping cross-cutting affiliations, wide-spread literacy, adequate and equitably distributed personal incomes and the development of a widely shared sense of national identity.[34]

Views on nation, nation-building and democracy tend to be rather static. Societies are dynamic and while a person, community, or ethnic group may in one instance identify with a certain aspect of ethnic identity, they may in another identify with the ideals of the so-called "nation one" model, and in yet another with the socialist or democratic ideas (of "nation two") promoted by certain

interest groups. One may even find people maintaining simultaneously two opposing views, such as socialist and democratic
values. Within this confusing context Africans are forced to make
choices causing internal conflict. Although one's experience of
identity, group-association, cultural boundedness, ethnic linkage,
and so on have become volatile, some rather fixed cores remain.

The idea of culture is also not a self-enclosed whole.[35] It is not
so that each nation has only one culture and each culture forms a
different nation. What is socially produced by an individual does
not necessarily belong to his or her culture and to all of its members. Differences within a culture are also not secondary to differences between cultures. Culture is a sign system open to other sign
systems.

South Africans will never be a nation in the idealistic sense of
the word. South Africa may, however, become a people united by
mutually shared values and interests. However, the ideal of becoming a united people must be promoted by a process of bonding
and a commitment to values like respect, freedom, diversity, interdependence, and shared sacrifices. In this context one should opt
for symbols like the rainbow people, capturing the idea of interdependence and difference. The development of an over-arching
identity in a multicultural context is only possible if a culture of
recognition can be established. Recognition of the individual and
collective other seems to be prerequisite for peaceful co-existence.

5. Bridging the Individual-Collective Gap

The danger of reducing complex issues to binary either/or
choices is very real. One cannot divide humans into certain categories and give legal rights and other forms of recognition to selective categories. The private/public, and personal identity/collective
identities are some of these category distinctions. Habermas doubts
whether a theory of rights that is so individualistically constructed
can deal with struggles of recognition where collective identities
are at stake.[36]

5.1. The Dialogical Self: More Than a Romantic Molding of Identity

Under the influence of the German philosopher Herder and Romanticism, the ideal of personal molding has often been stressed. I must be true to myself in a very peculiar way that fits my person. I should not mold[37] my life to the demands of external conformity, but according to my own judgment. This became the background to the modern notion of authenticity.[38]

It is, however, not possible for the individual to mold him/herself in isolation from the surrounding context. For Taylor the crucial feature of human life is its fundamentally *dialogical* character.[39] We define our identity always in dialogue with, and sometimes in a struggle against, the things our significant others would like to see in us. A human being and his/her context cannot be severed. Being dialogically constituted does not mean only that I have a way of being that is peculiar to me, but that in developing myself I must fight against the family, organized religion, society, the school, the state—all the forces of convention. Dialogue shapes the identity I develop as I grow up, but the very material out of which I form this identity is provided by my society.[40]

5.2. The Politics of Equal Dignity vs. the Politics of Difference

Appiah tries to link the public and personal aspects of identity.[41] He argues that if what matters about me is my individual and authentic self, then contemporary talk of identity should include large categories like gender, ethnicity, nationality, race, and sexuality in identity talk. Major collective identities such as religion, gender, ethnicity, race, sexuality, demand recognition. Habermas considers that marginalized cultural forms of life require guarantees of status and survival—a kind of collective right that shatters the outmoded self-understanding of the democratic constitutional state, which is tailored to individual rights.[42]

The influence of the collective as it comes to the fore in, for example, national ideals, community values, a specific group mentality, peer pressures, and so on, cannot be underestimated. The politics of universal dignity fought for forms of non-discrimination that were quite "blind" to the ways in which citizens differ. The modern notion of identity has given rise to a politics of difference. Equal dignity implies that the unique identity of every individual or group has to be recognized. This does not mean that we should view non-discrimination as requiring that we make these differences the basis for differential treatment.[43] In Appiah's view, it will not be enough to require treatment with equal dignity despite being black, for that would require a concession that being black counted naturally against one's dignity. And so one would end up being treated as a black.[44] Taylor formulates the problem as follows: the possibility that the Zulus, while having the same potential for cultural formation as anyone else, might nevertheless have come up with a culture less valuable than others is ruled out from the start.[45] Even to entertain this possibility is to deny human equality. The demand for equal recognition extends beyond an acknowledgment of the equal value of all human potential, and includes the equal value of what humans have made of this potential fact. The development of each culture or group has its own sufficient ground. This view must, however, also allow an apartheid culture to exist, because it is a legitimate form of development. Recognition cannot come to fulfilment when, as in the case of apartheid, it leads to dissociation and a lack of interaction. Recognition implies interdependence. For Hegel we can only flourish to the extent that we are recognized. Each consciousness seeks recognition in another, and this is not a sign of a lack of virtue. The normal conception of honor as hierarchical is crucially flawed because it cannot answer the need that sends people after recognition in the first place. Those who fail to win remain unrecognized, and those who win are also frustrated because they win recognition from losers, whose acknowledgment is not really valuable, since they are no longer free, self-supporting subjects on the same level as the winners.[46]

The challenge remains, thus, to combine the politics of equal dignity with the politics of difference, and to deal with difference, with marginalization, without threatening different points of view. It simply has to be done since societies are becoming increasingly multicultural and more porous. People are being confronted with differences more than ever before.[47] South African communities have to cope with this multiplicity. We must all guard our right to be ourselves both on the individual and the group level, and simultaneously accept our interdependence. A natural process of exposure, of interaction and evolutionary growth can ensure living differently, in harmony. It is in the interest of all to react when minority or oppressed cultures are being forced to mirror those is power.

6. The Role of Religion as Common Denominator Binding People Together

Another answer to the question as to what our common humanity is, as it is expressed in plurality, may be found in religion.[48] Religion binds most people in this country together. Religion is perhaps more typical of African identity than the dark skin of most Africans. Religion is a key factor in determining African identity and interrelating most ethnic and cultural groups on the continent. Religion has always occupied a central position in the life of most African peoples. It is an integrated part of African life. Religion, more than any other binding force, whether technology or a free-market system, a constitution or democracy, has the potential to become a common element binding people together. Religion may, however, also become a dividing force as white fundamentalism, exclusivity, and intolerance in particular may prevent white churches from opening up to African religion. A theological movement away from the domination of Western theological ideas to the rediscovery of traditional religious values is an important contribution to redefining African identity. A re-discovery and exposition of African myths and medicine, rituals and customs, community life and worldview, relationships, hopes and fears are resurfacing in African religious discourse and writing.

African religion, like African identity, is no unitary, fixed entity, but manifold, dynamic, and in a process of change.[49] Although many similarities may be found in African traditional religion, the religion of the AIC's and of mainline churches, African religions, like African identity, remain complex, multi-layered, dynamic, and with a history of contradiction, contestation and innovation.[50] Religions in Africa are African. The Christian religion, inculturated in various forms, is a very important part of authentic African identity. Theologies developed by Africans can never be entirely African, as theology developed by Westerners cannot be entirely Western.[51] Liberation theology has developed in a very specific context of interaction and critique with Western involvement in

Africa. This has influenced Western theology decisively. This process of interaction and mutual influence should be allowed to continue in an evolutionary and spontaneous manner.

Churches and religious groups may contribute significantly to mutual understanding and the discovery of mutual interests. They may succeed in opening people up to one another and contribute to a spontaneous encounter between different people on an existential and very human level.

The challenge in the process of transition is to create an environment where polynational societies, comprising free and differing individuals, can freely interact and influence each other in all spheres of life, where commitment to common causes does not prevent the maintenance of differing personal opinions and styles of living. This would be the beginning of creating a world without foreigners.[52]

Different groups have different contributions to make. There must, however, be an attitude of recognition and an acceptance of interdependence. If one must think along color lines it may be said that whites, although a minority group, enjoy the advantage of literacy, employment, access to land and production sources, and relative affluence. The black majority, on the other hand, has the advantage of governing the country, the potential of a rich cultural and religious sediment, and the prospect of trying to narrow the educational and prosperity gap. If one must think along ethnic lines there is a multiplicity of cultural inputs that can be made, of technological expertise; this diversity is an important guarantee against domination from any specific group. If one is to think along religious lines there is a rich variety of traditions which may differ radically in some respects, but also enjoy strong similarities. Religious people share ethical commonalities which make them a powerful pressure group able to decisively influence political decision-making.

The prerequisite remains openness, recognition, tolerance, mutual empowerment and respect. The realization of these and similar virtues makes the establishment of a harmonious nation a possibility.

NOTES

1. One can think of the fact that the ANC agreed to the deal because it could not match the white government's military power at the time, and that the white government accepted because of the economic pressures and because they believed that they had not too much to lose. The outgoing white government was sure of maintaining a free-market system and it probably believed that it could retain power through coalition with some ethnic groups.

2. The fact that, after the election of a democratic representative government, massive illegal immigration from African countries was and still is tolerated and not seriously addressed, points to more than simply inefficiency or a lack of will to curb it. It must be seen as an expression of Pan-Africanism, black nationalism, and black consciousness. Africans, being accustomed to multi-ethnicity, may resent immigrants taking up job opportunities, but apparently do not experience cultural differences as a serious problem (see also J. Habermas, "Struggles for Recognition in the Democratic Constitutional State," in A. Gutman [ed.], *Multiculturalism: Examining the Politics of Recognition* [Princeton: Princeton University Press, 1994], pp. 118, 135-142).

3. J. Kristeva, *Nations without Nationalism* (New York: Columbia University Press, 1993), p. 42.

4. The precedence of economic over cultural values can be seen in the fact that the failure of the Reconstruction and Development Programme has received much attention in contrast to the little attention given to the success of the ANC government to rectify the position and rights of women.

5. George Haymes once said: "the African does not exist except in the minds of those who have never seen the people" (quoted by N.E. Bloch-Hoell, "African Identity: European Invention or Genuine African Character?" *Mission Studies*, ix[1] [1992]:105).

6. M. Reuver, F. Solms and G. Huizer (eds), *The Ecumenical Movement Tomorrow* (Kampen: Kok, 1993), pp. 273-274.

7. *Multi Party Democracy News*, Oct. 1996, 5/2:8.

8. A.B. Pasteur and I.L. Toldson, *Roots of Soul: The Psychology of Black Expressiveness* (New York: Anchor Press, 1982), p. 71.

9. C. Taylor, "The Politics of Recognition," in A. Gutman (ed), *Multiculturalism: Examining the Politics of Recognition* (Princeton: Princeton University Press, 1994), p. 65.

10. J.S. Pobee, "Africa in Search of Identity," in M. Reuver, F. Solms and G. Huizer (eds.), *The Ecumenical Movement Tomorrow* (Kampen: Kok, 1993), p. 397; Bloch-Hoell, "African Identity," *op. cit.*, p. 102.

11. C. Carolus Carolus, *Transformation in South Africa: The Role of Civil Society and the Church in the Reconstruction and Development Programme* (EFSA

Institute for Theological and Interdisciplinary Research, 1994), p. 2.

12. Taylor, "The Politics of Recognition," *op. cit.*, p. 38; C.W. Du Toit, "Empowerment of the Poor," in C.W. Du Toit (ed.), *Empowering the Poor* (Pretoria: Unisa, 1996), pp. 10-37.

13. Y. Turaki, "Culture and Modernization in Africa: A Methodological Approach," in *Cultural Diversity in Africa: Embarrassment or Opportunity?* PU for CHE, No. 40 (1991):134-135.

14. The notion of personal identity in which personality, confessional, linguistic, behavioral and sexual issues come to the fore cannot be separated from national and ethnic identity, and constitute an even more important aspect of identity than the latter.

15. Kristeva, *Nations without Nationalism*, *op. cit.*, pp. 2-3.

16. The hatred of others is symbolized by the Greek myth of the Danaides. The Danaides were foreign to the Greeks because they—being descendants of Io, priestess of Hera, who gave birth in Egypt to their ancestor Danaüs—were born outside Greece, did not speak the language, and had strange customs. The women who were not amenable to Greek customs were obdurate in marriage. The Danaides refused to marry their cousins and the women ended up murdering their husbands on their wedding night. The myth symbolizes the transition from endogamous to exogamous society, in which one selects a spouse from a "foreign country"—outside the family, the clan, the lineage. The Egyptian Danaides testify to the beginnings of civic protection for the foreigner in ancient Greece (see Kristeva, *Nations without Nationalism*, *op. cit.*, pp. 17-19).

17. Kristeva, *Nations without Nationalism*, *op. cit.*, pp. 20, 22.

18. Bloch-Hoell, "African Identity," *op. cit.*, p. 101.

19. Pobee, "Africa in Search of Identity," *op. cit.*, p. 388.

20. *Ibid.*, p. 394.

21. *Ibid.*, p. 390.

22. *Ibid.*, p. 392.

23. *Ibid.*, pp. 393, 395.

24. *Ibid.*, p. 395.

25. *Ibid.*, pp. 396-398.

26. Pasteur and Toldson, *Roots of Soul*, *op. cit.*, p. 93.

27. C.W. Du Toit, "Dealing with the Past," in H.R. Botman and R.M. Peterson (eds.), *To Remember and to Heal* (Cape Town: Human and Rosseau, 1996), pp. 123-126).

28. N. Smart, *Worldviews: Crosscultural Explorations of Human Beliefs* (New Jersey: Prentice Hall, 1995), pp. 44-47.

29. J. Degenaar, *Nations and Nationalism: The Myth of a South African Nation* Occasional Papers No. 40 (Stellenbosch: IDASA, 1992), pp. 1-20.

30. *Ibid.*, p. 9.

31. *Ibid.*, p. 2.

32. *Ibid.*, p. 2.
33. *Ibid.*, p. 8.
34. *Ibid.*, p. 11.
35. *Ibid.*, p. 7.
36. Habermas, "Struggles for Recognition," *op. cit.*, p. 107.
37. Herder applied his concept of the individual self not only to the individual person among other persons, but also to the culture-bearing people among other peoples. Just like individuals, a *Volk* should be true to itself (Taylor, "The Politics of Recognition," *op. cit.*, p. 31).
38. Taylor, "The Politics of Recognition," *op. cit.*, pp. 30-31.
39. *Ibid.*, pp. 32-33.
40. K.A. Appiah, "Identity, Authenticity, Survival: Multicultural Societies and Social Reproduction," in Gutman, *Multiculturalism, op. cit.*, p. 154.
41. *Ibid.*, pp. 149, 151.
42. Habermas, "Struggles for Recognition," *op. cit.*, p. 109.
43. Taylor, "The Politics of Recognition," *op. cit.*, pp. 38-39.
44. Appiah, "Identity, Authenticity, Survival," *op. cit.*, p. 161.
45. Taylor, "The Politics of Recognition," *op. cit.*, pp. 42-43.
46. *Ibid.*, p. 50.
47. *Ibid.*, p. 63.
48. Pobee, "Africa in Search of Identity," *op. cit.*, p. 387.
49. This is emphasized by the oral nature of African religion. Genuine African theology is oral theology, according to Bloch-Hoell ("African Identity," *op. cit.*, p. 105). African hymns, prayers, liturgies and stories are often improvised in a creative and enthusiastic manner.
50. Bloch-Hoell, "African Identity," *op. cit.*, pp. 100, 102.
51. *Ibid.*, p. 103; see also A. Wessels, *Kerstening en ontkerstening van Europa: Wisselwerking tussen evangelie en cultuur* (Baarn: Ten Have, 1994), pp. 211ff.
52. Kristeva, *Nations without Nationalism, op. cit.*, p. 36.

South Africa's Search for Peace and Unity

Albert Jan Venter

Chair, Department of Political Studies
Rand Afrikaans University
Johannesburg, South Africa

Introduction

After 340 years of white domination, some of it under colonialism, and some under indigenous Afrikaner-led *apart-ism*, Nelson Mandela was finally sworn in on 10 May 1994 as South Africa's first democratically elected black president. Much bloodshed, violence and social turmoil preceded this epoch-making event. South Africa has seen a great deal of social and political violence throughout its modern history. The political transformation witnessed during the last six years was no exception. The violence which accompanied democratization has its direct antecedents in the black armed struggle for liberation which began in 1960. Thousands of lives, most of them blacks, were lost in this struggle. Since 1985, with the beginning of the township revolt against the P.W. Botha government, up to the end of 1993, almost 17,000 lives were lost.[1]

South Africa is a deeply divided society, characterized by ethnic, class, social, racial, linguistic and religious cleavages. While its social segmentations are not uniquely grave in the world of today, they do not augur well for its survival as a liberal democratic state. The post-electoral euphoria, brought about by the nature of the elections, its acceptance by almost the whole population, and the emotional moments surrounding the inauguration of Mandela, has tended to downplay these divisions. The aim of this essay is to reflect on some of the more salient cleavages of South African society and to offer a prognosis on a relatively peaceful and successful democratization process. The scope of this essay does not allow a treatment of all the possible divisions and their likely resolution. It will concentrate on the Afrikaner right-wing, the incipient Zulu nationalism and some of the marked ideological and economic cleavages in government and other political forces. The underlying assumption on which the essay is premised is that the divisions and schisms of societies that undergo rapid transformation, tend to have a decisive influence on the strategies of change followed by the leaders of the new order. *The leaders of the new order have to work with what they inherit.*[2]

The White Right-Wing

Prior to the 1994 general election the Afrikaner-dominated white right-wing was united by a fear and rejection of the African National Congress-South African Communist Party-Congress of South African Trade Unions Alliance (ANC-SACP-COSATU), but hopelessly divided on what the best counter strategy was to be. The Conservative Party (CP) under Dr. F. Hartzenberg, an uninspiring leader, led the formation of a provisional *volksregering* (people's government) and boycotted the election. Hartzenberg has now accepted the reality of the new power dispensation in South Africa by stating that the CP does not want to disturb the peace in present (January 1996) South Africa. Under his direction, the Afrikaner-volksfront has entered into negotiations with the government with a view to acquiring a white Afrikaner *Volkstaat*. Politically the CP was wiped out in the November 1995 local government elections.

The principle of self-determination was added to the new South African constitution in last-minute bargaining during February of 1994 between the National Party, ANC and Afrikanervolksfront. The problem with the practical realization of the principle is that Afrikaners who wish to live in a *Volkstaat* are mostly those who reside among an overwhelming majority of black people. Examples of such areas are the Northern Province, North West Province, Mpumalanga and the western areas of kwaZulu-Natal. The numbers against Afrikaans whites in these areas are overwhelming: about 3 percent whites, not all Afrikaners, live among a black population comprising 97 percent of all people in the aforementioned areas.[3] There is no practical way to delineate a geographically and economically meaningful white *Volkstaat* in these or virtually any other area of South Africa.

The leader of the neo-conservative Afrikaner party, the Freedom Front, General Constand Viljoen, is the one figure who could unite the white right-wing. Viljoen seems to find excellent rapport with president Mandela and vice-president Mbeki. As a practical soldier, he realizes the cost of a (civil) war and has expressed himself in favor of a negotiated resolution on the demand for a *Volkstaat*. Having broken away from the Afrikaner-volksfront to start the Freedom Front and capturing nine seats in the National Assembly in the 1994 general election, Viljoen emerged as the real leader of the moderate white right-wing. The main obstacle to right-wing unity is the lack of a coherent practical policy regarding the establishment of the central symbolism of a *Volkstaat, Boerestaat, or Volksrepubliek*. Fundamentalist right-wingers like Jaap Marais of the Herstigte National Party still see the Verwoerdian "white state" with 87 percent of the land in white hands, as the state of the Afrikaner *Volk*. The neo-Nazi inspired Afrikaner Weerstandsbeweging (AWB) led by Eugene Terre-blanche wants the reestablishment of the Transvaal Republic of 19th-century British Colonial times, despite the fact that the area is populated by an almost four to one majority of blacks against whites and that it no longer exists as a political entity. Most other white right-wingers have accepted the fact that a *Volkstaat* would by definition have to be an *Afrikaner-stan*, a much smaller piece of the South African territory. But their dilemma is to answer the question where to find an area to establish such a state.

The main problem facing right-wing supporters is the same problem that undid apartheid: the peoples of South Africa are intermingled and the white Afrikaners are a diluted and spread-out part of this population, roughly 3 million out of a population of 40 million. Afrikaners do not physically occupy an exclusive part of South Africa's territory. The overwhelming majority of Afrikaners live and work in an industrialized and urban environment. They have become an urbanized bourgeoisie, interspersed throughout South Africa with other white South Africans of English, Portuguese and other European descent. Any plan that delimits an equitable portion of the land to Afrikaners will immediately place the majority of them outside that territory.

A just portion of land for Afrikaners on a strict per capita basis would amount to the following: The white Afrikaners constitute about 3 million people. In the April 1994 elections, the Freedom Front captured 424,555 votes (2.17 percent of the poll), most of which were at the expense of the Conservative Party. At a guess, about 250,000 CP supporters boycotted the elections, which means that about 700,000 adult whites could support the principle of a *Volkstaat*. Adding children under voting age one could estimate that a case could be made that this constituency represents about a million people. This means 1 million out of 40 million South Africans, or 2.5 percent of the total South African population. South Africa's land area comprises ca. 122 million hectares. Thus the *Volkstaat* should proportionally not consist of more than about 3 million hectares, an area roughly one-third the size of the present Free State province.

However, the right-wing dilemma is that South African white farmers, numbering only around 70,000, already own almost 70 percent of South Africa's total land area, or 86 million hectares. Almost 80 percent of these farmers are Afrikaners. A majority probably supports the idea of a *Volkstaat*, since the Afrikaner right-wing support is traditionally very strong among these people. The amount of land that the conservative Afrikaner white farmers would have to relinquish to move to the *Volkstaat* physically—at a guess about 83 million hectares out of 86 million hectares, as the above calculation suggests—is simply asking too much materially. Moreover, Afrikaners are almost 90 percent urbanized and are economically dependent on South Africa's urban industrialist economy. It is doubtful that the bulk of urbanized bourgeois supporters of the CP and FF will support, let alone be able or willing to materially sustain the consequences of a small Afrikaner *Volkstaat*.

One possible viable option for an Afrikaner *Volkstaat* is the so-called Boshoff plan of *Orania* somewhere in the remote, semi-desert, arid and sparsely populated North Cape Province. At present it consists of one small town (population ca. 400). *Orania* is simply a small town and does not represent a specifically delimited territory that could support a nation-in-the-making. The *Orania* project is more an ideological symbol than a practical, delimited and identifiable potential *Volkstaat*. Conservative Afrikaners have little material, historic or emotional interest in this territory. *Orania* simply does not have the political symbolism and economic potential to sustain a federal, let alone sovereign and independent, Afrikaner *Volkstaat*. At most a part of that territory could be declared a possible area of Afrikaner paramountcy, without derogating the rights of non-Afrikaner people already resident in the area.

The right-wing whites want what they cannot maintain physically: the exclusive political control of the areas of their present domicile, about 70 percent of South Africa's territory. This I suggest is an insurmountable problem and right-wing unity will remain unattainable. It is already clear that the Conservative Party of Hartzenberg and the Freedom Front of Viljoen are finding it difficult to cooperate in the post-election process of negotiating a *Volkstaat* with the ANC-Government. Hartzenberg and the CP refuse to sit in the *Volkstaat* Council, a statutory body provided for in the new constitution and dominated by Viljoen's Freedom Front. The right-wing will not be able to produce a mutually acceptable map for the *Volkstaat*. Most of the white right-wing supporters have strong middle-class material interests in participating in the wider South African state. These structural circumstances will force them to accommodate themselves to the post April 1994 political realities. What resistance remains would be of nuisance value: right-wing terrorist action which could be contained by the new state.

The ANC-IFP Rivalry

One of the most worrying schisms in South African politics is the rivalry between the ANC and the Inkatha Freedom Party (IFP) in the East Rand black townships and the "killing fields" of kwaZulu-Natal. The IFP has a significant support base: in the April 1994 elections it captured 10 percent of the national vote and 50 percent of the vote in kwaZulu-Natal. In the April 1996 local government elections this support was solidified at around 44 percent of the popular vote. However, these elections clearly demonstrated that the IFP has a rural power base. It lost out heavily in the urbanized areas of the province. Its party ideology is a conservative and capitalist-oriented one, with some symbolic Zulu-nationalism disguised in the form of allegiance to the Zulu monarchy added. While the IFP cannot play the role of a national party in South African politics, it has majority regional support in kwaZulu-Natal and cannot be ignored or left out of any political settlement. The ANC-government faces a dilemma in this regard. No long-term political accommodation in South Africa is possible without the cooperation of the IFP.

Resolving the dilemma will be difficult. When one takes the material and economic realities of South Africa into consideration, it is clear that the long-term structural conditions of a settlement are already available. This settlement centers around the strategic High-veld area of South Africa. Ranging from Witbank in the eastern high-veld, Pretoria in the north, the West Gauteng goldfields and maize producing areas, the Sasol-Vereeniging chemical-industrial complex and the Free State maize and goldfields, the area yields almost half of South Africa's gross domestic product. This geo-economic reality of the "Golden Crescent" has already forced the NP and the ANC to accommodate themselves into an arrangement at the system level of the new polity—the participation as partners in the new political order.

The ANC-Alliance cannot afford a black-on-black ethnic race war and accommodating the IFP is a necessary condition in avoiding such a war. The ANC also benefited from the deal regarding the Golden Crescent; it now effectively and legitimately controls the central state. The central state has the material resources and physical means to make kwaZulu-Natal comply with central direction on matters of national interest. Buthelezi and the IFP also have an interest in reaching accommodation with the new masters of the central state: kwaZulu-Natal is a poor and underdeveloped area of South Africa. The same reasons for not accepting "independence" under apartheid still apply: kwaZulu-Natal is too weak to go it alone. The province produces about 16 percent of the GNP, but is very densely populated, with a low per capita income.

The survival of kwaZulu-Natal depends as a necessary condition on the financial support and military tolerance of the central South African state.

The power shift in South African politics since the 1994 elections has only brought about a partial truce between the ANC and IFP in the two main theaters of conflict: the East Rand black townships and the disputed areas of kwaZulu-Natal. The rivalry and bitterness preceding the elections have not disappeared. In the provincial government of kwaZulu-Natal, it took almost a month to form a coalition cabinet. One of the major stumbling blocks was that the ANC wanted to have control of the provincial police portfolio. Only difficult negotiations between the ANC and IFP national leadership were able to resolve the allocation of provincial executive portfolios. There was a disagreement on the choice of administrative capital as well and after two years the ANC and the IFP have not been able to agree on a provincial constitution for the territory. Such constitution as has been drawn up for the province has been rejected by the Constitutional Court as unconstitutional. Neither has peace been restored to kwa-Zulu-Natal. Anti-IFP rhetoric from ANC leaders such as former ANC youth league leader and government member, Peter Mokaba, threatens the fragile peace in kwaZulu-Natal. Mokaba said on 16 June 1994 in Durban that the ANC would "use its national majority to break the IFP."[4] Killings and faction fighting between political rivals in the ANC and IFP have continued unabatedly since 1994 and more than 2000 people have been killed since the instauration of the Government of National Unity (GNU) in May 1994. In the Constitutional Assembly which drew up a new and permanent constitution for the country, the IFP withdrew from the process, insisting that a pre-electoral promise of international mediation regarding the future of the Zulu monarchy in the kwaZulu-Natal province first be fulfilled. Few signs of a lasting accord between the ANC and the IFP have been established, despite the relatively peaceful local government elections of May 1996.

Other African Schisms: Traditionalists, the Black Consciousness Movement

While the 1994 polls showed strong support for the ANC at the popular level, the traditional African leadership will have to be treated sensitively. Nowhere is this better illustrated than in kwa-Zulu-Natal where the Zulu king remains a strong cultural influence, transcending the schisms between the modernized and ANC-supporting Zulus, and traditional IFP-supporting sectors of Zulu society. Part of the last-minute deals in April 1994 to ensure IFP participation in the elections entailed assurances that the Zulu king would be the constitutional monarch of the new province of kwaZulu-Natal. On 25 April 1994 1.2 million hectares of land was also transferred to the Zulu king as ultimate trustee, in one of the final acts of departure by former state president F. W. de Klerk. This act was condemned by the ANC and led to a cabinet investigation. While de Klerk acted within his powers as state president, it caused dissatisfaction in the ANC as being an underhanded last-minute piece of pork barrel politics by de Klerk to canvass traditionalist Zulu support for the National Party and the IFP at the expense of the ANC.

There are about 10,000 traditional chieftains in South Africa who exercise substantial influence and material patronage over communal tribal land. These interests have been accommodated partially in the form of advisory houses of traditional leaders at provincial and national levels in the new constitution. In addition Mrs. Stella Sigcau, a member of the Transkei nobility, and a member of the ANC-affiliated Contralesa (Conference of traditional leaders of South Africa) has been appointed to the Cabinet of the GNU. However, a number of traditional African leaders are pressing for a greater role in government and control of funds at the local government level.[5] A clash on this issue with the modernizing elements of the ANC is likely. After two and a half years the issue of the political status of traditional leaders has not yet been resolved.

The smaller Africanist, black consciousness-inspired parties on the left of the South African political spectrum, namely the Pan Africanist Congress of Azania (PAC) and the Azanian Peoples Organization (Azapo), are ideological predators on the relatively moderate ANC-SACP-Cosatu Alliance. One can expect them to try and exploit ANC concessions to the "white settler establishment." They have a constituency among the disaffected black youth and relish the symbolism of ideological purists. One can expect them to play the role of a perfectionist opposition now that the ANC partakes of real political power and its concomitant political responsibilities. While ostensibly committed to the ideals of non-racism, the two parties promote the ideology of black power and black consciousness, if not outright black racism. They could become ideological spoilers in the post election reconstruction towards national unity: outbidding the ANC in its commitment to the reconstruction and development program and exploiting divisions in that party. The president of Azapo, Ithumeleng Mosala, has already claimed that the ANC in government is "weak kneed" on the question of celebrating the 16th of June (the commemoration of the start of the Soweto uprising in 1976).[6] However, the first two years of ANC-in-government has not yet led to a significant increase in the influence of these two parties: they were routed in the November 1995 local government elections.

Contradictions in the ANC Support Base

The ANC is a rainbow coalition born of opposition against white oppression. With the advent of government responsibility, contradictions in this alliance have already developed. Some of the salient contradictions can be found in its alliance with organized labor. The organized labor movement in the form of the Cosatu labor federation represents material privilege against the high proportion of poor and structurally unemployed black people who are at present a natural ANC constituency. The poor may become disillusioned with the ANC alliance with the privileged employed and become targets of political entrepreneurs. The jobless are literally desirous of the (ANC-supporting) employees' collective material benefits. This contradiction was sublimated by the overall requirements of the black liberation struggle but has become salient since the freedom elections have taken place. The unemployed have started to seek rewards for their electoral support, and not much has been forthcoming.

Moreover, there are schisms in the ANC-Cosatu Alliance as well.

The ANC-government faces a daunting task in integrating South Africa into the international political economy. South Africa has extremely high trade tariff walls. Being a signatory to the Uruguay round of the GATT, these tariff walls will have to come down. Its concomitant spin-offs will be rationalization of, among others, the heavily protected motor and textile industries which are protected by import tariffs of as high as 110 percent. These tariffs have been cut by more than 60 percent and job losses have occurred in both sectors. These industries are also among those in which ANC-affiliated unions are the strongest, namely the National Union of Metal Workers of South Africa (Numsa) and the South African Clothing and Textile Workers Union (Sactwu). The Cosatu federation decided at its 1993 conference that it would keep a distance from the ANC-in-Government. Should heavy job losses occur in these industries due to GATT-required changes in tariff protection, the ANC-Cosatu Alliance would be severely strained. In addition, the GNU drive for the privatization of state enterprises ("restructuring") has led to serious disagreement between the Cosatu and ANC leadership: Cosatu is trying to protect its membership against possible job losses in the privatization of state enterprises, while the ANC, as governing party, needs the resources that can be unlocked by this program. President Mandela stated emphatically in May 1996 that privatization was "government policy" and that this would not be changed. On economic policy the ANC government has turned to center right with its GEAR (Growth, Employment and Redistribution) program.

Moreover, ANC member of parliament Jeremy Cronin, a foremost intellectual in the South African Communist Party, wrote in the June 1994 issue of the ANC mouthpiece, *Mayibuye,* that the ANC has to continue its role as freedom movement. The Communists in the ANC Alliance have become ideologically sidelined, and their latest writings indicate that they are without a coherent ideological or practical program of action[7] and that, if necessary, internal schisms in the ANC are to be promoted to keep the ANC government leadership in line.[8]

The Position of the National Party

The National Party (NP) will have to look for conservative ideological partners that can deliver some black votes. The April 1994 election was to a great extent an ethnic census. The National Party got an insignificant proportion of African votes; the ANC an insignificant white proportion. The only really established black party that could become an NP ally is the IFP. Up to the elections it was not eager to accept the NP's geo-economic accommodation with the ANC. As argued above, however, the IFP will not become a national force in black politics. It cannot capture the economic Golden Crescent, where the ANC holds the loyalty of the greatest majority of black voters and is likely to maintain that loyalty. The NP is strong among South African white capitalist interests, the white bourgeoisie and the emerging "colored" and Indian bourgeoisie. The NP and IFP are possible ideological allies. (Both are conservative parties sharing the capitalist ideology.) However, the pre-election relationship between the two parties was severely strained, and these schisms would need to be healed before significant cooperation could take place. Their relationship in the GNU cabinet did not turn out to be one of an alliance against ANC-generated pressure. Up to now, the IFP leader Buthelezi's sense of betrayal by the de Klerk government in September of 1992 has prevented any serious alignment between the IFP and NP occurring.[9] The NP has embarked on a serious rethinking of its political positioning in South Africa with a view to capturing significant African support.[10] It sees itself as an economically neo-conservative Christian democratic party in the European sense of the word.

Schisms in the Government of National Unity

The Government of National Unity was formed in early May 1994 and had a constitutional mandate to rule for five years. At its inception it was composed of 19 ANC members, 7 Nationalists and 4 members from the IFP. As a government of national unity, the cabinet had the political support of 377 members of Parliament (94 percent), and as such could be depicted as a "grand coalition"; more accurately, the Latin epithet *"coalitionis magna grandiosis"* would fit its composition. The cabinet had to accommodate a number of schisms, the most obvious being the ideological distance between the three political parties represented. Unifying these ideological differences required all of President Mandela's leadership and statesman's skills. On the ideological left were Communist Party members such as Mac Maharaj and Sydney Mufamadi. Leftwing ANC members include Kader Asmal, Pallo Jordan, Jay Naidoo and Tito Mboweni. Moderate ANC members include Deputy President Mbeki and Dullah Omar. Moderate center right members (the NP's) were De Klerk, Dawie de Villiers, Roelf Meyer and R.F. "Pik" Botha. Conservative members of the Cabinet include the IFP's Buthelezi and Sipho Mzimela. Such a wide ideological divide is unusual in coalition cabinets. South Africa's transition to democracy required such a wide representation of ideological views, but it had obvious potential for conflict and *immobilism*. The GNU was deeply divided from the outset. First, the National Party was forced to accept a de facto ruling by the ANC's National Executive Committee regarding the allocation of cabinet posts. This meant that Mandela had to renege on a deal in which the NP would have had access to one of the security ministries. Second, Deputy President de Klerk's judgment on transferring 1.2 million hectares of land to the Zulu king two days before the election and rendering executive clemency to 70 murderers and some members of the security forces put a strain on cabinet relations. Both these actions of de Klerk were subject to cabinet review. The committee which reviewed the land deal cleared de Klerk from acting improperly, preventing a possible early rift in the cabinet.[11] However, in 1995 there were further upheavals in the cabinet, between Buthelezi and Mandela and between De Klerk and Mandela. In November 1995 Mandela called De Klerk's leadership a "joke." Publicly, however, Mandela has given South Africans the assurance that the GNU is working well and that these issues are "party politicking."[12]

Within the ranks of the ANC itself, some division set in regarding the allocation of cabinet portfolios. The senior *exile* members of the ANC were clearly favored above the internal and younger resistance leaders, such as Cyril Ramaphosa. The role of the ANC's National Executive Committee (NEC) and the cabinet is still unclear. The NEC played a crucial role in the decisions regarding the composition of the new cabinet. Whether the NEC will play a behind the scenes role in ANC decisions in the cabinet could compromise the principle of cabinet unity and collective responsibility. Furthermore, the South African Communist Party through an elected member of Parliament, Jeremy Cronin, severely criticized the high salary increases of the new Mandela government, calling the salaries banal in view of the plight of South Africa's poor blacks and poorly paid black civil servants.[13]

Moreover, there was some initial disagreement between senior commanders of the South African National Defence Force (SANDF) and Defence Minister Modise on the question of appointing high level former ANC Liberation Army (MK) commanders to senior defence force positions. The ANC nominees were allegedly rejected on the grounds that they lacked suitable academic and military qualifications to be able to discharge the duties required of their commands, *inter alia* Chief of Staff of the Defence Force (deputy commander) and Chief of Military Intelligence. These issues have since been resolved.[14]

There was some difference of opinion between the National Party and the ANC on the concept of a Truth and Reconciliation Commission to unearth the sordid details of crimes and wrongdoings during the apartheid era. This Commission faces many political obstacles. Neither the ANC nor the National Party and its former government employees have clean moral consciences regarding the years of struggle since 1960. Truth Commission revelations have already opened up wounds on all sides. Moreover, senior police and defense force officers are discomfitted by the concept of a truth commission that may one-sidedly name and blame former government security staff for atrocities during the period of struggle. They patently point out that ANC leaders do not have a clear moral slate as far as human rights abuses are concerned. In 1993 the ANC-appointed Motsuenyane Commission found a number of senior ANC members blameworthy of human rights abuses. Among the more prominent of those found to carry accountability for human rights abuses in ANC army camps were Joe Modise, present Minister of Defence, Jacob Zuma, kwaZulu-Natal leader of the ANC, and Alfred Nzo, Minister of Foreign Affairs. These leaders were only mildly criticized for their actions, and were rescued by the ANC National Executive Committee, which accepted collective responsibility for the alleged abuses.[15] The Claus Barbie agonies in France and the revelations of the Stasi files of the former German Democratic Republic serve as reminders of the divisiveness of such efforts at revealing "the truth." The Commission for Truth and Reconciliation started its work in 1996 under the chairmanship of Archbishop and Nobel laureate Desmond Tutu. Former Defence Force and Police Generals were charged in the Durban supreme court in December 1995 with common-law complicity in murders allegedly committed in 1987. They were found not-guilty in early October of 1996.[16] At present only time will tell whether this commission could bring about reconciliation in South Africa. At the time of this writing the Commission was admonished by a full bench of the Appeal Court in Bloemfontein for not following the rules of natural justice. Police officers had taken the Truth Commission on appeal for not giving them adequate warning that their names were to be mentioned in hearings in front of the Commission. The implications of this ruling could be serious for all the work the Commission has done so far. At the time of this writing the issue was still unresolved by the Commission.

Mangosuthu Buthelezi, leader of the IFP and minister for Home Affairs, was reluctant to join the cabinet. The conflict between the ANC and the IFP in Natal has strained the relationship between the Buthelezi and the ANC-in-the-Cabinet. The ANC-inspired South African Prisoners' Organization for Human Rights (Sapohr) has demanded the resignation of Mzimela, IFP cabinet member and minister responsible for correctional services during the prison rampage of the week ending 12 June 1994.[17] Furthermore, Buthelezi had to publicly apologize for bursting into the *Agenda* Studios of the South African Broadcasting Corporation (SABC) in September 1994. He was perturbed by a debate presented by the studio regarding the struggle between the ANC and IFP for the Zulu king's loyalty. Buthelezi has also taken the IFP out of the Constitutional Assembly negotiations regarding a final constitutional text, but has decided to remain in the cabinet for the time being. The final constitution was accepted in February 1997 without the formal approval or cooperation of the IFP.

There is a further potential problem with the ANC-in-government. The party holds very strong views on a centralized and powerful state. This view follows the outdated 19th-century conception of the mono-state: central control over the population in terms of the culture to be followed, the national language spoken, the homogenization of museums, history books, national myths, sports bodies, monuments and so on. There is much thinking in the ANC that comes down to a "rage to control," which in essence holds that the ruling political party should monopolize civil society. The adherents of this line of thought will try to apply ANC hegemony to all parts of South African social life. An effort on the part of the ANC to extend its hegemony over civil society is bound to cause conflict and severe counter-reactions from various smaller interest groups.

From the above exposition it follows that the Government of National Unity, while having been instrumental in managing the peaceful transfer of political power, was also threatened by potentially serious schisms. It therefore came as no big surprise that the National Party left the GNU in May 1996, having lost the argument with the ANC to continue the GNU post 1999. After Mandela goes, the many divisive issues will need to be addressed and could well go off kilter. South Africa is not yet a consolidated democracy, neither have its many social problems and schisms been healed.

Ethnic Nationalism: Death Knell for South Africa?

Ethnicity and ethnic consciousness, contrary to the expectation of many liberal theorists of nation building, is reviving and rampant on a world-wide scale. The list of ethnic conflicts is seemingly endless, and not only confined to "backward" Third World ethnically divided states. Globally, "ethnic genies" are surging out of their enchanted lamps. Belgium, Canada, France, Britain, Australia, Switzerland, Spain, Czechoslovakia, Yugoslavia (Bosnia), the old USSR, India, Bangladesh, Sri Lanka, Nigeria, Somalia, Burundi, Indonesia, Malaysia, Iraq, Syria and Turkey. One can even have the place names alliterate: Biafra, Bangladesh, Burundi, Brussels, Beirut and Belfast.

In post-Second World War ethnically divided societies, ethnic conflict has been exacerbated by the role of the state in society. The actions of the state have been used to condition ethnic groups into responses of ethnic mobilization. In ethnically divided societies the state has neither been a non-autonomous executive committee of the capitalist classes, nor the neutral arbiter in service of society espoused by early liberal political theorists. In the post World War II, de-colonized, ethnically divided states a single ethnic group took control of the state and used its powers to exercise hegemony over other ethnic groups. It is more true to say that in many instances the state was the executive committee of the dominant ethnic group. Numerous states have found it useful to recruit their armies, police, judiciary and civil servants predominantly or disproportionately from one ethnic community. In states with coherent and organized ethnic groups, dominant ethnic classes have been able to enhance and preserve their dominance through state power. Malaysia, Sri Lanka, the Serbs of Yugoslavia, the Tutsi-dominated state of Burundi, and Zaire under Mobutu, as well as the National Party governments of South Africa between 1948-94 are classic examples.[18]

Where does this leave South Africa and its future as a non-racial society? The Afrikaans community is a classic example of one where state policies, from the 1910 Botha and Smuts governments onwards, aided ethnic mobilization and the eventual capture of state power by the Afrikaner nationalists. After 1948 the state was used to advance the material as well as symbolic interests of Afrikaners and to manipulate black ethnic identity. This exercise started to unravel by 1978 and we have witnessed a transfer of state power to a dominant and numerically superior race group: black Africans.

The Africans are divided among ethnic lines, although these are at present neither salient nor being exploited politically in South Africa. What is interesting here is that the winning party in this group is ideologically committed to some form of ethnically neutral, but racially representative state. The ANC conspicuously avoids the beating of African tribal drums. Its official ideology is progressivist and developmentalist: to it tribalism and parochialism are anathema. Moreover, in the April 1994 national elections as well as the November 1995 local polls, the ANC was universally supported by black voters from all black ethnic groups. It garnered overwhelming majorities among all black ethnic groups except the Zulus. In black politics, the ANC is a truly transethnic party.

What has to be decided in the post-apartheid era of a black-dominated government and political order is whether the ANC can maintain its stance of an ethnically neutral state. Some elements in South African society—the IFP, the *Volkstaters*—already perceive a threat to their ethnic identity in the new political order. Should it become clearer in time that in effect the supposedly ethnically neutral state is but a Xhosa- and African-dominated state, a reactionary ethnic response is likely. Support for the ANC could be transformed by ethnic entrepreneurs into mobilization of the various African and black subcultures against the ANC. Some evidence of such mobilization is emerging in the Western Cape where the ANC is facing continuous problems of reconciling the material interests of the Coloureds and Africans in their constituency. Indeed, this is immobilizing the ANC in that province, with the National Party capitalizing on the ANC's impotence regarding the contradictions in its support base in this province.

Mutatis mutandis a white reactionary response is possible if the ethnically neutral state is perceived and experienced as a de facto black-dominated and -manipulated state. The challenge to the new ANC masters is to remain true to their ideal of a non-racial state with which all ethnic communities can identify. The debate and struggle for control of the Jacobin faction in the ANC versus the old time liberal pluralists will be crucial in deciding the ethnic neutrality of the state, in contrast to an ethnically dominated central state.

Will Economic Pragmatism Preclude Ethnic Mobilization?

An elegant argument that economic pragmatism will preclude ethnic mobilization in South Africa is put forward by Heribert Adam. He argues that precisely because of its history of minority domination and extreme racial discrimination, together with an interdependent economy and interspersed population, South Africa is "well on the way toward eradicating tribalism in favor of common statehood." He cites the following evidence: the main parties (ANC, IFP, NP) promote an inclusive South African nationalism. The exclusivists from right and left, the Conservative Party, Pan African Congress and the Azanian Peoples Organization, are relatively insignificant minorities. He finds acceptance by the main players that the institutions of a future South Africa will have to reflect the state's ethnic diversity. And South Africa's people confront each other as equals. The blacks are not the detribalized slaves of the United States, while the whites have no other homeland and do not see themselves as settlers (*pace* PAC).[19]

Adam admits that there is no South African nation at present but he is sanguine about its development in the future. Black and white South Africans will be able to celebrate their common South African-ness because both groups will benefit from unity. Compromise in South Africa is likely because all will be winners. In his view the fundamental cleavages in South Africa do not revolve around race or culture, but around social equality. Rather than ethnicity, it is class (jobs, income, property)—the material conditions of life—that matters most to all South Africans: "The chances of a future South African democracy and stability do not falter on incompatible identities but *depend mainly on the promise of greater material equality in a common economy*" (emphasis added).[20]

Should one accept that there is nothing primordial or inevitable about ethno-nationalism in divided societies, as Adam argues so eloquently, some of the possible future developments in South Africa's economy should be anticipated. For it is the ability of the economy to deliver "greater material equality" that will, in Adam's labor, preclude South Africa from being swooped up in a vortex of violent and divisive ethno-nationalism.

In South Africa, as in other capitalist societies, economic power and privilege have been concentrated in the hands of a few. The gap between white and black wealth in South Africa is one of the most inequitable in the world. The Gini coefficient, an indicator of the distribution of wealth, in South Africa moves along an index of *circa* 0.68 compared to a Gini of *circa* 0.4 - 0.45 for developed Western societies. Even comparable societies such as that of Brazil and Mexico, have Gini's of *circa* 0.53. The redress of this inequality will be the major challenge of a democratic South Africa in the next 50-odd years.

It would technically be possible to identify no more than 400 white members of the South African parastatal and business elite who are effectively the controllers of well over 80 percent of the economy as a whole. This concentration, together with the expansion of communications capacities, has increased the ability of South African capital to influence events to suit their purposes. In the global economy capital has become extremely mobile, to such an extent that South Africa can and has been threatened by withdrawal by local as well as overseas capitalist interests. This threat was effectively carried out during the so-called debt stand-still between 1986-1994. The same threat was used against the nationalization policies of the African National Congress and has been used against the GNU. The so-called Mexico phenomenon of January 1995, when global investment capital abandoned Mexico and forced down the value of the *peso*, is a further illustration of the mobility of global capital. But it goes further than this. The mobility of capital is likely to be a threat against the workers of South Africa as well: should they "price themselves out of the market" the threat would be that international and local capital will take their investments to more profitable societies, for instance in the Pacific Rim States. As things stand at the moment, South African labor costs compare unfavourably with that in the Pacific Rim states, which have better technically trained, and at present more docile, workers.

It is clear that a more equitable political economy, needed to stabilize a future democratic South Africa, will be at fundamental odds with the tenets of a Hong Kong-style unfettered free-market economy. There is a cardinal contradiction between the needs of unimpeded profit-driven private enterprise and the need to improve the conditions of life of the poor members of South African society. Business and economic leaders have been putting heavy pressure on the South African GNU for minimal regulation and maximum profits. Moreover, the international context of capitalism is such that the threat of "divestment" from the South African economy is ever-present. There is currently no coherent international agency to regulate world economic affairs. More than the international political system, the international economic system is a Hobbessian *homo homini lupus*.

The type of economic system that present-day free marketeers strive for, one of maximal competition and minimal state interven-tion, can but have deleterious and nefarious side effects on the South African political economy. The "buy low, sell high" dictum that is the organizing metaphor of the free market ultimately and logically must lead either to a clamor for monopolistic protection or to product degradation. In South Africa business already receives ample protection from the government. The side effects of continued local oligopolism on the South African human population would be that present inequalities will be continued and that the major issue and conflict in South Africa will be resource-based and clad in race and color. This would not augur well for the future, particularly for nation-building.

In the global context the new South African government finds itself in a decidedly capitalist-dominated environment in which the national economy will be under pressure. The role of multinational capital will put into stark focus the economic inadequacies of the state. Should the South African government become unable to provide the two most basic functions of a state: differential treatment of its citizens against the outside world and their protection, it will be seriously weakened. For there would be no reason to expect the continued allegiance of its citizens to an institution that fails them. Under such circumstances the economically most powerful group in the country (the whites and their class allies among the other race groups) would threaten either to leave or to take over the state by force.

South Africa is heavily dependent on international trade (*circa* 60 percent of its Gross Domestic Product) and direct foreign investment for economic expansion. Its overreliance on gold as a foreign exchange earner (*circa* 33 percent of total export sales) makes it vulnerable to foreign economic pressure as well as the general state of the global economy. Moreover, the present free enterprise policies of the World Bank and the International Monetary Fund, which are now followed in South Africa, will force the South African government to keep to fairly strict free-market oriented monetary and fiscal policies. Failing this, little international aid will flow to South Africa. It is also clear that the *deus ex machina* of wealthy Japanese investors or conscience-stricken American and European philanthropic foundations will not be economic saviors of poor South Africans. Thus the South African government does not have many economic options outside a free-market oriented economy.

Accepting the hypothesis that egalitarian policies would in general benefit all South Africans by stabilizing its new democratic institutions, the capacities of the state and its socialized parastatal enterprises should be utilized to benefit all of South Africa's population, especially the poorer black section, in order to facilitate greater economic egalitarianism. This argument does not mean that an economy can be centrally planned and directed. This is a logical and epistemological impossibility. The thesis is simply that South Africa's so called "public sector" has an enormous capacity to improve the lives of its (mainly) black impoverished citizens. Responsible management of this sector is a *sine qua non* for South Africa's future well being.

The Crime Rate

South Africa at present is going through a phase of grave public concern regarding the crime rate. The figures regarding violent as well as white-collar crime are shocking: In a populace of 40 million, 18,000 murders, 20,000 attempted murders, 44,000 drug-related offences, 55,000 cases of fraud, 95,000 vehicle thefts, 96,000 robberies, 276,000 burglaries, 7,000 cases of arson and 157,000 serious assaults were reported in 1994. Moreover, police claim that there are 278 organized crime syndicates in South Africa, the majority of which specialize in serious crimes such as drug-dealing, vehicle thefts and illegal trade in endangered animal and plant species. Likewise South Africa is under-policed by international standards, with less than two police officers per 1000 of the population. The Police Service was delegitimized by its application of apartheid laws in the past and is seriously understaffed and poorly paid—leading to significant figures of fraud and rogue officers in the police service. The black people of South Africa bear the brunt of serious and violent crimes, while the richer whites are victims of burglaries and motor vehicle theft. Crime has become one of the most salient issues among foreign investors when contemplating direct foreign investment in South Africa. There are no short-term answers or quick fixes regarding the so-called crime problem in South Africa. The Government is acutely aware of the problem and ongoing attention is being given to the issue. Among others: a larger police budget, restructuring and demilitarizing the police, civilian control over the police force, retraining of police officers, specific anti-crime drives in large cities, anti-corruption units and the Office of Serious Economic crimes, prison reform, inner city business fora to combat crime in specific crime-ridden areas, and the list could be continued. The fight against crime will be a continuing issue until such time as South Africa's economic performance over time has increased significantly and the police and justice systems overhauled and made more efficient to prevent "crime from paying." South Africans are going to have to live with this issue and take a greater part in protecting their assets and their persons.

The Role of the Church in Overcoming the Divisions

I am not qualified to write on the role of a religious institution like "the Church" in overcoming the deep divisions of South African society. There is no guarantee that religious institutions or the religiosity of their followers can facilitate peace in a deeply divided society. Some evidence points the other way: conflicts in history as well as in the present time have quite often been religiously inspired and legitimated. The examples are well known: the medieval Christian crusades against Islam, the Catholic Inquisition against Protestants and apostate Catholics, the 30 Years' War (1618-1648) in Europe, the present conflict in Northern Ireland, the Bosnian conflict, Chechnya in Russia, the Islam-Hindu conflict in India in 1948 which threatens to revive at present, and so on *da capo al fine*. In South Africa apartheid was given moral legitimacy and credence by the three Afrikaans Reformed "sister" churches.

What can be said is that the Dutch Reformed Church (NGK), the largest single denomination among Afrikaners (38 percent of Afrikaners nominally are NGK members), and her sister churches, the *Hervormde* as well as *Gereformeerde* Churches, can play a conciliatory role by accepting and confessing, as the institutional successors to earlier synods, to the wrongs they supported by giving moral credence to the apartheid policies of the National Party Governments since 1948. These churches, however, face a practical and material dilemma. At present they are the only really well-institutionalized cultural networks left in which their Afrikaans adherents find spiritual solace. Many Afrikaners still do not accept that the Churches should "confess on their knees" regarding their role in the apartheid era. Many still perceive apartheid as a well meaning, benign, though paternalistic, attempt to regulate racial conflict, to Christianize, educate and "develop" the black tribes of South Africa. (I use this terminology advisedly in an analytic sense to connote the meaning attached to apartheid by some Afrikaners.) Confessing to the sin of apartheid would mean to many Afrikaners that their last Afrikaans institution has been sullied by grovelling before the new political order. The General Synodal Commission of the NG Church decided in the week of 31 October 1996 "that the time was not ripe to make a submission to the Truth and Reconciliation Commission." Spokesmen for the *Gereformeerde* as well as *Hervormde* Churches respectively said that their churches were not planning any confessions to the TRC.[21]

In January 1997 the National Synod of the *Gereformeerde Kerke* in Potochefstroom decided not to make an "apartheid confession of guilt" and, instead, to refer the matter of guilt and confession regarding apartheid back to the constituent congregations of the Church. The National Synod of 1991 did however declare apartheid as a sin. Ironically a local congregation of this church in the Northern Province town of Nylstroom refused to admit a black member of the church to become a member of the congregation. (He was a member of a black congregation of the *Gereformeerde Kerk* in another town, but had moved to Nylstroom.) So much for the local congregation's actions.

The official journal of the NG Church, *Die Kerkbode (The Church Messenger)*, reiterated in an editorial at the beginning of 1997 that churches would have to rethink their attitude to the Truth Commission in the light of some of the *fauxs pas* committed by members of this Commission, in particular by its deputy chairman, Dr. Alex Boraine. It is clear that the church is sceptical of the conciliatory role of the TRC, and its attitude clearly delegitimizes the TRC in the eyes of ordinary Afrikaans members.[22]

Moreover, the actions of the liberation movement during the struggle, among other things to target military strongpoints in civilian areas and to argue that innocent people inevitably get hurt in such crossfire, strengthens the attitude of many Afrikaners that neither party (NP or ANC) is blameless of human rights abuses. Likewise the fact that the ANC as well as the PAC sought military and material solace from the Communist bloc during the struggle

fills many white, Christian South Africans with scepticism regarding their commitment to liberal democratic values. The ANC's
intellectual commitment towards abolition of the death penalty and
abortion on demand goes against the moral sensitivities of these
white Christians who hold conservative opinions on such matters.
In their opinion these are grave moral wrongs which mitigate
against the new political leadership's commitment towards "human
rights." The attitude of leading ANC personalities that the mis-
deeds perpetrated during the struggle were part of a just war is
neither helpful nor constructive. NP Leaders are complaining that
the Truth and Reconciliation Commission is one-sided in its deal-
ings with the past and that it has thus far neglected human rights
abuses by the liberation movement.[23]

And so one could go on supplying argument and counter-
argument. A heartfelt confession regarding apartheid may well tear
the Afrikaans churches apart, leading many of the faithful to join
other churches, the obvious one being the *Afrikaanse Protestantse
Kerk,* which is Calvinist Dutch Reformed in confession, but bla-
tantly an exclusive church for white Afrikaners. A full confession,
an earnest and sincere expression of regret and guilt by the three
established Afrikaans Churches will almost certainly lead to a conciliatory attitude from the black community. I am not convinced
that the church leadership is ready for such a move. Professor
Adrio König recently admonished the NGK-leadership for not
confessing and expressing their genuine and unqualified regret at
the pain caused by apartheid.[24] Public confession of sin is, in any
case, not a particularly well-established tradition in Calvinism.

Japanese governments since 1945 have found it hard to apologize to the East Asian nations for the atrocities of World War II,
only issuing a guarded apology three years ago. The Afrikaner
political order was not defeated in a devastating war. The rapprochement between black and white led by de Klerk and Mandela
followed a perception and judgment that a war about South
Africa's future would be futile and unwinnable for either side. The
Afrikaner establishment attitude in my judgment is that it has
conceded power to the ANC peacefully and orderly and that no
further apology is necessary. In their opinion, the human rights
abuses of the of the past are much regretted, but the ANC is not
entirely blameless for having opted for the armed struggle and

allying itself with Communist regimes. The future is seen as more important than the past and it is felt that bygones should be bygones. That is not the attitude of the black elite. They see the apartheid policies of the past as a crime against humanity and hold that a full confession of guilt by the NP-Afrikaner-white establishment is indispensable before the past can be forgiven.[25] The Truth and Reconciliation Commission was set up to accomplish just that task. It is not entirely clear at present, March 1997, whether such a full confession of guilt will be forthcoming from either the present political or religious Afrikaans leadership. This issue may well haunt South Africa for a generation of more. Adolescent whites already disclaim responsibility for apartheid as the "sins of their parents." The next generation of Afrikaans church and political leaders may well be the ones to express a full and sincere expression of guilt and sorrow regarding apartheid. During that period, much can go wrong in South Africa.

Conclusion

This essay has alluded to the deep divisions in South African society and to some of the structural conditions that are affected by and mutually reinforce these divisions. The question is whether these divisions could be managed in order to keep South Africa from tearing itself apart. There is some reason to be sanguine. The inclusivity of the political settlement, the fact that a constitutional compromise could be negotiated between the major contenders for power by themselves, and even-handed leadership at crucial junctures during the past seven years are positive indicators for a unified future. South Africa is fortunate that the main parties to the settlement are well-institutionalized with considerable depth of leadership. The constitutional machinery provided for—namely an interim grand coalition, proportional representation, some form of segmental autonomy for conservative Afrikaners through the *Volkstaatraad*, the semi-federal nature of the constitution to accommodate regional interests, special majorities to amend the constitution and the Constitutional Court to safeguard individual and cultural rights—all augur well for a cohesive future. President Mandela's magnanimity in victory and his concerted efforts at peacemaking are felicitous circumstances surrounding the beginning of South Africa's search for a democratic political order.

As the essay highlighted, the road to unity will not be smooth. The role of the Afrikaans churches in effecting reconciliation seems weak. The many deep divisions of South African society cannot be healed overnight. The main hindrance to unity, in my judgment, and as argued above, will not be the extraordinary ideological, party political, racial and cultural differences in South Africa. The main obstacle to be overcome will be to obtain more equitable distribution of material resources. If we accept the thesis that national unity and non-racialism will depend on specific germane material circumstances, the political leadership should focus on restructuring the conditions of material distribution in South Africa. It has been pointed out above that predominantly free-market economic policies would exacerbate the conflict. It would create material conditions of inequality unsuitable for racial conflict regulation. The point is simply this: the normative commitment of any South African political economy cannot be unfettered free marketism. It has to be a commitment towards fostering economic equality. This will, in my judgment, create the conditions of greater material equality and lead to democratic stability. If the economy cannot deliver the material needs of South African society, the alternative will not bear contemplation.

NOTES

1. Anton Harber and Barbara Ludman (editors), *A-Z of South African Politics* (Johannesburg: Penguin 1994), p. 296.
2. See Theda Skocpol, "Old Regime Legacies and Communist Revolutions in Russia and China," in Jack Goldstone (editor), *Revolutions* (New York: Harcourt, 1986), pp. 218-238.
3. Harber *et al.*, *op. cit.*, pp. 282, 283.
4. Johannesburg, *Star*, 17 June 1994.
5. Johannesburg, *Sunday Times*, 19 June 1994.
6. Johannesburg, *Star*, 16 June 1994.
7. Cf. R.W. Johnson in *Focus Letter, Helen Suzman Foundation*, No. 4, October 1996, p. 5.
8. Johannesburg, *Mayibuye*, June 1994.
9. In September 1992 a record of understanding between the ANC and the de Klerk government was reached to bring forward the stalled negotiations between the two parties. Buthelezi accused the two parties of "ganging up against the IFP."

10. Johannesburg, *Rapport*, 14 January 1996
11. Johannesburg, *Star*, 15 June 1994.
12. Personal briefing by Mandela to the author, Pretoria, 28 November 1995.
13. Johannesburg, *Beeld*, 8 June 1994.
14. Johannesburg, *Sunday Times*, 19 June 1994.
15. Johannesburg, *Beeld*, 31 August 1993.
16. Johannesburg, *Rapport*, 4 December 1995.
17. Johannesburg, *Beeld*, 10 June 1994.
18. David Brown, "Ethnic Revival: Perspectives on State and Society," *Third World Quarterly*, October 1989.
19. Heribert Adam, "Nationalism, Nation Building and Non-Racialism," in Nic Rhoodie, *et al.* (editors), *Democratic Nation-Building* (Pretoria: HSRC-Publishers, 1994), pp. 37-51.
20. *Ibid.*, p. 49.
21. Cf. *Beeld*, 1 November 1996.
22. Cf. *Beeld*, 31 January 1997.
23. Cf. *Beeld*, 1 November 1996.
24. *Beeld*, 15 November 1996.
25. *Beeld*, 12 October 1996.

Religion and Democracy in South Africa:

Can Religion Facilitate the Cause of Democracy in South Africa?

L. D. Jafta
University of South Africa

To what extent is the South African government democratic and what role can religion play in a democratic South Africa? It is my position that Western models of democracy have their values and are to be appreciated, but there also is a form of democracy emanating from African soil. This form of African democracy has a contribution to make, more especially because traditional African world view does not separate between the religious and the secular spheres. My answer to the question whether or not religion has a role to play is positive. I believe that religion facilitates the cause of democracy, provided that religion is rightfully used.

There are many faces of democracy. Which best suits South Africa? The model of democracy which emanated from the Greek City States had its own limitations, especially regarding women, foreigners and children. Although it was the basis of and influenced the formation of democracies in the rest of the world, it had glaring weaknesses.

In his book *Democracy: Prospects for South Africa*, J. N. Cloete describes eight models of democracy in the world as follows: direct democracy, representative democracy, participatory democracy, social democracy, consociational democracy, liberal democracy, people's democracy and pluralist democracy. Cloete describes how these forms of democracy function in the world and how they differ from each other. It is beyond the scope of this paper to analyze them. The interesting thing about all of them is that no one is altogether satisfactory. Nevertheless, compared to non-democratic forms of government, democracy is still preferable. Sir Winston Churchill is reported to have said that democracy tops all forms of government, and the next to democracy is a distant second.

The religious principles of the sixteenth-century Reformation are the foundation of the modern democracies. While Christianity cannot be equated with democracy per se, Protestant religious principles were the building blocks of modern democracy. The Calvinistic emphasis on the sovereignty of God, which can be described as the point of departure for the Reformed tradition, is foundational for democracy. The sovereignty and Providence of God, which are so basic in the formulation of the American constitution, are a typical example of this Protestant doctrine.

The following paragraphs discuss the concept of the sovereignty of God and the ramifications of that concept for other religions. Law, it will be seen, is not a prerogative of any one person. It is the gift of God to humanity and must be handled as such.

There are many Reformed Tradition Christians in South Africa. If they can take their roots seriously once more, the young democracy in South Africa will have many supporters. Democracy, as we know it today, is rooted in the awareness of an Almighty God who creates all human beings equal. A renewed awareness of that God can make democracy work. It is in the light of this awareness of the Creator God that I argue that religion can facilitate the cause of democracy.

The other doctrine to which both Catholics and Protestants subscribe, which is foundational for democracy, is the doctrine of original sin. According to this doctrine, no human being is perfect. No one, therefore, can make correct decisions alone. The king, the chief, the president, etc., are as greedy, egocentric, power hungry as anybody else. In the light of this doctrine, democracy is good government.

The doctrine of the Revelation of God also supports democracy. According to this doctrine, God revealed and continues to reveal Himself to us. Governments, with all their imperfections, are orders of creation, a revelation of God. The imperfections themselves reveal that we are finite beings and that there is an infinite one who is not like us.

The relevance of the doctrines mentioned above to democracy must not lead the reader into thinking that without them there would be no democracy. As indicated before, the Greek City State did practice a form of direct democracy. The British Industrial Revolution influenced the birth of democracy. It is, therefore, safe to say that religion did not start democracy but historically influenced it.

Professor William Makgoba, in a Sunday *Times* article, poses serious questions on the integrity of Western democracy. He argues that liberal democracy is not suitable for South Africa because it is based on European culture. Makgoba opts for a democracy based on African values, particularly the concept of *UBUNTU*. Makgoba argues that the Western liberal type of democracy tends to ignore other groups' values and cultures. Makgoba further argues that Western liberal democracy is not suitable for South Africa because it was conceived in countries where there were not as many cultures as there are in Africa.

Democracy from the Traditional African Perspective

The traditional African worldview has a contribution to offer to this debate on democracy. There is in traditional African society a continuum between democracy and kingship or chieftainship. The patriarchal, African lifestyle extends from the family unit through the extended family to the community. The chief, in fact, is an extension of the family father. But family decisions not taken solely by the father, though theoretically he is the one who decides. The same procedure applies to the chief. The mother has a very powerful role, though mainly in the background. Such an influence can be more powerful than the one in front. Thus patriarchy should not be taken as absolute domination by the father of the family. Neither should the voice of the chief be taken as absolute. It is with this background that African democracy must be understood.

Issues affecting the community are first discussed at the community level in a small *imbizo* (community meeting). Beyond that is the tribal *imbizo*, where anyone is free to express himself as long as he or she adheres to the tribal rules of debate and acknowledges the tribal customs and taboos. A typical example of this is found in the famous novel *Ityala Lamawele* by S. E. K. Mqhayi which has been televised recently.

The role of the king or chief is unique. Like a bishop in the early church, the king, who always inherits the position, is the symbol of unity. There is an aura of oneness emanating from him which binds his people together. This is the most important role of the king and this is the reason heredity is taken so seriously.

The traditional African worldview is obviously religious. Professor John Mbiti[1] humorously says that "Africans are notoriously religious." There is no separation of the sacred and the secular. All life is undergirded by religion. The chief is both political and religious. Kingship itself is a divine office. In the novel *Ityala Lamawele*, which has already been alluded to, the author, Mqhayi, writes:

> Yivani sizwe sinibaliselie. Ngemihla yakudala
> mini kwavelintaba, kwabekw'umntu wamnye woku
> phatabanye. Kwathiwa ke lomntu ngumntu wegazi,
> Kwathiwa loo mntu yinkonyane yohlanga, Kwathiwa
> loo mntu makathotyelwe luluntu. Aze athi yena
> athobele u Qamata. Apho kuya kuvela imitheto nez-
> imiselo, Ayakuth 'akuzigwenxa, kungalelelani Kube
> ziziphiti - phiti nokuphambana koluntu
> Ibe nguqulukubhode ukuphambana komhlaba.[2]

Translation:

> Listen, countrymen, let us tell you of the olden days when mountains were created. One person was installed to rule over others and that person was called the Calf of the Nation. And it was

decided that person would be obeyed by everyone, and he in turn obey Qamata, where laws and regulations would be promulgated, and disobedience to them would cause havoc and confusion.

Mqhayi's poem reveals much in terms of traditional African governance. While the poem basically relates to the Xhosa ethnic group, the sentiments expressed in it extend to all African ethnic groups. The chief referred to is hereditary (*wegazi*). He is the son of the people who must be obeyed by everybody. He, in turn, must obey Qamata (name of the Deity). All rules and regulations ultimately come from Qamata. What this means is that kings, chiefs and councillors are basically mediators for Qamata. If the kings fail to obey the Deity, only confusion will result.

What is important in the governance just described is that there is a healthy relationship between the office of the king/chief and the lower levels of society. The king maintains the dignity and the unity of the kingdom in his person. The divinity of his office extends to his personality. The kingdom is wrapped and symbolized in him. On the other hand, democracy is allowed to take place because he never decides alone. There are also diviners (*izanuse*) and the medicine men (*amagqirha*) who constantly advise the king in the execution of his duties. Not the least are the ancestors (the living dead) who continue to be invisible advisors.

In the traditional African worldview described above, religion has the most important role to play. It fosters morality. There are ethical codes, undergirded by religion, which must be obeyed. The religious awe around the king is because the king himself respects the Deity, as we are made aware in Mqhayi's poem. The new South Africa can learn something here, i.e., that when the president of the country takes his or her religion seriously, issues of morality will be treated with the dignity they deserve. A multi-cultural society like South Africa requires a symbol of unity which will make every cultural group feel at home.

Between the traditional African kingship and democracy there is a continuum which can be a model for South African democracy. While running away from rigid autocratic kingship, we must be careful not to land into a loose democracy where everyone irresponsibly does what one wants to do, irrespective of the feelings and aspirations of others. We do not want irresponsible democracy, neither do we want autocracy. The traditional African continuum, therefore, makes sense and there is much to learn from it.

The ancestors, who have been alluded to in passing, are guardians of the tradition from the past through the present and into the future. They are consulted when serious decisions have to be taken. Needless to say, that continuity from the past to the present is vital for every generation. We do not build from a vacuum. Ancestors are a reminder of our past and our future. But in the African tradition, it is in the religious atmosphere that these living dead are evoked. The diviner and the medicine men are mediators between the living and the living dead.

Traditional African worldview is undergirded by *UBUNTU*—a difficult concept to define. Among other things, this concept means kindness, humaneness, godliness, compassion, understanding, etc. Individuality is superseded by the sense of belonging to a community, to others. You are, because there are others. If South African democracy can take this African concept of *UBUNTU* seriously, we all would be living in a safe, just and friendly environment. Our young democracy would not only be responsible, it would also be godly.

Monitoring and Protesting the Abuses of Power

"Power corrupts and absolute power corrupts absolutely" (Lord Acton, 1834 -1901). History is replete with abuses of power from all classes of society. People want to cling to power by all means possible. Power hunger cuts across racial, sexual and cultural boundaries.

In pre-colonial times, African ethnic groups vied for power and were involved in internecine wars in order to have control over other groups. In South Africa this led to the so-called Mfecane or Difaqane wars in which powerful groups defeated the weaker ones.

The arrival of the colonial powers crystallized the human hunger for power. Through the barrel of the gun Africans were dispossessed of their land from the seventeenth century onwards. Through false treaties which were agreed upon and signed when one of the parties to the treaty was unaware of the implications of the treaty, the race to power started resulting in the dispossession of the land of those who were nòt familiar with treaties. The 1948 elections which placed the National Party on top were won by power-hungry people who, once they assumed power, maintained it by all means possible. The entire apartheid system was uncontrolled hunger for power at the expense of basic human rights. That story is well documented and does not need to be elaborated here. The issue before us is: How do we avoid apartheid atrocities being repeated in the New South Africa? How can abuse of power be prevented from happening and what signs should we look for when there is suspicion of the abuse of power?

Monitoring the use of power and protesting against its abuse is the responsibility of all South Africans. A democratically elected government is responsible and accountable to all who voted for it. In spite of minor discrepancies here and there, the 1994 South African elections were declared to be fair and free. The democratic government is, therefore, in place. The preamble[3] to the constitution of South Africa which was adopted by the constitutional Assembly in May 1996 prepares all South Africans for a democratic future.

> We, the people of South Africa,
>> recognise the injustices of the past,
>> honour those who suffered for justice
>>> and freedom in our land,
>> respect those who have worked to build
>>> and develop our country,
>> believe that South Africa belongs to all
>> who live in it, united in our diversity.
> We, therefore, through our freely elected
>> representatives, adopt this constitution
>> as the supreme law of the Republic so as to
>> heal the divisions of the past and establish
>> a society based on democratic values, social
>> justice and fundamental human rights;
>> lay the foundations for a democratic and
>> open society in which government is based on
>> the will of the people and every citizen is
>> equally protected by law;
>> improve the quality of life for all citizens
>> and free the potential of each person
>> build a united and democratic South Africa

able to take its rightful place as a sovereign
state in the family of nations.
May God protect our people.

While this constitution does not purport to be religious, every
line of it can be said to be grounded on religious principles. There
is nothing in it which can be described as irreligious. Words like
"democratic" and "injustice," which appear more than once, are,
of course, secular words with religious connotations. The last sentence, "May God protect our people," is obviously religious. The
chief executive officer in every nation is like the defender of the
constitution, irrespective of his or her religious or non-religious
position.

The American constitution is an interesting study. When
Thomas Jefferson was president of the United States, his church-
manship was questionable, yet Jefferson was very aware of a
Supreme Being on whom the American constitution was grounded.
Jefferson believed in the laws of nature, which are God-given, and
in the basic human rights which are given to everybody. Denial of
those rights, in Jefferson's theory, is tantamount to denying God
himself. "We hold these truths to be self evident...," so says the
American constitution. One does not necessarily need a formal
teaching to know that one has these rights. The inscription on the
American coin, "in God we trust," is consistent with the ethos of the
constitution.

The South African constitution, on the other hand, is not as
overtly religious as the American one. But one cannot miss the religious ethos behind the words. The anthem, as has been said
already, is religious. The role of religion also is built in the constitution itself. Religion must protect and promote the South
African constitution as long as that constitution is upholding basic
human rights. It is common knowledge that God was invoked in
the struggle to dismantle apartheid. That same God must also be
invoked in the defense of the South African constitution and the
democratic principles it upholds. The presence of a number of
clergy in national and provincial governments is applauded, albeit
with reservations. It is good to have such men and women where
laws are made and where religious principles are needed. One
wonders, however, if the Constantinian church in which the

religious principles were compromised in order to foster selfish political aims, is not brought in through the back door. The parliamentary procedures, language and remunerations can very easily compromise the religious language and turn the prophet into an oppressor. The larger religious body must watch out for false prophets who, in the name of the struggle, find themselves in chambers where national laws are made but have lost accountability to the grassroots.

Facilitating Reconciliation and Conciliation

This is the most opportune time for religious bodies to reconcile and engage the citizens of South Africa. The Truth and Reconciliation Committee is already in place, although there are suspicions from both left and right whether such a committee will achieve the desired results. It is believed that after the revelations have been made and evil doers exposed, those offended will forgive the offenders and thus reconciliation will take place. The offenders not only fear the reprisals of those offended but feel that the Truth Committee is witch hunting, more especially those who worked in the previous government in order to achieve political gains. This is, however, only a perception from those who fear being called to appear before the commission. The reservations of those offended are that if the offenders are not punished, the ends of justice will not be met; that the culprits will go free after the confessions have been made and amnesty given to those labeled as political offenders in the old dispensation. Does it meet the ends of justice to allow such perpetrators of evil to go free, even if they have made confessions? How does reconciliation take place between the offenders who are still benefiting from the fruits of the racist laws and the offended who are suffering loss of loved ones, property and financial support? True reconciliation can only happen amongst equals. This means that those who were deprived through the operations of the offenders, must be compensated by those offenders. When financial and social egalitarianism has been achieved, then reconciliation can take place.

Conciliation is a step beyond reconciliation. When former enemies have been reconciled, then they must conciliate. They need to be brought together and made to learn how to live together and to respect one another. Previously, they were far apart, not necessarily in terms of proximity but in terms of accepting one another as human beings. The biblical concept of neighbor goes beyond the next door neighbor to any human being in God's world.

There are areas in South Africa where young people, on their own, started a reconciliation process even before the Government of National Unity came into being. The Imbali Reconciliation, Rehabilitation and Reconstruction program which was started by young people in the late eighties when violence in Natal was at its height, is a typical example of such a venture. Religious bodies can support such ventures.

A number of people in parliament, liberation movements, political parties, guerrilla gangs, including thousands of people who cannot be religiously labeled, are affiliates of religious groups. Religion can appeal to the conscience of all these people and awaken the righteous anger in them.

But reconciliation without restitution is a non starter. That is what Bonhoeffer calls cheap grace. A meaningful reconciliation for South Africa must be accompanied by restitution, more especially that of the land to offset the growing menace of squatter camps. There cannot be true reconciliation until people's land has been restored to them. In his article on "The Significance of Land in the Old Testament," Gunther Wittenberg[4] described the value of land for the Israelites:

> ...land is the inheritance of the fathers; it is the property which was handed from generation to generation as symbolised by the family tomb. It provides for the basic foundation for the life of Israel's peasant community.

The majority of blacks in South Africa are peasants, some of whom live in remote rural areas. Land and livestock are all they have. To deprive them of their land, as chief Albert Luthuli once said, is like depriving them of their soul. No true reconciliation can take place in South Africa until this land has been brought back to its rightful owners.

There are at least three types of reconciliation required for the New South Africa. The first one concerns races. The previous regime emphasized racial differences. Racial superiority was deeply entrenched in the minds of the whites, while the opposite was true of the blacks. Some blacks still believe that they are racially inferior to whites.

The second dimension that should be in the agenda of religious groups is political tolerance. The political conflicts between the ANC and the IFP prior to the 1994 elections were unnecessarily violent. This was partly due to political ignorance and partly due to the third force, which not only facilitated the conflicts but also rejoiced in perpetrating them. People's political choices must be respected. It is everybody's democratic right to live where one wants to be and to vote for the party of one's choice. Political defeat must be welcomed with humility.

The third dimension of reconciliation borders around what can be called tribal conflicts. This, however, must be seen in the light of the political conflicts. The continent of Africa, which has over 800 tribes, has experienced this problem. The unrest in Rwanda, which resulted in numerous refugees, deaths and displacements, was exacerbated by tribal differences and greed for power.

In all the three cases enumerated above, religion has a role to play. The political and tribal conflicts can be dealt with by appealing to the African concept of *UBUNTU*. This is a religious and secular term with various shades of meaning, e.g., goodness, divinity, compassion, love, etc.

Transformation of Institutions, Policies and Values

The introduction of the Government of National Unity and the process of agreeing upon a new constitution which, we believe, embraces democratic principles, are only the beginning of a long road to democracy. Transformation goes beyond reformation. What is required in South Africa is a complete overhaul of all structures. If South Africa only reforms, it will only be patching as if one is pouring new wine in old wine skins. There is nothing reformable in the old apartheid structures which were nationally and internationally condemned by people of good will.

Transformation means going back to the drawing board by all the parties concerned, to jointly determine the rules of the game and to agree on the parameters and duration of the game. The stake holders on the drawing board meet as equals and with mutual respect. The inequalities of the apartheid regime resulted in some people having access to better education and to financial resources which others did not have. To reverse that order means consciously elevating those who previously had no access to those resources. This means, in some cases, that normal procedures will be sidelined and that a deliberate choice of a black over a white candidate for an office will be made. This, of course, will cause an uproar, more especially if the white candidate has better qualifications. The motive behind this deliberate exercise is to redress the imbalances of the past.

Many South African whites slipped into the New South Africa without confessing their guilt in participating in the apartheid regime. They have had no remorse, no confession that they not only benefited but also consciously supported it and participated in a system designed to destroy others. The same whites want to compete with the disadvantaged people for positions in the New South Africa. If they are sensitive to the pain to which their fellow black South Africans were exposed, they would exercise caution when both races compete for the same positions.

Affirmative action is not racism in reverse, as some whites seem to suggest. It is rather a means towards an end. It is an attempt to correct the imbalances of the past. It is putting on the map those who previously were not on that map. It is a means, a method, a vehicle towards a goal.

Tertiary institutions like universities and technicons are educational institutions which desperately need transformation. Promotions and appointments in these institutions must be made in the light of affirmative action. Not so long ago, some positions in work places in South Africa were reserved for whites only. Many whites availed themselves of these opportunities and quickly climbed up the ladder and secured for themselves comfortable positions at the expense of their black brothers and sisters. How can blacks who did not have these privileges now be expected to favorably compete with their white counterparts using the same rules as if the situation had always been as it is now? This is what affirmative action is supposed to address.

But the transformation of institutions without transforming the policies governing those institutions is a fruitless exercise. The policies of the institutions must change to allow for the transformation to take place. It is not enough to say that the doors of the institutions are opened for all the citizens of the country and that the sky is the limit. It is not enough to say that the market is open to everybody. The reality is that those who were prepared by the previous government will run first to the market and get the best fish while those who were not prepared by the same government still have psychological hang ups about the market, let alone that they may not even have the fishing instruments. Apartheid damaged blacks' self esteem. It was drilled into their minds that they were inferior. The tendency for many blacks during the apartheid days was to take the back seat even if the front seat was vacant. This is the depth of the psychological damage.

Religion and the Transformation Process

The role of religion in this transformation process is to appeal to the consciences of the privileged and underprivileged. But the religious message to the privileged and the underprivileged is not the same, although they all lived in the same country. Their past histories were different. Their past experiences are different and they enter the New South Africa at different social levels. One knows white residential areas while the other knows township life. Religion must relate to these different realities and the message must be relevant. The Old Testament has numerous good examples of challenges to the rich and also relevant messages to the poor. The context is proper in each case. There is precision in the direction of the message. To the white person, religion must remind him/her of the privileges enjoyed in the past and that contrition, repentance and confession require restitution.

The appeal to conscience is religion's strongest weapon. It was conscience which troubled Martin Luther in the sixteenth century and which made the Reformation (in Europe) a success. Luther was first troubled by his own conscience. He could not sit and watch the problems of his day go unchallenged. He had a message for both the religious status quo and for the peasants of his day. Luther identified the religious status quo as the main source of the evils of his day. But the peasants were not perfect either. Their outbursts which resulted in them taking the law into their own hands angered the politically conservative Luther. The lesson South Africans should learn from Luther is first, that neither the privileged nor the underprivileged is perfect. They both need religion to appeal to their conscience. Luther's stand on this issue made him vulnerable from the peasants' side; he was already vulnerable from the religious status quo. Second, Luther attacked the problem at its source. Religiously motivated people should not be satisfied with secondary solutions. They should trace and attack primary sources of problems, even if it leads to confrontations.

Conclusion

The subtopic of this paper asked: "Can religion facilitate the cause of democracy?" The answer is positive. Religion can, and indeed, should facilitate the cause of democracy. The starting point is the sovereignty of the Deity to which all religions subscribe.

> All religions imply in one way or another that man does not, and cannot, stand alone, that he is vitally related with and even dependent on powers in nature and society external to himself. Dimly or clearly, he knows that he is not an independent center of force capable of standing apart from the world.[5]

It is clear from Noss' statement that religion, whether primitive or modern, expresses a deep yearning from humans not to stand alone but to be responsible and accountable to a Deity who is the ultimate owner of the cosmos. Rudolf Otto, in his famous study, *The Idea of the Holy*, bases the idea of the holy upon an encounter with what he describes as a *"mysterium et fascion"* and finds awareness of it in all religions. Whether the Deity is the creation of our minds, as Feuerbach would say, or exists in the form of a person to whom we can relate, or is in the form of a Spirit, is beside the point.

Human beings are basically threatened by seen and unseen forces and want a Deity on whom they can lean—a Being who runs the society with justice and who can subdue these threatening forces and thus make the society secure. The Deity may be remote and work with or through intermediaries, e.g., ancestors, kings, princes, rulers, presidents, etc.

This essay has concentrated on democracy as a form or type of government which South Africa has embraced since the last National elections. Imperfect as any form of government is, South

Africa has chosen the democratic route, which she considers to be the best. We need to be reminded of John H. Yoder[6]:

> Yoder's words in this regard that democracy is the best form of organisation, is true domestically for our society, and until something better comes up, I shall agree that it would be best for many other societies as well.

In a country experiencing rapid social changes like South Africa, religion may provide a feeling of security and assurance for many who need to be affirmed and assured. Neighborhoods which used to be white only, are now mixed. Schools which used to be white only, are now non-racial. Dividing walls have been pulled down in post offices, banks and buses. No South African can be excluded on the basis of color. Government policies are trying to be as inclusive as possible. These rapid changes pose many threats to whites who thought they would rule forever. Religion can, therefore, function as security. It can assure people that beyond the rapid changes there is a Deity who does not change. The awareness of that Deity can allay the fears and stabilize the society.

NOTES

1. J.S. Mbiti, *African Religions and Philosophy* (New York: Doubleday and Co., 1969), p. 1.
2. S.E.K. Mqhayi, *Ityala Lamawele* (Alice: Lovedale Press, 1914), p. 27.
3. Republic of South Africa, Constitutional Assembly as Adopted on May 1996, p. 2.
4. G.H. Wittenberg, "The Significance of Land in the Old Testament," in *The Journal of Theology for Southern Africa*, Dec. 1997, No. 77, pp. 58-59.
5. J.B. Noss, *Mans's Religions* (New York: Macmillan Publishers, 1974), p. 2.
6. J.H. Yoder, "Christianity and Democracy," in a symposium in *Center Journal*, Summer 1982, Vol. 1, No. 3, p. 83.

The Function of Islam in the South African Political Process:

Defining a Community in a Nation

Abdulkader Tayob
Department of Religious Studies
University of Cape Town
Rondebosch, South Africa

Islam in the political process in South Africa takes on two broad images. The first image regards Islam in South Africa as part of international religious resurgence in general, and fundamentalist Islam in particular. Since 1996, when an anti-crime organization like People against Gangsterism and Druglords (PAGAD) took Islamic symbols to the streets, this image has become dominant. South African intelligence reports connected the activity of the PAGAD to international Islamic militancy: "recent events in the Western Cape were in part driven by the phenomenon of Islamic militancy" which is "a hyper orthodox and distinct interpretation of the Islamic faith which is predisposed to the use of violence and subversion as a means to, firstly, impose certain religious beliefs, behavioral codes on all society; and secondly, challenge and ultimately seek to overthrow any non-Islamic political system

in order to establish a a theocracy based on their unique understanding of the concept."[1] An opposing thesis places Islam in
South Africa in the ranks of the liberation process. In this view,
barring a few exceptions, Muslims generally played a positive role
in the transformation of the country. As early as 1977, Nelson
Mandela visited the shrine of Shaykh Matura on Robben Island to
pay tribute to the role of Muslims in the struggle against colonialism and oppression. Since then, many scholars have highlighted
the role of Muslims in the liberation struggle. Without denying
the presence of collaborators and neutral fence-sitters, Lubbe reg-
istered a history of anti-colonial and anti-apartheid figures in
South African Muslim history: "both in terms of past involvement
and present protest, it is therefore clear that on the basis of the
very principles of Islam, Muslims are opposed to apartheid."[2]

Both these theses contribute to a particular understanding of
Islam in the political process in South Africa. Both, however,
seemed to place the history of Islam in the context of the dominant themes without an analysis of the processes within the religion. In this contribution, the role of Muslims in the political
process examines the discourses within the community on the
nation and its forms. I draw here on the idea that religion ought
to be regarded as a discourse by which religious actors fashion a
new world view out of the given elements within a religion.[3] Such
an approach focuses on the productive way in which religious actors interact, consciously and unconsciously, in the production of
approaches and orientations within religions. In this way, the
developments within Muslim society may then be appraised in
relation to the new nation. For the purpose of this paper, I intend
to examine how various groups among Muslims in South Africa
tried to construct relations between Muslims and the nation, and
Muslims and the new state. Such an examination shall highlight
two important facets of contemporary Muslim discourse. On the
one hand, it will illustrate the dynamic nature in which Muslims
construct an understanding of the Muslim community. Each
group or organization proposed a distinct conception of *ummah*,
the universal Islamic society, as well as its South African part. On
the other hand, the group or organization also posited a distinct
notion of the post-apartheid nation and state.

Islam and Nationalism

World religions like Islam tend to be regarded as potential threats to modern political formations in general and nationalism in particular. This is also true of Christianity and Buddhism, but the particular "nature" of Islam in the twentieth century makes this religion particularly suspect. Islam has a powerful concept of *ummah*, community spanning across race, language and ethnicity, which potentially threatened the nation and all patriotic sentiments. This essentialist notion has guided observation of political developments in Muslim societies. Thus, for example, Lewis described the dominant place of Islam as ideology in the pre-modern period: "descent, language, and habitation were all of secondary importance, and it is only during the last century that, under European influence, the concept of the political nation has begun to make headway."[4] According to Lewis, moreover, only the essential character of Islam appealed to the masses of Muslims in the modern world. Even before the rise of militant Islam, he declared that Islamic movements alone were authentic: "The religious orders alone spring from the native soil, and express the passions of the submerged masses of the population."[5] Needless to say, this observation suppressed or ignored the dynamics of pre-modern Islamic history, including the successive challenges to the caliphate by Persian, Turkish and regional sentiments. Another approach to illustrating the extreme contradictions between Islam and the modern nation is to search for justification in the life of the Prophet Muhammad, beyond the actual experience of Muslims in the past fourteen centuries. In this way, the researcher takes the place of the ideal Islamic jurist, and posits a possible reason why Muslims should be objecting to the idea of nation. Vatikiotis, in particular, followed this approach and found that the concept of the nation-state clashed with the Medina constitution where "ultimate authority or legitimacy for acts of the community rested not with the tribal chiefs as before, but with the one deity, Allah, and His Prophet, Muhammad."[6] Thus, he concludes, "the nation-state is...a concept alien to Islam."[7] Modern political developments are similarly brushed aside in order to unveil the "authentic" and "true" Islamic position. Schulze has correctly identified the *ummah* as a symbol in Arab politics, equally powerful as "a means for political order and orientation" in pan-Arabism and pan-Islamism.[8] However, most scholars take this to mean that no significant difference exists between twentieth-century invocation of Islam and that of the earlier caliphs. And even when contemporary Muslim scholars try to do so, their attempts are placed against the universal character of Islam. Nagel finds the Syrian Muhammad al-Mubarak's idea of multiple *umam* (plural of *ummah*) consisting of a variety of nations "not convincing because the message of the Prophet Muhammad from the beginning had a universal character, and Islam hinders the development of nation states while in opposition to Christianity, it wants also to establish power and state."[9] In one sweep, Nagel assumes essential characteristics for Islam and Christianity: the one universal and hungry for power, and the other not so in spite of centuries of perhaps misguided authority in the form of the Vatican. It is not surprising, therefore, that Nagel finds Mawdudi to be more representative of Islamic ideology.[10] According to Nagel, by rejecting the nation-state, Mawdudi and others ensure that the "original understanding of *ummah* continues to thrive, strengthened by the situation that a number of post-war international organizations were established."[11] Needless to say, such analyses relegate Muslim choices to the overpowering influence of a past, and the useless attempts of the present. Whatever they do, Muslims are condemned to live in the past. The fact of the matter, however, is that even the most eloquent advocates of this form of Islamic ideology have not been able to break the boundaries of the state set by recent colonial and post-colonial history. Forms of political organization, religious and otherwise, have been competing to define political entities in which people find themselves. The notion of an *ummah* is in this sense a powerful symbol of community which political groups invoke. Careful attention to the concept as invoked in the twentieth century reveals that the symbol is expected to bear the burdens of contemporary needs, and is thus subject to redefinition and re-invention. Thus, for better or worse, the Muslim brothers in many Arab countries remain identified with national bodies in spite of their common rhetoric of Islamic ideology. Similarly, Saudi Arabia, Pakistan and Iran, prominent representatives of Islamic political ideologies, remain divided and also generate intense 'national' symbols within their boundaries. The soccer and cricket teams of Saudi Arabia and Pakistan respectively are just two examples which define the national ethos of these countries in very dynamic ways.

The South African *Ummah*

During the past two decades, South Africa has gone through a period of rapid transformation. The momentum against apartheid increased from around the mid-seventies, and eventually led to political reforms and changes in 1990. After a period of intense negotiations, the first democratic elections in April 1994 ushered a new era for all the people of South Africa. Muslims in South Africa have been in this country for over 300 years, and they built institutions and communities in the context of colonialism and apartheid. Such institutions were generally concerned with the preservation of the Muslim identity, often very specifically located in the different regions, and often in the face of tremendous legal and social obstacles. Rituals and organizations strove to protect the Muslim in the face of these difficulties. The period of negotiations and the first democratic elections posed a number of challenges to such conceptualizations. The negotiations and elections changed the old political order, and thereby Muslims' relations with the state. It also raised questions about political values such as democracy, and the general leadership of the whole South African Muslim community. In one way or another, the new context provided an opportunity for Muslims to redefine the notion of *ummah* for themselves in South Africa. From 1990 onwards, Muslims across a broad spectrum organized extraordinary gatherings, and produced important documents to grapple with these notions. An analysis of these documents reveals some of the key dynamics of defining an *ummah* in South Africa at the end of the twentieth century. The following documents will be used in the analysis:

1. **The Struggle**, F. Esack (Cape Town: Call of Islam, 1988).
    This booklet was produced by the Call of Islam (est. 1984) wherein the author outlined an Islamic ethic against apartheid. Of particular concern was his grappling with the Muslim community which did not espouse the values of justice, and did not resist apartheid.

2. National Muslim Conference: Western Cape Convening Committee (1990)

The pamphlet prepared the groundwork for a national Muslim conference. It outlined the history of Muslim struggle against oppression in South Africa, and situated the challenges to democracy and negotiations for Muslims.

3. The MJC Speaks (1990)

The undated pamphlet by the Muslim Judicial Council, a group representing religious leaders in Cape Town, expressed its position in relation to celebrating the pilgrimage Id (Id al-Adha) with the pilgrims in Mecca. The importance of this document lies in the fact that the Council claimed to be the "most representative group of *ulama* in South Africa," a statement which was not only important in relation to ritual decisions but contemporary political ones as well.

4. "A Muslim Response to Albie Sach's 'To believe or not to believe'—the perils of the third option," by Imam A. Rashied Omar, pp. 49-52. In *Believers in the Future: Proceedings of the National Inter-faith Conference on Religion-State Relations, December 2-4 1990, Johannesburg* (Cape Town: WCRP, South African Chapter, 1991)

The author, Imam at the Claremont Main Road Mosque, reminded the conference of pluralism within religious traditions as well as non-religious ideologies. Secondly, he focused on the ambiguous record of religious tradition in relation to apartheid, and appealed for confessions from this quarter as well.

5. Islamic Workshop on "The Draft Declaration on the Rights and Obligations of Religious People," for October 25, 1992, by Qiblah

This pamphlet was produced by Qiblah, a prominent anti-apartheid organization which, however, has rejected democratic alternatives. It called Muslims to a discussion on a proposed document that would suggest a model relationship among religions, and between religious traditions and the state in the country. The workshop's announcement clearly rejected this document by pointing out some of the problems that "genuine religion" would not tolerate.

6. **"The Holy Grail of Democracy,"** *Ar-Rasheed*, vol. 1, no. 12 (Shabaan 1412/March 1992)

This editorial reflects on the West's acceptance of the coup in Algeria while supporting democratization elsewhere. Democracy, according to the editorial, was simply a convenient political tool for the subjugation of Muslims.

7. **"Transvaal and Natal Jamiat's Memo to Codesa,"** *Ar-Rasheed*, vol. 1, no. 12 (Shabaan 1412/March 1992)

The Transvaal and Natal Jamiats are regional guilds of religious scholars following the Deobandi religious outlook from India. The organizations excluded religious leaders from the Sunni Jamiat, as well as the eclectic Muslim Judicial Council. As representative of the Muslim community and its religious leaders, the Jamiats requested full observer status during the negotiations. They also took the opportunity to remind the negotiating teams of Muslims' rights and obligations towards the new nation.

8. **The Role of Muslims in the New South Africa**, Mohamed Shoaib Omar (1994)

Mr. Omar, a practicing attorney closely aligned to the Jamiat al-Ulama in Durban, wrote this essay outlining the two-fold responsibility of Muslims in the new South Africa. First, Muslims had a responsibility towards the transformation of the society, and second, an opportunity for maintaining their Islamic identity and spreading Islam.

9. **Sheikh Yusuf Tricentenary Commemoration Committee: Draft Mission Statement** (1994)

The committee, headed by social worker and community historian Achmat Davids, was responsible for a highly successful tricentenary celebration in 1994. It attracted thousands of Cape Muslims to ceremonies, marches and mass rallies. The statement, inspired by Davids, is a good example of how the Commemoration Committee regarded the meeting of Muslim and South African history.

10. **"Muslim Personal Law,"** *Ar-Rasheed*, vol. 2, no. 8, September 1994/Rabi-at-Thaani 1415

The statement reminds Muslims of the opportunity provided

in the constitution to implement Muslim Personal Law. It presents the acceptance and implementation of Muslim Personal Law as a responsibility given by God.

11. **"Qiblah: Muslims and the Elections,"** by Imam Achmad Cassiem, in *Boorhaanol Islam,* Meelad-un-Nabi edition, vol. 28, no. 4 (January 1994), pp. 29-32.

This was a pre-election issue of the magazine in which Cassiem and others clarified their views on the first democratic elections. In this article, Cassiem situated the Muslims in the context of the oppressed of South Africa, but called upon Muslims to make unanimous decisions based on unity without being "mesmerized" by the 1994 April elections.

12. **Proposed Constitution: People Against Gangsterism and Drugs (PAGAD) National Conference**, March 1997

PAGAD burst on the South African scene in August 1996 when it marched onto the house of a notorious drug-dealer, and killed him. Photographers and television cameras relayed this image all over the world. PAGAD's Islamic connections are clear from the slogans and symbols it uses.

It is clear from these documents that Muslims were divided on a number of issues in relation to the emerging South African nation. However, one notion that persists across the spectrum is the recognition of a community located geographically in southern Africa. This is true of Cassiem, who insists that "it is first of all necessary to locate the Muslims in the context of South Africa.... The Muslims are indissolubly part of the oppressed people; they do not desire, nor demand, nor expect preferential treatment either from the oppressor nor the oppressed" (Document 11:29). In his contribution, Esack brings into sharp relief the reality of the "community" and the goals of liberation. Even though covered by "lots of muck" which is "embarrassing" and "painful," the activist has no choice but to be in this community (Document 1:69). On the leadership level, the documents reveal an acute desire or aspiration to represent the South African Muslim community. In this case, the Muslim Judicial Council declared that it was "the widest and most representative group of *ulama* and

Imams in South Africa," while the Jamiats of Transvaal and Natal rightly claim that they too "represent a broad cross-section of the Muslim community in South Africa" (Documents 3 and 7). In one way or another, the reality of South Africa informs the discourse of both politically oriented groupings (Call of Islam and Qiblah) as well as religious leadership groups. The latter have been regional groupings which have now come to adopt the South African nation as their point of reference. This is a point that also comes out very clearly in Shoaib Omar's essay when he argued for Muslims making a contribution to South Africa as such. The Muslim community, as part of the *ummah* in a geographical region, seemed to have grappled with the idea of a nation without too much difficulty. Unlike the predictions of the purist Islamic rhetoric cited earlier in this essay, Muslims do not seem to see a fundamental contradiction between the South African nation and their community as part of the *ummah*. This does not mean that there are not any fundamental differences among Muslims on what they regard as their responsibility towards the South African nation. This is, however, true of Muslims as it is true of other communities in South Africa. A careful look at these differences provides evidence of how Muslims grapple with this issue of the nation. For South Africa particularly, the dividing line between South Africa under apartheid and democracy provides some contrasting scenarios of how the 'nation' is conceptualized by various Muslim groupings.

The attitude towards South Africa can be divided between two approaches. The first, represented in varying degrees by Cassiem, Esack, the National Muslim Conference and the Tricentenary Celebrations Committee, adopts South Africa as a nation with a unique Islamic history and destiny. Both Cassiem and Esack regard themselves as part of the oppressed in the country; the former embarrassed about the lack of justice among Muslims, but the latter identifying all Muslims as part of the oppressed. The National Muslim Conference and the Tricentenary Celebrations Committee gave it a special narrative focus. Concluding a history of Islamic political struggle in South Africa, Davids captures the sentiment of the National Muslim Conference pamphlet with eloquence:

The Muslims of South Africa have a history of struggling against political injustices. Our hope, as the present generation, lies in the continued struggle against injustice. On us, therefore, rests the onus to ensure that justice prevails for all people in this country. In this struggle lies our salvation and our coexistence in a happy, just, equitable, democratic South Africa of the future.

Similarly, the Tricentenary Celebrations Committee seeks a similar meeting of destinies for Islam and South Africa, when it proposed:

To promote the spirit of the pioneers of Islam in South Africa through highlighting the admirable social conscience prevalent in early Muslim history....

This approach clearly mythologizes the history of struggle and political liberation, where the past seems to be moving inexorably towards the new democracy. The destiny of Muslims was locked with the destiny of the nation. This position becomes even clearer when contrasted with the position of the Jamiats. Here, one does not find any celebration of a common history. The Jamiat Memo speaks of the religious needs of the Muslims, particularly "full recognition in South African courts of law" of Muslim personal law. Similarly, Omar's eloquent essay urges Muslims to participate in the new political dispensation, and contribute meaningfully to it, but does not allude to a South African Muslim history of establishing such a dispensation. On the contrary, in the Foreword to M. S. Omar's essay (Document 8), the President of the Jamiatul Ulema Natal, Maulana Yunus Patel, states that "people of intellect, wisdom and knowledge could not make their rightful contribution towards the full and proper development of South Africa because they happened to be of the wrong colour." Whereas the Tricentenary could easily compile a list of such contributions, the Jamiat stands apart from that history. Most clearly, Document 10 (Muslim Personal Law) of *Ar-Rasheed* (Jamiatul Ulama Transvaal) spells out this contractual relationship between Muslims and South Africa. It deals with the difficult period in the past when the Jamiats were "negotiating for the enactment of Muslim Personal Law in South Africa." The article applauds the success of these "negotiations" in 1986 out of which a 1990 report was ready, but "owing to the political changes taking place at the time, the report and subsequent research and implementation of Muslims Personal Law was shelved until a new dispensation was in place." The use of "negotiations" is interesting as the article tries to legitimate the 1986 collusion with the Apartheid State. Such "negotiations" were a form of cooption which the apartheid state exercised among willing groups in black, colored and Indian communities. More importantly for this essay, however, is the manner in which these bodies representing religious leaders deal with the new state. Just as they had concerned themselves with the affairs of the Muslims in the apartheid state, they now wrote to the negotiating teams and made demands for the "basic religious needs" of the Muslims. In terms of history and destiny, they are as far removed from the emerging new nation as the earlier groups were part thereof. This does not mean, however, that their concerns and demands were illegitimate. The point being made here is how two groups of Muslims positioned themselves in relation to South Africa at the end of the apartheid era: the one saw its destiny merging with the symbols of the new nation, while the second chose to establish a formal, legal relationship with the new state. Both were dedicated to the changes taking place, but they had different expectations of and commitment to the new nation.

Strange as it may seem, my analysis has so far placed Esack, A. Rashied Omar, Cassiem and Davids in one group. With regard to the documents selected for analysis, however, there exist a number of differences among these as well. The principal disagreement lies in the acceptance of democracy as a fundamental principle of governance. Cassiem, in contrast with most of the other documents cited, supports democracy conditionally:

> ...this also means that if "Democracy" opposes Islam, then Islam opposes democracy. For example, if by so-called democratic procedures the majority of citizens in a country support the legalization of marijuana, Muslims will oppose that democratic decision. (Document 11)

In this statement, Cassiem cannot see how Muslims could endorse the democratic alternative for South Africa. This sentiment was also addressed from another angle by the *ar-Rashied* when it portrays democracy as the political tool of the West (Document 6, "The Holy Grail of Democracy"). This suspicion of democracy is evident in many other international Islamic movements as well. The unconditional acceptance of democracy as the basic framework for legislation and governance has often been regarded as a fundamental theological problem for Muslims. The sovereignty of God as the sole legislator could not be compromised by the will of the people, or any other democratic right or freedom. This is a widespread sentiment among Muslims as well as observers, and has not been directly addressed by those endorsing democracy in South Africa. A brief examination of this challenge, however, indicates that modern political theorists have inadequately dealt with what they perceive to be the problem of democracy. The assumption is that if an issue is clearly stated in the Qur'an or the normative example of the Prophet Muhammad, then no parliament may legislate contrary to such an issue. For example, since intoxicating substances were regarded as harmful and prohibited in Islam, no laws may be enacted which allow people to consume them. However, Muslims have neglected some fundamental implications of this approach. If democratic procedures reflect the desire of the people, whether Muslim or not, to do that which is harmful or evil according to Islam, how do Muslims respond? What do Muslims do with a majority decision that alcoholic substances may be consumed? Presumably, protagonists of an Islamic solution argue that the strong arm of the law would be used to enforce Islamic law. Irrespective of the wishes of the majority, the law of God has to reign supreme, and the instruments of the state will be used to enforce the law. Upon careful reflection, however, this approach towards non-practicing Muslims or non-believing citizens in a country is fraught with difficulties, not least from the Islamic tradition itself. Such an authoritarian and mechanical approach to enforce compliance falls in the face of the ethical teachings of Islam. For the purpose of this essay, the following Prophetic statement, which is often used to invoke an authoritarian approach to Islam, makes for interesting reading:

> Whoever of you sees an evil action, let him change it with his hand; and if he is not able to do so, then with his tongue; and if

he is not able to do so, then with his heart—and that is the weakest faith.[12]

Clearly, the statement advocates a constructive approach to ridding society of evil, but equally allows for other approaches as well. Islamists choose to adopt the first part of the statement as the manifesto of an Islamic approach to politics. Such a choice is open to question, and certainly makes a mockery of the broad ethical guideline contained in the statement. This approach to democracy, however, conceals another problem which Cassiem and other contemporary Muslims do not address. Real power lies theoretically in the hands of the religious elite who have the capacity to interpret the will of God for people. Mawdudi, the most important theorist of this ideal, underscores the authority of this elite: "every Muslim who is capable and qualified to give sound opinion on matters of Islamic law, is entitled to interpret the law of God when such interpretation becomes necessary."[13] It is this absolute authority to which Cassiem and the Jamiats allude, in essence their own authority, when they speak about the limits of democracy. A. Rashied Omar's response to Albie Sachs poses this fundamental problem when he asked the most eminent theorist in the African National Congress how the state would relate to the pluralism inherent within religious communities (Document 4). This is a legitimate question in itself, and has not been adequately addressed by either the state or by religious communities themselves. With respect to this essay, however, Omar's question underscores a fundamental dilemma at the heart of Islamic leadership mechanisms within Islam in general, and Islam in South Africa in particular. In the absence of a central authority that regulates religious leaders and leadership, the Islamic tradition recognizes leaders within fairly broad parameters. Leadership arises out of knowledge expressed in education and ritual settings. In the past, such expertise and ritual leadership was recognized by the state and accordingly rewarded. In South Africa, in the absence of an Islamic state, leaders equipped with some Islamic disciplinary expertise were recognized and accepted by the people. Not surprisingly, expertise on the one hand and community acceptance on the other, resulted in a great deal of diversity in religious leadership. More than any other group in

South Africa, the Muslim Judicial Council reflects and admits to this diversity:

> The community appoints its own imams. We are the collective of people who—through their *masajid*, Islamic institutions and through the religious service to the community came to be in the MJC. Any person whose community appoints him as an Imaam or who has studied Islam at any of the recognized institutions is welcome to apply for membership. (Document 3, p. 18)

The problem that Omar asks, and which Cassiem and the Jamiats cannot answer, is how and which religious leadership, vested with full authority in an ideal Islamic state, would address issues of governance. It seems that Islam stipulates knowledge as a minimum requirement for eligibility, but that the community or society as a whole should supplement this recognition of their leadership. The latter factor, the recognition of leadership, has not been adequately dealt with in modern Islamic thought. The democratic method, espoused by many Muslim organizations in South Africa, poses a possible solution to this problem, but Cassiem and the Jamiats are more ambitious.

The Jamiat letter addressed to the chief negotiating teams of South Africa offered their services "to discuss the feasibility and the practicality of establishing a fully-constituted Islamic Court of South Africa" (Document 7). Cassiem is even more ambitious as he speaks from a more dynamic national position examined above. Consequently, he regards the Muslims as playing a vanguard role in South Africa. Reflecting on the 1994 elections, Cassiem revealed how he viewed the destiny of Islam leading the destiny of the oppressed:

> If Muslims cannot unite then how on earth are the amorphous oppressed masses going to do it! We should not be mesmerized by the 27th April 1994 but pursue our goal of unity of the Muslims AND the unity of the oppressed masses. For after all, it is the oppressors who are the minority. (Document 11, p. 32)

Cassiem seemed to be expecting the liberation of South Africa to take place under the leadership of the Muslims. This sentiment, inspired no doubt by Cassiem, was reflected in the preamble of PAGAD's constitution. Re-constituting a verse of the Qur'an, the anti-crime organization configures the goal of South Africa in Islamic terms: "You are the best of people evolved for mankind, enjoining what is right, forbidding what is wrong and believing in the Creator and followers of the books: Zaboor (David); Taurat (Moses); Bible (Jesus); Qur'an (Muhammad S.A.W.). All those persons who thus surrender themselves to the will of God are welded into a community and that is how the Society comes into being" (Document 12). The preamble takes a verse of the Qur'an (3: 110) and re-reads it in the context of a post-apartheid South Africa that is aware of religious pluralism. Cassiem's sentiments of leading the South African oppressed are clearly evident in this reading. It reflects his ambition within the South African nation. Thus, a guarded rejection of democracy is really a dissimulated bid for leadership over all Muslims for the Jamiats and over the oppressed South Africans for Cassiem.

Conclusion

This essay has argued that cultural and religious communities in South Africa often face judgment and evaluation in terms of their concurrence with national and developmental themes. Such approaches are useful for evaluating the extent to which such communities have matched or evolved according to such criteria. Focusing on the final conclusions and desired expectations, such approaches, however, ignore the processes and discourses within cultural and religious traditions. Thus, for example, Islam in South Africa is regarded as universally and potentially militant, or part of the liberation movement. Moreover, the Islamic religion is regarded as essentially hostile to the nation. Such generalizations and conclusions miss the important nuances within Muslim discourses. Taking a careful look at a variety of documents produced at the close of apartheid, it is very clear that the presumptions about Muslims and Islam are unfounded. These documents revealed the debates and arguments among Muslim leaders and organizations. One group of Muslims, generally youth who were engaged in the anti-apartheid struggle, constructed a mythology where the Muslim community and the South African nation converged. Religious leaders, exemplified by the Jamiats in the old

Transvaal and Natal, were more aloof, and chose to lead the South African Muslims and represent them in negotiations with the state. These contrasting mythological and contractual models divided the Muslims in their attitude towards the nation. With regard to post-apartheid South Africa, Muslims were re-divided between those who opposed or resisted democracy, and those who endorsed it as the foundation of the new nation. The former, consisting of both youth as well as religious leaders, draw easily on modern Islamic political theory developed elsewhere in the Islamic world. Those in favor of democracy have not directly addressed the democratic challenges to religion in general, and Islamic thought in particular. They have been content to join the pro-democracy chorus, but refrained from addressing the challenges lurking in anti-democratic discourse in modern Islamic thought. Clearly, there are signs of such a debate as Muslims develop their destiny as part of South Africa. Much more, however, needs to be done.

NOTES

1. Cabinet Secretariat, Minutes of the Cabinet Committee for Security and Intelligence Affairs: 15 August 1996.
2. G. Lubbe, "Christians, Muslims and Liberation in South Africa," *Journal of Theology for Southern Africa* 56 (1986):28.
3. I have developed this analysis in more detail in an unpublished publication entitled "Mosques, Imams and Sermons in South Africa." (T. Asad, *Genealogies of Religion: Discipline and Reasons of Power in Christianity and Islam* [Baltimore, 1993]. T. Asad, "The Idea of an Anthropology of Islam," Occasional Papers Series [Washington, D.C., 1986]).
4. B. Lewis, *The Middle East and the West* (New York, 1966 [first published 1964]), p. 71.
5. *Ibid.*
6. P.J. Vatikiotis, *Islam and the State* (London, 1987), p. 36.
7. *Ibid*, p. 38.
8. R. Schulze, "Panislamismus oder Panarabismus? Die Suche nach der Grossen Einheit," in *Die Welten des Islam: Neunundzwanzig Vorschlaege, das Unvertraute zu Verstehen* (1993), p. 171.
9. P. Antes, K. Duran, T. Nagel and W. Walther, *Der Islam: Religion-Ethik-Politik* (Stuttgart, 1991), pp. 39-40.
10. *Ibid.*, p. 40.
11. *Ibid.*, p. 42.

12. Narrated by Muslim and reproduced in Al-Nawawi's *Forty Hadith*, translated by Exxedin Ibrahim and Denys Johnson-Davies (Damascus: The Holy Koran Publishing House, 1976), p. 110.
13. A.A. Mawdoodi, "Political Theory of Islam," in *Islam: Its Meaning and Message*, with a foreword by Saleem Azzam (London: 1976), p. 161.

The Role of Hinduism in Addressing Human Rights Issues in South Africa

Pratap Kumar

Head, Department of Science of Religion
University of Durban-Westville
Durban, South Africa

In the present essay, I shall provide first a general discussion of human rights within the general framework of traditional Hinduism. Secondly, I shall attempt to highlight some of the contributions of modern Hindu thinkers in India and in South Africa to the discussion on human rights. Thirdly, I shall identify in a sketchy way some issues that Hindus need to come to grips with in their effort to address the broader issues of human rights.

It is a matter of choice whether one looks at Hinduism in the light of human rights or human rights in the light of Hinduism. Although the problem of human rights is as old as the human race, the universal struggle for human rights via the many lobby groups is certainly a modern phenomenon. And Hinduism being one of the very ancient religions of the world, perhaps one would have to use different hermeneutic tools than the ones that modern discourse would require. To look at Hinduism in the light of the modern struggle for human rights would mean that one has to

evaluate Hindu sociology in the light of the human rights issues of
contemporary society. This would further mean that one would have
to force traditional Hinduism to address some of the peculiarly
modern issues, such as modern war crimes, treatment of prisoners,
treatment of sick in the hospitals, dealing with the senior citizens
in our society and so on. Most of these problems are not peculiarly
modern, but their modern manifestations are certainly unique. On
the other hand, to look at human rights issues in the light of
Hinduism would mean that the emphasis is on human rights questions within Hindu society rather than on the teachings of Hinduism. In other words, Hindu teachings are simply the background
against which a discussion of human rights is pursued. It is the
latter approach, i.e., to look at human rights issues against a general ethos of the Hindus, that I would like to take in this present
essay. As such, I shall not present a list of Hindu teachings on
human rights but rather reflect on how modern Hindus have dealt
with human rights issues using traditional resources.

Let me provide some preliminary comments on Hindu society
in general. First, like many traditional religions, Hinduism is largely patriarchal in its approach to human society. Its social fabric,
based on many variables such as *Jati* (family/birth), *Gotra* (kin), *Kula*
(clan/tribe) and *Varna* (color/race),[1] is conducive to many social
inequities that most societies have suffered in the past and continue
to suffer. This means, in the context of ritual, the priesthood and
patronage of the ritual is by and large male-centered. As such, the
spiritual emancipation of a woman is tied up with her male companion. Exception to this may be found in the devotional traditions of
the Hindus, and the so-called popular traditions which are essentially non-brahmanical. Secondly, Hindu society is essentially hierarchical. What makes the social hierarchy within Hindu society
significant is its rootedness in ritual. Rules of ritual clearly define
an individual's place in society by a list of prohibitions and injunctions.[2] From the various mundane issues such as interdining or
marital relations to the spiritual details dealing with officiating the
various rituals, all such activities are regulated by rules. In other
words, the place of an individual in the society is largely defined by
the injunctions of the ritual.

Thus in a general sense, Hindu society does not stand in any
particularly favorable position in so far as human rights issues are

concerned. It is a society structured to provide coherence to the world of ritual, for within the complex of ritual, social roles are predetermined and no mobility is allowed outside those social boundaries. Hence, one acquires a social status, be that higher or lower, by virtue of birth. It is precisely this lack of mobility that led many western scholars to doubt the relevance of such a social structure to the changing dynamics of the modern world. For instance, Max Weber found Hinduism and its allied traditions (such as Buddhism or Jainism) to be incompatible with the modern capitalist worldview.[3] Louis Dumont saw in Hindu society an absence of the notion of the individual as known in western society. Western society with its emphasis on the value of equality (*homo equalis*) gave rise to the modern notion of the individual as equal and on a par with everyone in the society. On the other hand, the traditional societies such as Hindu society are based on the value of holism with an emphasis on hierarchy (*homo hierarchycus*).[4] These assumptions, however, have been challenged by other social scientists.[5] Nevertheless, in response to western criticisms, many contemporary Hindu thinkers moved away from the ritualistic mode of society and attempted to find solutions to the problems of modern society within the philosophical and theological literature. I shall return to these thinkers later on.

Let me explore some of the areas within Hindu scriptures which provide some basis for consideration of human rights. Like many religious texts, the Hindu mythological and ritual texts are full of references to the universal theme of victory over evil. The ancient Vedic texts refer to the battle between the god Indra and the demon Vritra. Indra's many similar victories over the demons inaugurate a theme that finds resonance throughout the subsequent religious literature of the Hindus. The story of the Ramayana and that of the Mahabharata take the theme to its theological heights. Although both epics display by and large a patriarchal society, modern scholars with feminist leanings have been able to tease out many themes that tended to uphold the rights of women. Thus, Sita of the Ramayana and Draupadi of the Mahabharata stand as symbols of not only trials and tribulations but also triumphs of women in the primarily male-dominant society.

The single most important theme that provided scope for human rights issues is the doctrine of Dharma that reverberates

throughout the two epics mentioned above. Although the notion
of Dharma, in its original association with ritual, connoted mainly
ritual obligations to be carried out by individuals in the process of
their spiritual emancipation, its meaning and significance have
been expanded within the epic texts and other mythological texts
to include the universal good and moral duty. As such, the central
part of the epic Mahabharata, viz., the Bhagavadgita, is devoted
entirely to the discourse on Dharma. For the first time in its
theological development, the doctrine of Dharma is associated with
the idea of the divine incarnation. Thus, Vishnu becomes incar-
nated whenever and wherever there is a threat to the well being
(Dharma) of human society (Bhagavadgita, 4:7-8). The many mythological texts of the Hindus abound in this theme.

Hindu theology generally understands the world in a cyclical
fashion. Creation, sustenance and dissolution follow each other in
a continuous cycle, and as such the decline and deterioration of
human society is inevitable and functions so that a new world order
is created again. Both mythological and ritual texts often point out
that the very process of creation is undertaken by the creator god
Brahma with a view to provide final emancipation for human
beings.[6] In other words, the human world is created in order for
past karmic activities to be exhausted so that souls find their final
emancipation. Thus, the notion of Karma has played a vital role in
defining social action within the Hindu worldview. The Bhagavadgita epitomizes the doctrine of Karma when it suggests that one
should abandon attachment and desire for the reward of action
(Bhagavadgita, 18:9, 24, 66). Hindu theology further understands
that the world order proceeds from the *Sattvic* (pure) mode in
which highest spiritual values are upheld to the *Tamasic* (dark/
impure) mode in which evildoers and their actions predominate.
Thus, the world is divided into four phases—in the first phase,
Dharma walks with four legs, in the second phase it walks with
three, then with two and finally with one. This indicates the grad-
ual decline of human values and spiritual qualities required for
one's final emancipation. The pursuit of Dharma by the righteous
is undertaken with the above constraints.

It is against this kind of Hindu worldview that one has to
understand the struggle for human rights. Within this traditional
Hindu worldview, contemporary Hindu thinkers sought to find

various models that would allow a meaningful discussion of human rights in our modern world. I shall enumerate a few of those models here. The most dominant model that was explored by contemporary Hindu thinkers such as Dr. S. Radhakrishnan is found in the non-dualist philosophical model provided by Sankara of the 8th century. Within this model, the empirical world is totally negated as Maya and thus all contradictions of our human society are to be overcome by realizing one's real identity as Brahman. Thus, the proponents of this model did not call into question many social inequities present in Hindu society, but rather chose to work within the framework of the social divisions of the Hindus. Thinkers like Dr. Radhakrishnan argued that the only way to overcome the inequities present in human society is to work towards their elimination in the future by focusing on the present rather than on the past. He reinterpreted the notion of Karma as something that is future-oriented rather than past-oriented.[7]

A second model is found in the qualified non-dual philosophy of Ramanuja, who sought to address the problem of the world through the analogy of body-soul. Unlike Sankara, Ramanuja did not negate the world as Maya but rather sought to see it as part of the divine being. In other words, the world is understood as the body of God.[8] Within this model, there is scope for equality of all within the being of God. Ramanuja was not particularly opposed to social disparities present in his time but rather accepted them as given. However, the occasional radical departures he made, by proclaiming to everyone what was given to him as a secret teaching by his teacher,[9] indicated his willingness to go beyond the social norms to address the problems of his time.

A third model is found within the devotional traditions of the Hindus. The devotional theology provides a better scope both for the overcoming of social inequities as well as providing greater promise for the emancipation of women. Devotional traditions placed human beings from all social backgrounds including men and women on a par before God. With its emphasis on grace and divine accessibility, devotional Hinduism has provided a basis for equality of all before God. Both the Vaishnava saints and the Saiva saints of the periods between the 4th and 9th centuries, most of whom were non-Brahmins, radically departed from the traditional social boundaries of purity and approached God as just and righteous, merciful and bounteous, a God who cares for all human beings regardless of their social rank. One of the most outspoken sectarian groups on the issue of social equality is the sect called Virasaivism (literally it means those who are ardent or heroic worshipers of Siva) which flourished between the 12th and the 15th centuries in the state of Karnataka, India. They have provided perhaps the strongest criticism of the traditional concepts of purity and rules of conduct which guided the social organization of Hindu society.[10] In the state of Gujarat, the Swami Narayana sect[11] led the struggle against social inequality.

The beginnings of the struggle against many social evils in contemporary times in India may be seen with the rise of Raja Rammohan Roy in the 18th century. His opposition to the practice of *Sati* (burning of young widows on the pyre of their dead husbands) and child marriage is well known. Rammohan Roy is considered the father of modern India because of his contribution to social reform. While Roy led the movement against Hindu traditional orthopraxy in the 18th century, the Sarvodaya movement[6] led the struggle of the poor farmers to obtain land in the early 20th century. The rich farmers in India were encouraged to donate large segments of unused land to subsistence farmers so as to enable them to become self-sufficient. In the 19th century, the Brahma Samaj, the Arya Samaj and many other movements, though predominantly religious, also focussed on the social problems of the day. These movements certainly enabled the depressed classes in India to have access to the religious centers, which had been prohibited to the lower classes of Hindu society.

On the political front, the 19th- and the early 20th-century Nationalist Movement led by many Hindu intellectuals drew its inspiration from religious texts like the Gita. The role of the Gita in the Nationalist Movement during the struggle for freedom in India is very significant. The Gita was first translated into English by Charles Wilkins in the 18th century (1778) and a hundred years later Edwin Arnold provided a poetic rendering of the text. It was this text that the famous Mahatma Gandhi read while he was a law student in England. Ironic as it may seem, the European intelligentsia, by their translations of Hindu sacred literature, prepared the way for modern Hindus to participate in the human rights discussion. As far as we know, the Gita was the first Hindu religious text that Gandhi had read, although his knowledge of Hinduism was based on many mythological and epic stories that he had heard from his family during the early years of his life. However, the Gita was to remain his close companion during his struggle for justice and equality in South Africa and subsequently during his struggle for freedom in India. I shall return to Gandhi in South Africa shortly. Another freedom fighter who based his struggle on the Gita was Bala Gangadhar Tilak (B. G. Tilak). His commentary on the Gita is oriented toward political action motivated to eventually force the British to submit to the Indian demand for freedom and democracy. The quintessence of India's freedom lay in the free democratic society which goes beyond the traditional social boundaries to include equality of all social groups and both men and women. Underlining the need for equality and fairness, in many of his speeches Gandhi urged Indian society to provide equal status to women and the depressed classes. The Hindu leaders of the Nationalist Movement, viz., Gandhi, Tilak, Aurobindo, Nehru, Vallabhai Patel and others saw the basis of their struggle for freedom within their vast spiritual tradition, epitomized by the text of the Gita.

All these ideals which the freedom fighters upheld were transferred into the constitution of India. The chairman of the Indian constitutional committee, B. R. Ambedkar, a man from the depressed classes, ensured that the historically disadvantaged communities in India received fair treatment within the bounds of the basic principles of democracy. Thus, the fundamental human rights of justice, equality, education, freedom of speech and religion, etc., have been guaranteed under the provisions of the constitution. In other words, for the first time India systematically moved away from the Hindu religious orthodoxy that controlled Hindu society. The process of secularization has thus begun.

The Hindu attitude toward the *modern* values of justice, equality and freedom has not been antagonistic because of its tradition of tolerance. Nonetheless it has not been easy to overcome the many traditional biases of the past, especially in relation to the issues of social hierarchy and the status of women. The traditional Hindu attitude had to be reconciled with these new developments in Indian society vis-à-vis the new constitution. Most significantly, the pop-culture of music, theater, cinema, especially television, interdining in restaurants, mass-media, mass-transport system (railways, airlines), etc., all have radically altered the many traditional perceptions and attitudes of Hindus. The traditional rules of purity could not be accommodated within the bounds of the emerging modern India. The diaspora Hindus in America, Britain, Canada, Australia, South Africa and in many other countries have problematized many traditional Hindu values in relation to women, marriage, dowry, social divisions, etc. (not to mention many of the traditional ritual obligations which they would have had to carry on if they were to live in India), because of their interaction with western values. All of these factors have cumulatively impacted on the concept of human rights within Hindu society. Modern society has forced traditional Hinduism to level the playing fields between men and women, between various social groups, between orthodoxy and heterodoxy and most importantly between sacred and secular. In other words, the issues that were once considered sacred (e.g., place of women in the society, marriage, profession, etc.) are now seen as part of the secular world. A serious concern with human rights is now thrust on Hinduism because of the many changes taking place in the modern world.

Let me now turn to explore the issues that became important for Hindus in South Africa. The beginning of the human rights struggle for Hindus in South Africa began with their arrival in 1860. The lure of "gold" for "chillies" did not materialize as they were promised in India when the indentured Indians were mustered into the ships that brought them to Natal under the most inhuman conditions. Many women and children died of diseases such as malaria during and after the arduous journey. Upon arrival they were made to live in conditions that were detrimental to their health and morale. The indentured Indians had to face unacceptable levels of ill-treatment and hardship. Some of the problems that the indentured laborers had to face were: 1) the remunerations guaranteed in their contracts were not honored; 2) most employers forced them to work long hours and almost seven days a week; 3) the living conditions, such as housing, sanitation, and health facilities were deplorable by any standard; 4) once the indentured laborers became free and self-supporting through small-scale farming, trading, domestic service, etc., they were subjected to unacceptable levels of taxation. The most fundamental human rights of the indentured Indians were denied. By the time Gandhi arrived in South Africa in 1893, the situation was ripe for a struggle for human rights. Gandhi's involvement with the South African Indian struggle for justice and equality began with his own humiliating experience on the train at Pietermaritzburg. Very soon he realized that his real job was not the one for which he was brought to South Africa by a Muslim merchant (i.e., to provide legal service to Dada Abdualla, a Muslim merchant, in settling a business dispute) but to fight the injustices meted out to the Indians in South Africa. Many indentured Indians began to approach him with complaints of ill-treatment such as whipping at their work place.[7]

Not only were the Indians persecuted at work, but their movement was controlled by strict laws. They had to carry passes wherever they went, and they could only move within a certain jurisdiction. This led Gandhi to organize a mass protest in which many Indians burnt their passes in defiance of the unjust laws of the government. Gandhi also protested against the tax levied on the Indians.

One very crucial issue that Gandhi took up against the white government was the marriage act which virtually reduced the Indian women and their children to the status of illegitimacy. More than 75 percent of the indentured Indians and the passenger Indians were Hindus. One of the first things that happened to them was the allocation of the indentured Indians to various employers. Although in many instances people from the same village were allocated to one employer, it wasn't always the case. People of differing languages and social ranks were mixed together. Secondly, the initial period after the indenture tenure saw people moving into locations where their native affiliations to language and social rank could not be continued. The resulting implications are many. One of the most striking problems was how to practice monogamy in a meaningful sense. Not only were Indians forced to live far away from their immediate families, but also there were fewer women as compared to men. This situation led to men competing for partners in marriage. Soon afterwards, the British government made sure to send an adequate number of women to work in the sugar cane plantations in South Africa. With the increase in the number of women, the practice of polygamy began to become

common among many Hindus. This situation presented a problem
to the South African government and they passed legislation which
forced Indians to register their marriages with the registrar of
marriages. But what the Euro-centered South African government
did not see was the fact that the Hindu marriage could not be
proven to be valid through documentation because the Hindu
priests did not have the necessary licensing power to register
Hindu marriages. The resulting mess was that all Indian marriages
were considered legally invalid. The original idea of the Indian
Marriage Act was to control polygamy but it also affected negatively those who were monogamous. In other words, the act in
question effectively denied the validity of every single Hindu marriage. This was the greatest assault on the dignity of Hindus, both
men and women, for it made their children, as Gandhi later put it,
"illegitimate." Gandhi opposed the Marriage Act vehemently. Only
a few years ago the South African Marriage Act was modified to
recognize non-Christian marriages as legally valid.

As pointed out earlier, the Gita was to provide Gandhi with a
sense of direction throughout his struggle in South Africa, even
though his struggle was not exclusively for the sake of Hindus.
While his struggle for justice and equality went beyond the bounds
of the Hindu society, his spiritual resources were largely Hindu,
though he also paid attention to the scriptures of Muslims and
Christians. Gandhi maintained constant dialogue with Christians
and Muslims on many religious issues throughout his struggle in
South Africa. Nonetheless, he was convinced that it was possible to
find sufficient spiritual strength and direction within Hindu religious sources to launch a sustained battle for human rights.

In addition to Gandhi's contribution to the struggle for the
rights of Indians in South Africa, many other Hindus continued
the struggle for human rights in South Africa alongside their
Muslim and Christian partners. Both Bhai Paramanand, who arrived in 1905, and Swami Shankaranand, who arrived in 1908,
contributed enormously to the concerns of Hindus. Initially they
were concerned with the issue of Hindu conversion to other faiths.
But soon their work went beyond the religious sphere. Bhai
Paramanand laid the foundation for the future growth of Arya
Samaj which was to play a vital role in the field of Indian education. He also established the Hindu Young Men Association.

Swami Shankaranand's work, on the other hand, resulted in the establishment of the Hindu Maha Sabha, which was to represent the Hindus in dealing with many of their religious issues, such as the demand for religious holidays, etc. Swami Bhavani Dayal was perhaps more politically involved than his predecessors. He participated in the Passive Resistance campaign of Gandhi. He was also elected president of the Natal Indian Congress. Other significant personalities who contributed to the struggle included Shastri, Sir Kurma Reddy and Rama Rao, all of whom were representatives of the Government of India. They were able to lobby for educational facilities for Indians in South Africa.

This resume of the South African Hindu contribution to the struggle for justice and equality in a country where segregation laws inhibited their progress points to the fact that Hindus were able to find adequate religious resources to deal with the situation. The struggle of South African Hindus cannot be separated from the political struggle of Indians and Blacks in general. Their progress and well being is tied up with all the disadvantaged people of South Africa.

While historically the Hindu South Africans, along with their African and other partners, fought for their freedom from the white minority rule, the contemporary struggle of the Hindus is more related to their internal problems. These have to do with the abuse of women, children, the aged and other disadvantaged people in that community. Even though Hindus in South Africa have lived under western conditions and assimilated many, often good, western values, Hindus have a long way to go in regard to some of their traditional biases in relation to women. For example, Hindu women in South Africa still do not have equal property inheritance rights on a par with men. Although on the issue of dowry Hindu women have come a long way,[8] the issue of property inheritance still bogs them down. The age-old tradition of passing on property and other assets to the male children and not dividing the estate equally among both male and female children is still common. This requires urgent attention if human rights issues are to be addressed meaningfully by Hindus.

A second issue has to do with family violence. In cases of family violence women are often the victims. In general, family violence is the result of many traditional assumptions that men have about women and that women have about men. For instance, Hindu women assume it is okay for men to drink either at home or in public places. At the initial stages, these assumptions are never questioned by either partner. But as the problem of drinking becomes unbearable, it is women who suffer the consequences more than men. In this context it is noteworthy to mention what Shahid Refai reports on an Indian woman he encountered in India:

> During a train journey in India, I witnessed a brutal beating of a young Indian woman by her husband from whom she was separated. She was commuting to a primary school where she was a teacher, and her enraged husband boarded the train at a station. He was following her. First he used abusive language then took his shoes out and started to beat her.... I wanted to call the police and to report this, but the passengers and the woman herself objected. She said he would kill her if he heard of my action.[9]

This incident, though reported from India, aptly reflects many such cases among South African Hindu families.

Thirdly, even though modern Hindu women are increasingly becoming involved in many professions, many traditional assumptions relating to the role of women in the family have not changed. For instance, a working woman would still have to come home and fix dinner for the family. It is assumed that it is a woman's duty to cook and feed the family. This has radically affected the working conditions of women in our modern world. Whereas men work only in their work place, women are forced to work both at work as well as at home. Even women who remain as housewives spend an average of 18 hours providing the necessary conditions for the smooth running of the entire family—e.g., for the husband to go to work, for the children to go to school, and so on.

One could go on listing many of these modern issues facing men and women in Hindu society. South African Hindus need to come to grips with these modern issues. In dealing with these issues, modern Hindus need to look for resources not only within their traditions but also beyond. As Hindus increasingly become exposed to modernity and global communities, they need to reassess many traditional assumptions relating to family and society. It is not sufficient to rely solely on traditional resources; Hindus need to be open to other cultures. Often orthodox Hindus are skeptical about western responses to the social evils that have and continue to plague Hindu society. In a recent internet discussion on "Indian women and violence," Shahid Refai alluded to the role played by the American missionary women and the British government in the 19th century to eradicate "female infanticide." However, V. Rajagopal of the University of Wisconsin at Madison objected to such reliance on "alien" sources to respond to the Indian (Hindu) problems. He says,

> These are issues about which a lot of debate has already taken place. I am not very comfortable with the invocation of missionary materials by people who want to talk about "amelioration" of Indian women. I have no doubt that a great deal remains to be done, before Indian women attain a status of equality with men. But Indian people can draw from their own cultural resources, as well as what they need to learn from contact with "modernity" in raising the status of women in their own society, and can very well do without inputs from missionaries, American or otherwise.

Such a closed attitude, I believe, is often not very constructive. It is the constant willingness to appropriate positive values and ideas from other cultures that allows Hindus to deal with human rights issues. In fact, one of the strengths of Hinduism is its ability to assimilate ideas from other cultures and religions. That is how Hinduism has survived many centuries in the past and stood the tide of many countercultures and traditions which emerged from India (e.g., Buddhism, Jainism, etc.) as well as those that came from the outside (e.g., Islam and Christianity). Although human beings are culture specific and may belong to one or the other religious tradition, human rights issues cannot remain culture specific. They transcend the boundaries of all cultures and religions and touch the very core of our human society. Human rights violations are wrong by any standards. And no cultural excuses should be proffered either to scuttle the issues or to sidestep the problems which we as human beings face. And Hindus, with all their diverse traditions, must live up to their philosophical and religious ideals. This means Hindu religious authorities have a major role to play on the political and economic front to lobby for the rights of human beings. It is in doing so that Hindus will be able to give credibility to their age-old traditions.

NOTES

1. I have provided approximate social equivalents. While Varna is an external category, the first three (Jati, Gotra, and Kula) are internal categories and may be understood in that order as I have presented. None of the above are equal to the term "caste" which the Portuguese had used for their society and then wrongly identified the Indian phenomenon with that term.
2. See P. Kumar, "Ritual as the Defining Factor of Identity: A Case of the Srivaishnavas," in *Journal for the Study of Religion* (Forthcoming).
3. Max Weber, *The Religion of India*, translated and edited by Hans H. Gerth and Don Martindale (New York: The Free Press, 1958).
4. Louis Dumont, *Homo hierarchycus* (London: Paladin, 1972).
5. See André Béteille, "Individualism and Equality," in *Current Anthropology*, Vol. 27, No. 2, April 1986, pp. 121-134. Also see Mattison Mines and Vijayalakshmi Gourishankar, "Individuality, Achievement, and the Institutional Big-man: Putting the Individual Back into Conceptualizations of Indian Society," unpublished paper (University of California, Santa Barbara, n.d).
6. In a medieval ritual text called Ananda Samhita, the creation of the world is initiated by Brahma at the request of Vishnu so that he (Vishnu) can incarnate himself in the world and save the suffering souls from their bondage. See Ananda Samhita, "Oh the lotus born one, I have a desire to travel in the world to establish order and fulfil the Vedic scriptures and to ensure that the creation of the universe proceeds without division" (4:9). "People are tired, less Sattvic and less intelligent and so they do not know the Vyuha, Vibhava and Antaryamin manifestations (of mine). They are indeed confused. To give them the meditation (technique), and for the accessibility of my devotees and for the compassion of the whole world, Oh four-faced one, in the form of Arca I incarnate in this world along with Hri (Bhudevi) and Lakshmi" (4:10-12). Translation of the text is mine.
7. See S. Radhakrishnan, *The Hindu View of Life* (New York: George Allen and Unwin Ltd., 1957), pp. 61ff.
8. See J.B. Carman, *The Theology of Ramanuja* (New Haven: Yale University Press, 1974).
9. See Ramanuja, *The Vedanta Sutras*, tr. by George Tibaut (Delhi: Motilala Banarsidass, 1971, SBE series).
10. For more details on Virasaivas see Jan Peter Schouten, *Revolution of the Mystics: On the Social Aspects of Virasaivism* (Kampen, Netherlands: Kok Pharos Publishing House, 1991).
11. See R.B. Williams, *A New Face of Hinduism: The Swaminarayana Religion* (Cambridge, UK: Cambridge University Press, 1984).
12. The Sarvodaya movement was led by Gandhi's associate Vinoba. See V.

Bisoondayal, "Gandhi and Vinoba," in *Mahatma Gandhi: 125 Years*, ed. by B.R. Nanda (New Delhi: Indian Council for Cultural Relations, 1995), pp. 166ff.

13. See Y.S. Meer, *Documents of Indentured Labor: Natal 1851-1917* (Durban: Institute of Black Research, 1980), p. 690 (Document 66).

14. Bala Pillay, *British Indians in the Transvaal: Trade, Politics, and Imperial Relations (1885-1906)* (London: Longman Group Ltd., 1976), pp. 112ff.

15. Meer, *op. cit.*

16. Pillay, *op. cit.*

17. Here I shall limit my comments to Hindus, although the same could be said about the Muslim community who also suffered equally.

18. See P. Kumar, *Hinduism in South Africa* [monograph] (Durban: University of Durban-Westville, 1995), Ch. 3.

19. As far as the dowry situation in India is concerned it is still very deplorable. Often Hindu parents in India prefer male children in view of the dowry-related problems. Note the figures: According the World Bank report (quoted in India Abroad, August 9, 1996) there were 6000 abortions in Mumbai (Bombay) of whom only 2 were males. It also reported that there were 4.2 million female child deaths and about 1.2 female babies were aborted, and 6000 brides were burned. (This information is taken from Shaid Refai, "Indian women and violence," discussion on H-Asia Net list (an internet list for Asian History and Culture), Fri., 20 Sept. 1996. Although dowry is not a problem in South Africa according to my field survey between 1991 and 1993, a higher percentage preferred sons to daughters rather than daughters to sons. See P. Kumar, *Hinduism in South Africa* (New Delhi: New Age Publications [forthcoming]).

20. Shaid Refai, "Indian Women and Violence," discussion on H-Asia Net list (an internet list for Asian History and Culture), Fri., 20 Sept. 1996.

21. *Ibid.*

22. V. Rajagopal, "Indian Women and Violence," discussion on H-Asia Net list (an internet list for Asian History and Culture), Sun., 22 Sept. 1996.

The Role of Religion in the Transformation of Namibian Society:

The Churches and Human Rights

Christo Lombard
Professor of Religious Studies
University of Namibia, Namibia

Introduction

In writing about Namibia after independence, and in assessing the role of the churches in the ongoing process of liberation, it is impossible to ignore the impact which the so-called SWAPO (South West Africa People's Organization) detainee issue has generated, and still may have on the shaping of a just and democratic culture in post-apartheid Namibia. Looking at this issue from the perspective of the churches as part of civil society, the crux of the matter lies in the fact that the ecumenical churches, that were standing firm in the struggle for justice and liberation in Namibia,[1] allowed the SWAPO movement, and present government, to cover up atrocities and human rights abuses perpetrated against large numbers of their own followers. Many Namibians are disappointed, if not disillusioned, with the churches and especially some church leaders, since they were expected to have acted as consistent custodians of truth and reconciliation—whatever the circumstances.

This inconsistent lapse of integrity could have been understood, if not excused, to some extent in those difficult years, when South African hegemony, torture, murder and abuse were running rampant in beleaguered Namibia. However, since Independence, more than enough has been revealed about SWAPO's own culture of authoritarianism and the churches' complicity in silencing voices of critique. It can thus be understood why a critical researcher writes sharply about "SWAPO and the churches: an international scandal."[2] Currently there are signs that forces within civil society, and within the churches, are strongly at work, and may force Namibians to reconsider their handling of the so-called "detainee and missing persons issue," and related key words such as "truth," "reconciliation" and "justice."

The detainee issue has become a test-case, not only for the churches' integrity and witness, but also for civil society as such. The overall Namibian handling of the detainee and missing persons issue may become the acid test determining the nation's future.[3] The central role of the Christian churches in this national dilemma is therefore the focus of this contribution.

The Prophetic Witness of the Churches During the Struggle

The Namibian churches have been hailed for their strong stance against the apartheid regime. Since the famous "Open Letter" of 1971, the churches fulfilled the typical role of "the voice of the voice-less," and the ecumenical movement in Namibia became the carrier of the message of hope, justice and freedom for the Namibians. That first prophetic statement served as an ice-breaker for many such statements to follow.

The words of the "Epistle to the Namibians," explaining to congregations all over the country why the churches simply had to speak out, receive increased prophetic significance in the current, post-independence Namibian "culture of silence"—a culture which in effect covers up the grave human rights abuses that took place under the SWAPO leadership in exile and helps ensure the firm political grip of the authoritarian leadership elite.[4] In this "Epistle," sent out by the Lutheran church leaders on June 30, 1971, the message was clear: "We are concerned about the future of this country and about the future of the various peoples who live here.... We feel that if we, as the Church, remain silent any longer, we will become liable for the life and future of our country and its people."[5] After the Open Letter to Vorster, the mainline churches, representing more than 80 percent of the Namibian population, consolidated their cooperation towards the liberation of the oppressed masses in Namibia and jointly launched a very impressive ecumenical program.

In 1974 an ecumenical Christian Centre was founded in Windhoek to provide a forum for ideas and strategies for the churches' participation in the struggle for independence, with the formidable Tauno Hatuikulipi (who went into exile in 1977 and is believed to have been murdered by SWAPO in January 1984) as Director.[6] The Lutheran and Anglican Bishops (Auala and Wood) successfully took legal action against the new practice of public floggings of suspected SWAPO members and sympathizers, implemented since 1974. In 1975 the Catholic Church issued a Statement of "Conditions for reconciliation in SWA," which included an end to the use of violence in keeping the majority down; equal human rights for all; a fair trial for all political prisoners; and free and fair elections of the true leaders. The Christian Centre helped publish a booklet, *Torture: A Cancer in Our Society*. In May 1977 the major churches issued a joint statement on torture in Namibia, with advice to victims.[7]

When reading the barrage of statements, prepared by the church leaders of Namibia, on behalf of "the voiceless" during the time of the struggle for independence, the overall impression is one of tremendous courage, commitment and clarity of purpose. After the establishment of the Council of Churches in Namibia (CCN) in 1978, a number of statements were sent to the South African Prime Minister, for instance on October 4, 1978, after SWAPO's acceptance of the Western peace plan for Namibia: "At this decisive time and mindful of the ongoing suffering of our people, we call upon you, Mr. Prime Minister, to accept this opportunity for peace under the guarantees provided by the United Nations. We feel compelled to caution that should your government not make use of this opportunity, you will be held responsible worldwide for the escalation of an unavoidable, terrible and tragic war in this country."[8] For a fair evaluation of the detainee crisis, especially as it developed on the basis of the "spy drama" within SWAPO in the eighties, these prophetic admonitions are extremely important.

Many similar bold actions were still to follow, such as the Maseru Statement of the Anglican church (July 1978), in which the Western Contact Group was criticized for their selfish interests in the Namibian dispute,[9] and for allowing South Africa to register voters without supervision of the UN, and with its army still fully deployed in Namibia. Ecumenical solidarity was strengthened through the Southern African Catholic Bishops' Conference *Report on Namibia* (published in May 1982), containing details of South African atrocities in Namibia.[10] Since Pope John Paul II's visit to the World Council of Churches (WCC) and the Lutheran World Federation (LWF) in Genève, in 1984, the central authority of the Roman Catholic Church has been strong in its support of the Namibian cause.

After the failure of the 1978 initiatives on UN Resolution 435, and the South African answer of "internal" elections and an "interim" government, the CCN suffered internal division, sparked by the escalating violence of the struggle for liberation and the ghosts of Marxist ideology observed within SWAPO.[11] However, these internal problems did not prevent the CCN from amplifying its voice in the international arena.[12] Whatever the analysis of the bigger political powers at work behind the scenes of the successful implementation of the UN Resolution 435 and SWAPO's subsequent hour of glory, these contributions by the CCN on behalf of all Namibians must be acknowledged as very direct moral and political factors that tipped the scales in favor of a peaceful settlement of the Namibian quest for independence.

Indeed, the churches in Namibia had to pay a heavy price for this involvement: false propaganda against the "liberation theologians" were put in motion; bishops were banned; pastors were detained, harassed and tortured; and infrastructures were destroyed.[13] In line with Bonhoeffer's three options for churches in their confrontation with a state abusing its political power, the Namibian churches questioned the legitimacy of South Africa's actions; came to the aid of victims of state action; and courageously took the ultimate step as well: "not just to bandage the victims under the wheel, but to put a spoke in the wheel itself through direct political action."[14]

The Namibian churches broke the silence with a strong prophetic voice, not only offering an ambulance service for the victims of oppression, but also serving as an avant-garde movement for social justice and political liberation; they fulfilled the role of an internal ally of SWAPO, even as an alternative political opposition to South Africa and its proxy representatives. Through their contacts in the LWF and the WCC, the ecumenical churches in Namibia created an international platform for the Namibian cause. However, the CCN always operated under scrutiny of SWAPO's external leadership, and eventually was affected by their leadership style. In its control of donor aid, development policies and practices before independence, and the political process in Namibia, the CCN developed the same paternalistic, top-down culture as the SWAPO movement itself.[15] The massive structures developed by the CCN before independence (for education, legal aid, contextual theology, community development, social services, youth work, women's affairs, displaced persons, etc.), will nonetheless always testify to the fact that its influence was not restricted to words only: the CCN has in fact become the prime implementor of the churches' involvement with the Namibian people in their cause of peace and justice.[16]

The Question of Prophetic Consistency

It is against this undeniable involvement of the churches in the Namibian struggle for liberation, that the question of consistency must now be addressed. Could the churches keep up the agendas of justice, human rights and prophetic criticism, after access to independence, as before? The Namibian church historian, Nambala, makes interesting remarks on this challenge: "The ministry of the church...is not caged. It is directed to all people of God, irrespective of their political affiliation. Moreover, the church is a 'thorn in the flesh' to those who love injustice and violate human rights. The church...indicates how SWAPO is 'godless' or 'godly.'" He concludes his book on the history of the church in Namibia: "It is important for the church to be constant and faithful.... We hope the church in Namibia will be wise enough to assess these things

rightly. But in the face of injustice a neutral stance will always be
evil. The hope is that the church in Namibia will in all situations
continue to be a voice of the voiceless and the oppressed."[17]

In their testimony during the WCC Programme to Combat
Racism Hearings on Namibia, the Namibian church leaders said:
"The stands taken by individual Christians, bishops, international
church bodies, and later by whole churches have also influenced
SWAPO's perception of Namibian society and the possible nature
of Namibia as an independent state. The churches do not believe
naively that SWAPO will bring a utopia to Namibia. They hope to
continue the positive relationships which have been developed.
However, there is also a realization that, as the churches in other
parts of Africa have shown, the churches may also have a prophetic
role to play in opposition to any new tyranny that may emerge."[18]

Peter Katjavivi (currently Vice-Chancellor of the University of
Namibia) was bitterly criticized by Paul Trewhela[19] for not even
mentioning the detainee issue in his book *Church and Liberation in
Namibia*, published in 1989, when there could not have been any
more doubt about the reality of severe human rights abuses by
SWAPO in exile or the knowledge about it in church circles in
Namibia and internationally. Katjavivi himself ends his introduc-
tory article with two quotations which jointly pose crucial questions
to both the churches and SWAPO: (a) "Only if the Church is, and
is seen to be, on the side of the revolution in Southern Africa,
suffering and sharing in the guilt of spilt blood, can the church
then, from within the situation, judge the situation, then judge the
revolution.... Revolution inevitably involves suffering, death, separation and the ruin of human lives.... It seems likely that only a
church within the revolution can help to humanise it...";[20] (b) "It
is only after being faithful to this overall imperative of truthful
confrontation, and after having defeated the system of injustice
and lies that the churches will be able to work towards a further
step of liberation—the work of Namibian nation-building in the
light of national reconciliation. Oppressor and oppressed, aggressor and aggressed cannot be reconciled by the Church except in
the context of a just society under the scrutiny of truth."[21]

The crucial questions, implicit in these striking quotations but
still largely unanswered, are the following: Are the churches, that
shared the suffering and the guilt of spilt blood in defeating the

previous system of injustice, now judging the revolution fearlessly as to its outcome? Are they taking the further steps towards nation-building and reconciling the aggressor and the aggressed, under the scrutiny of the truth, and in the context of a just society? Have the churches played their part, as before independence, to ensure this new context of justice, truth and reconciliation?[22]

The Churches and the New Post-Independence Challenges

The churches and the CCN shared in the euphoria that spontaneously swept through the previously suppressed Namibian society, once it became clear that the UN-supervised elections resulted in a democratically elected government, a model Constitution, the rule of law and, at least in principle, a peaceful and just society. A sense of accomplishment and vindication was naturally part of the festive mood of liberation. However, the CCN was not only immediately saddled with a challenging task, that of "Repatriation, Resettlement and Reconstruction" of more than 41,000 returnees (delegated to the so-called RRR, or 3Rs, Committee),[23] it also had to face the severe challenges of a new role and status in a liberated society.

Although donor funding still helped the CCN to retain a high profile during the first few years after independence, especially through the commendable work of the 3Rs Committee and the revamped Communication Unit,[24] it was already apparent after the Conference on the future role of the Church in Namibia (March 27-31, 1990), that a drastic financial and organizational re-orientation was inevitable for the CCN.[25] After five years of painful re-orientation, the year 1996 saw the inevitable implementation of these drastic prunings, resulting in a CCN with a core staffing of 10 instead of more than 50 (in the heyday even 89!) full-time members, and only a handful of "facilitating" clusters remaining.

In spite of these sobering realities, the CCN and its member churches managed to address many burning issues, such as the churches' contribution towards a democratic and human rights culture, as well as national reconciliation.[26] Important issues highlighted in the short lifespan of the CCN publication, *CCN Messenger*, were: children's rights, drug abuse, AIDS and disabled persons. A concise CCN Documentation was also dedicated to the ideological abuse of religion by right-wing political groups.[27] Initiatives indicative of the contextual involvement of the churches were the Day of Prayer and the Conference dealing with Unemployment, as well as the African Association for Liturgy, Music and Art (AFALMA) workshop and festival on the theme: "Worshipping God as Africans."[28] These initiatives, however, also illustrate the weakness of the CCN in addressing relevant issues: restricted by funding, resources, and perhaps also lacking vision, the churches after independence could hardly manage to move beyond fruitful debate at conferences, with scarce effective implementation of good recommendations.[29] Although the 1994 Report of the CCN General Secretary, Dr. Ngeno Nakamhela, still provides details of a variety of activities, the restrictions brought about by financial constraints shine through. From the report it is also clear that an ambiguous relationship with the SWAPO government needs urgent clarification.[30]

A positive development for the ecumenical movement in Namibia was the admission of the "apartheid churches," the Dutch Reformed Church and the Reformed Church, as observers at the CCN. This provides a new context for a truthful process of reconciliation, in which many outstanding issues related to these churches' pro-apartheid stand of the past can be addressed. In principle, however, it seems as though there is a determination from both sides to work through this agenda, which may contribute meaningfully to the process of national reconciliation.

Struggling to maintain the churches' contextual involvement, the CCN in crisis was dealt another severe blow by the so-called drought-relief and food-aid scam in which individuals from the FMLU (Food Management and Logistics Unit of the CCN) were implicated. The ongoing investigation also points to corruption and collaboration by high-ranking government officials and may still lead to court cases and indictments, but has not helped the image of the struggling Council itself.

To add to the woes of the CCN, the year 1996 has squarely placed the neglected detainee issue once again on the churches' agenda. It seems fair to say that this issue, more than any other single issue or event, has exposed dangerous cracks in the edifice of "independent Namibia." The policy of national reconciliation, to be tested for truthfulness and consistency, came under pressure. The churches' inadequate contribution towards the process of true reconciliation and reconstruction is all too obvious. The lack of the erstwhile prophetic stamina is tragically evident. Indecisiveness and uncertainty, even blatant differences about the way forward, seem to have replaced the conviction and courage of yesteryear.

The Churches and the Detainee Issue

With the evidence now available, it is evident that the Namibian churches and their ecumenical allies such as the LWF and the WCC received details of disappearances, detentions, and torture within SWAPO from impeccable sources, already in the mid-seventies. Considering retrospectively how differently the detainee issue could have developed if only the churches had addressed it with the same prophetic vigor deployed against the South African atrocities, it must be admitted that there are simply no excuses for the universal conspiracy of silence on this matter.

Consider, for example, the very clear language of Rev. Salatiel Ailonga, the first Namibian pastor-in-exile, who had to flee Zambia after taking up the detention issue with the SWAPO leadership, as addressed to Bishop Leonard Auala of the Lutheran Church in the North, in a letter dated May 24, 1977: "As you know, since 1976 there was a conflict among the Namibians in Zambia. This led to many members in SWAPO and my Chaplaincy being imprisoned on the request of SWAPO's leadership. First, eleven leading members of the Party and Youth League, then forty-eight from the front, talking on behalf of the soldiers, and later on over one thousand Namibians disappeared. In the wake of this I had to leave Zambia and since June 1976 I have been staying in Finland." After giving Bishop Auala many details—especially about who were involved and where they were imprisoned, including some SWAPO Youth League leaders who challenged the leadership in exile to call a congress and have democratic elections of leaders—he urgently requested his Bishop to find a way of seeing some of these people while attending an LWF conference in Dar-es-Salaam, Tanzania, as head of a Namibian delegation. This offered the perfect opportunity of not only addressing the issue, but also visiting places of detention, including Mboroma camp in Zambia, where the "over one thousand" were kept.

The rest of Ailonga's letter proved to be almost visionary in its prophetic clarity: "According to the proofs and my knowledge, this is not a purely political case or internal SWAPO affair. It is a case concerning the wellbeing of the Namibians and their human rights, which touches the church and its responsibility to a great extent. The imprisoned in Tanzania and Zambia are members of all churches, including Lutherans, Anglicans and Roman Catholics. The reason for the imprisonment is not yet known to the world, and there is no legal ground to hold people without trial. This needs to be said with all seriousness even at the present (LWF) meeting.... If there should be any fault or crime, not all the thousand could be held responsible. There is a reliable report that at Mboroma camp in August last year many people were shot at, many were wounded and some died.... In matters like these, which may have the most serious effect for the future, the church should not be silent. All these thousand may be lost within a short time and never to return to Namibia. But there are thousand of families, friends and relatives of these people, and their voice will be demanding an explanation. What will the answer of the church be? I would say that in every leadership, church or state, the leaders have to be led and shown the truth without fear or partiality. That shows not enmity, but love for the leaders you correct, because you care about what he is doing. If you as leaders of the church in Namibia will fail to go with love into the question in SWAPO, which is a small group, how will you be able to cope with the problems which will arise on a much larger basis within a free Namibia, be it under the leadership of SWAPO or someone else? I request you in all humility to take this matter seriously and prevent more vain bloodshed."

Parallel to this letter, which was also sent to the President of the Evangelical Lutheran Church (in Southern Namibia), and the President of the LWF, are the many occasions on which another well-known pastor-in-exile, Pastor Siegfried Groth, gave even more detailed accounts to church leaders from Namibia and abroad, of the same events reported by Pastor Ailonga.[31] Sensitive letters to and from and other confidential documents of Pastor Groth were included in the shock publication, *Namibia, A Struggle Betrayed* (1986), in which a detailed analysis is given of the ruthless suppression of the attempts by some SWAPO Youth League and People's Liberation Army of Namibia (PLAN) cadres towards democratic reform and consolidation of the struggle, by what has become known as the "Old Guard" SWAPO leadership. The publication of these documents broke the silence on the open secret of SWAPO's scandalous handling of criticism and dissent once and for all.[32]

A Committee of Parents was formed to act on behalf of the parents and relatives of "missing persons," and to seriously challenge SWAPO, the churches and the international allies of Namibia's liberation struggle to address the human rights abuses within SWAPO. Following a meeting between internal and external partners in the Namibian struggle held in Lusaka in 1984, where the partners from "home" were informed about many details of the crisis by numerous friends in exile, one would have expected the churches to support, and even spearhead, investigations into and counter-measures against these atrocities. However, this shameful truth could simply not be faced at that stage. It was played down, ignored and even opposed energetically in lieu of another "truth": "Some church leaders, while aware of SWAPO's abuses, believed that only SWAPO was capable of bringing peace, and that any public action by them on the detainees issue would have weakened the movement fatally, leaving the Democratic Turnhalle Alliance (DTA), backed and financed by South Africa, to win any UN-sponsored elections. They were not prepared to allow this to happen for the sake of exposing a few 'bad apples' in SWAPO. Their conviction that SWAPO and liberation were inseparable led them to sacrifice their religious principles on the altar of political expediency."[33] Once this political agenda was endorsed by the churches and other international partners, it became more and more difficult for them to admit and to confess their complicity, and to raise a new, critical voice. That is why the same pattern of discrediting efforts such as those of the Committee of Parents, has befallen similar critical voices and movements up to this day.

Fortunately, due to a convergence of important factors,[34] the quick turn of events leading to the implementation of the UN Peace Plan in 1989 also saw the return of at least 200 of the detained "spies" who publicly verified the earlier allegations of human rights abuses in SWAPO with gruesome details of their fate at the hand of the SWAPO security system.[35] The first response came from the Justice and Peace Commission of the Catholic Church on July 12, 1989, mentioning "great pain and deep disappointment" about the stories of suffering and torture, but also denouncing the misuse of the detainees' suffering for party-political gain (against SWAPO). After meeting with a group of detainees and SWAPO leaders (on August 23 and 24, 1989), the CCN Executive issued a cautious statement, conceding on the one hand that many of the victims of the vicious cycle of wars were innocent, but on the other hand also blaming apartheid for the suspicion and distrust that led to the destruction of the unity of the oppressed. While stressing the need for forgiveness as the basis of nation-building, the CCN leaders "failed to acknowledge their own failure to respond earlier"[36]—endorsing a policy of reconciliation in which confession and apology, as correlatives for forgiveness, are played down.

These double standards by the churches and international partners of SWAPO made it possible for a deadly pattern to develop: with SWAPO, from time to time under pressure of detailed revelations of internal problems, first strongly denying and then later admitting these in a very qualified way, only to allow the "silent complicity agenda" to prevent a public scrutiny of the underlying issues. This strategy in effect actively fostered the avoidance of a true confrontation with the darker side of the Namibian struggle for liberation. The pattern was illustrated in February 1986, when two senior SWAPO functionaries, Theo-Ben Gurirab and Hidipo Hamutenya (currently senior cabinet ministers), announced in London that SWAPO was detaining at least one hundred of its own members as South African spies, paving the way for the CCN's General Secretary, Dr. Shejavali, to brush aside the Committee of Parents' charges as mere allegations and defend SWAPO's right to protect its people from collaborators with the enemy. The same pattern was revealed after the shock revelations by ex-detainees, back home from Angola, when SWAPO reacted with a strongly worded election statement in the media, in July 1989, denying all allegations. To Mr. Gurirab was left the uncomfortable task of qualifying this hard-line stance by admitting publicly that "the issue of the former detainees was a painful subject affecting virtually every family in Namibia"; that it would not go away by being ignored; and that the time for dialogue on this painful issue has arrived. "At the end of the day we will have to sit around the fire and take inventories: who is alive, who is dead, how did it all happen? As a SWAPO leader, I will never defend the humiliation and suffering of torture. If the allegations are true, I apologize to the victims and to their parents and pledge to you now that the SWAPO leadership will take the necessary steps to bring those involved to book."[37]

The detainee issue became a hotly-debated election campaign topic. The Parents Committee and the Political Consultative Council[38] pursued the demands of justice as civil society action groups; political parties such as the Patriotic Unity Movement, launched by some ex-detainees, and the United Democratic Front put tremendous pressure on SWAPO and the churches to follow up on Gurirab's admission.[39] All these efforts, combined with the public outrage as reflected in the Namibian press, resulted in public statements from *inter alia* the Green Party in Germany, the UN, the LWF and the German Churches (EKD), condemning the human rights abuses of SWAPO in exile. However, this overt politicization of the issue again led to the negative effect of a renewed implementation of SWAPO's culture of silence and denial. It also diverted the praiseworthy policy of national reconciliation in a dangerous direction: one where those responsible for atrocities (the SWAPO security agents and the Koevoets of South Africa) could easily agree on a shallow conciliation of "forgive and forget," without truth and justice; one in which injustices of the past could simply be swept under the carpet, and the wounds of war be left to heal by themselves.[40]

Even Pastor Groth's publication, in the crucial election period (September 1989), *Menschenrechtsverletzungen in der namibischen Exil-SWAPO—die Verantwortung der Kirchen*, with 27 addenda of letters and relevant substantiating documents giving a clear picture of the complicity of the churches in promoting the deadly "culture of silence," was immediately attacked by colleagues from Germany: "Groth's statements did not support reconciliation, but division, suspicion and non-peace. With this publication he does not only discredit the party that, for decades, has carried the main burden of the liberation struggle, but also the churches in Namibia, who expect definite signs of solidarity from us."[41]

Today, looking back at this very intense period during Namibia's first free and fair elections, it is easy to see how proper pressure from the churches in Namibia could have redefined the whole process of reconciliation. Whatever the motivations and rationalizations at the time, SWAPO was let off the hook and allowed to continue its authoritarian and uncompromising culture and to take over the governing responsibility without having accounted for its own human rights abuses.

As Peter Koep argued in March 1992, SWAPO came closest to accepting responsibility for any abuses committed before independence during the run-up period to the elections, in 1989-90.[42] After winning the elections comfortably, just short of a two-thirds majority, the detainee issue was buried by SWAPO, and the "Butcher of Lubango" (the man in charge of "security"), Jesus Solomon Hauala, was appointed as Commander of the Namibian Army in October 1990. At that stage the protests of Dr. Shejavali, on behalf of the CCN, fell on deaf ears: the CCN style, of "discussing" such issues with the SWAPO leadership, had no effect. What Roy Enquist has aptly called "Politics of reconciliation, Namibian style," and Gwen Lister (editor of the influential daily paper, *The Namibian*) has called "reconciliation without any stocktaking exercise, without an attempt to come to terms with the past," was already firmly in place, with the churches' complicity.[43] Steve Titus' assessment is that in terms of the Kairos theology, the Namibian churches have lapsed into a "state theology," accompanied by a "church theology"—both of which compromise the churches' true prophetic witness.[44] In Steenkamp's judgment, the churches had fallen prey to the same authoritarian culture as their political partners, and thus could not speak the liberating word in time.[45] As with apartheid, religion once again could not break through an ideology of self-interest and could not liberate people to a culture of truth and justice. The churches were part and parcel of an international scandal, which cannot be rationalized.[46]

New Initiatives within Civil Society and New Hope for True Reconciliation

Just when it seemed as if Namibians had accepted living cynically with all the skeletons of war in the national cupboard, a book by pastor Siegfried Groth, first published in German[47] but soon also in English translation, stirred up the emotions, memories and discussions. In *Namibia—The Wall of Silence* (1995) Groth simply told the stories of approximately one hundred SWAPO detainees or dissidents and their struggles to survive the SWAPO security system, the torture chambers of Lubango and the desperation of people seemingly forgotten by the outside world. My review of the German edition of the book, in the *Windhoek Observer* of June 24, 1995, was given a provocative caption by the editor: "Shattering SWAPO's wall of silence," which inspired the English title of the book, and sparked an intense public interest. When the English translation became available towards the end of 1995, bookstores could not cope with the demand, and ex-detainees, hopeful that the issues involved will at last receive due attention in Namibia, started discussing the idea that the CCN should be approached to launch the book—using the opportunity to publicly confess the churches' guilt in this sad chapter and simultaneously initiate a process of national reconciliation and healing.

After an inspiring keynote address by the Namibian academic, Joseph Diescho, at the Annual General Meeting (AGM) of the CCN early in December 1995, the detainee issue was discussed seriously. Dr. Shejavali, the General Secretary of the CCN at the time when this issue first surfaced, before independence, openly admitted that he had been misled through the SWAPO counter-propaganda, such as the enforced videotaped "spy confessions." He also stated that the time had come for the churches to face the issue and come up with new initiatives to address it squarely. The AGM also noted a decision to this effect. In mid-January 1996 the CCN received a formal request, signed by forty-two ex-detainees, to launch the Groth book, described as "just the tip of an iceberg," which could be supplemented with many living testimonies as to the hell experienced in Lubango and other SWAPO detention centers. They also asked for an audience with the CCN Executive, to ensure that these church leaders were in a position to make a well-informed decision. Without meeting the ex-detainees, the CCN Executive issued a statement on February 19, 1996, explaining that the CCN had decided not to launch the book (which was seen as "a commercial venture"), but to organize a national conference "somewhere between May and July 1996," to address "the serious

issues raised by the author of the book...more fully." At the same
time the Executive encouraged leaders and ordinary members of
churches and the public at large to read the book for themselves.

In the meantime a new civil society movement, the *Breaking the
Wall of Silence Movement* (BWS) was growing rapidly. Since January
1996 a group of ex-detainees had been meeting regularly, and
soon elected a Committee to coordinate the new initiative. BWS
actively engaged in the ensuing public debate through the media.
A pledge was made that BWS would contribute, as far as possible,
towards the success of the proposed church conference, and the
negative utterances by some bishops about the Groth book were
challenged.[48]

Suddenly the nation realized that Namibia was confronted with
a very important unfinished agenda. A TV reporter of the National
Broadcasting Corporation screened a long interview with members
of the BWS Committee, some ex-detainees, and the General
Secretary of the CCN—all of whom spoke out straightforwardly on
the human rights abuses within SWAPO and the need to still
address this shameful history and its possible effects on post-
independent Namibia's political culture. The next evening, on
March 6, 1996, the nation was surprised when State President
Nujoma himself appeared on TV for an unscheduled attack on the
Groth book, speaking as "the President of SWAPO and the
Commander-in-Chief of the Namibia Defence armed force," and
denouncing the book as "false history." His fifteen-minute speech
was characterized by a scathing personal attack on the person of
Pastor Groth, who was described as "never a friend of SWAPO and
thus never a friend of Namibia's liberation struggle." The President stated that "Pastor Groth's agenda will only lead to bloodshed
in our country," something that will not be tolerated.[49] He also
construed Christo Lombard as someone "assigned to work as an
apostle of apartheid to ensure that Bantu education and white domination were perpetuated in Namibia," who "dutifully served that
apartheid system" and had to remember that he was not dismissed
from his work at the university because of the policy of national
reconciliation.[50] When I reacted in the media with a personal letter
to the President, pointing out that he had not addressed the real
issue at stake: the truth about SWAPO atrocities against Namibian
compatriots, a heated debate was sparked in the media.[51]

SWAPO, realizing that what was thought to be a buried issue was resurrected almost overnight, reacted with even stronger language, again playing the politics of fear-mongering: on March 12, 1996 Mr. Moses Garoeb, Secretary General of SWAPO, issued a statement on behalf of the Party, making it very clear who was in control: "SWAPO cannot allow this country to be made ungovernable and be turned into a chaotic and lawless society by irresponsible, unpatriotic elements and foreign remnants of fascism, and apartheid." An attack was also launched on the current General Secretary of the CCN, Rev. Nakamhela, who was described as "the nonentity unknown in the long journey to freedom of our people who is under the influence and control of renegades and foreign finance," and who "is viciously engaged in wanton destruction of the unity of the church, good relations between SWAPO and the church, the policy of national reconciliation, peace, stability and fomenting hatred among the people of this country." The offensive attitude of the statement, closing with calls to compatriots "to rise and defend the gains of our revolution," was supplemented by Garoeb's personal comments that perhaps Namibia needed "a new revolution," "a civil war," to sort out the issue.

It soon became evident, through the enormous reaction in the media, especially also in the so-called "radio chat shows," that SWAPO had miscalculated the national mood on the detainee issue, and that the personal attacks were counter-productive. In a spirited show of civil courage people simply spoke their minds. Even the SWAPO-affiliated umbrella body for NGOs, Nangof, responded critically.[52] The National Society for Human Rights (NSHR) energetically took up the agenda, responding with various media statements, such as: "Civil war against the truth?"[53] Many individuals, some of them strong SWAPO supporters, rallied on behalf of the detainees and the Groth book, but also religious bodies such as the local Quaker group, issued supportive statements. A debate on the merits of the Groth book was also sparked in German church circles.[54]

Amid these hectic debates the BWS Movement pushed ahead and organized a very successful launch of the Groth book, at a well-known hotel in central Windhoek, on March 30, 1996. The public interest at the launch, where hundreds of people had to be turned away because of limited space, but also after the launch, was simply enormous. The book was translated into Afrikaans in record time, and all English copies were time and again sold immediately upon arrival.[55] An Oshivambo translation is still in process. After the book launch and the ensuing debates in the Namibian media, the detainee issue also attracted international attention: the BBC made several in-depth broadcasts, and German, British, South African and American papers and church magazines published critical articles, covering the developing debate.[56]

The detainee saga saw a new twist when it became apparent that the CCN itself was divided on the viability of its own proposed conference. The division was brought about by the hesitance of some bishops, who are not always directly involved in the decisions of the CCN Executive. Having built up a sound relationship with SWAPO, and with President Nujoma personally, some church leaders showed reluctance to force the issue with SWAPO. The internal debate within the CCN, in which the unity of the ecumenical movement remains a serious consideration, resulted in a postponement of the proposed conference and the appointment of a special Committee.

At the last Annual General Meeting of the CCN, in December 1996, a proposition was accepted to dedicate 1997 as "A Year of God's Grace" in Namibia, and to mandate the General Secretary personally to take personal responsibility for a national conference on reconciliation, after meetings with all relevant parties. Significantly, also, Bishop Dumeni was elected as the new President of the CCN. There thus seems to be a new resoluteness about the role of the churches in contributing towards national reconciliation and the healing of the wounds.

An interesting development also came on Heroes Day (August 26), when SWAPO launched a book of its own, *Their Blood Waters Our Freedom*, containing the names of almost 8000 "heroes of the liberation struggle" who had paid the ultimate price. Before the content was known BWS and the NSHR cautiously welcomed the idea of SWAPO's accounting for those who died in their care during the struggle. Unfortunately, however, the book is still very controversial because of glaring omissions, repetitions, obvious mistakes, the inclusion of the names of people who were previously branded as spies and traitors (such as Tauno Hautuikulipi, the former Director of the Christian Centre), and then of course also the exclusion of other names.[57]

In the debate which followed this publication, the Prime Minister, Mr. Hage Geingob, challenged the opposition parties in the National Assembly, especially the DTA, who was responsible for the formation of an "interim government" under the auspices of South Africa, to also come clear on their own involvement with human rights abuses before independence. He charged them to account in similar fashion to the Namibian people, so that reconciliation would not only depend on SWAPO's one-sided revelations and confessions. This proposal was strongly supported by the Deputy Speaker, Dr. Zephaniah Kameeta (previously also a very influential church leader), who urged that the SWAPO book be corrected where necessary, and supplemented with the "Book Two," supplied by South Africa and the opposition parties. He proposed that the "revised book" should be supervised and published by a Government body, and should be "launched at a solemn occasion of forgiveness and reconciliation and the brave people of Namibia will close this chapter of our liberation history in unity."[58]

The Minister of Higher Education, Vocational Training, Science and Technology, Mr. Nahas Angula, made a remarkable contribution in parliament and in local papers when he described the "long, tortuous road" that led to independence, and pointed out that the ugly turn of events in the war could have been avoided if South Africa, and the internal parties in Namibia, had accepted SWAPO's cease-fire in the early 1980s, instead of forcing the Liberation Movement to react to their dirty war tricks and "Total Strategy against the Total Onslaught." His suggestion for a solution to the present impasse is simple: "In my view the best way to turn a new page on this issue is for those who were responsible for imposing the war on the Namibian people to come clean by opening their records truthfully and sincerely and to make available the names of those who worked for them.... I see no reason why they should not be able to give the list of all their agents." He said he did not want to simply shift the responsibility from SWAPO, but he wanted "a way to close the tragic chapter in the history of our country." He suggested that, while apartheid was discredited as a crime against humanity, and South Africa was fighting an illegal war against the Namibians, "at the end of the day...the people of Namibia have a right to demand the establishment of an International Tribunal to try the crimes of apartheid and illegal occupation." He ended by stating: "To those innocent people caught in the cross-fire, I want to say: 'Human is error, forgiveness divine.'"[59]

With the contributions by the Prime Minister, Dr. Kameeta and Minister Angula, there seemed to be some hope of a compromise solution. However, directly after an analysis of the role of fear in Namibian politics by Joseph Diescho,[60] and a call for dialogue rather than confrontation by the CCN President, SWAPO officially called for a boycott of any conferences organized by the CCN. As already mentioned, the CCN, however, now seems to be working independently on its own role and task in the process of national reconciliation, and it will be very interesting to see how the chemistry of the new CCN President, Bishop Dumeni, will influence the strategies and processes.

A Test-Case Still Waiting for a Solution

Whether Namibia will eventually go through a formal Truth and Reconciliation process, as South Africa has, remains to be seen. The BWS will probably proceed along its course of pushing for a meeting between SWAPO and the detainees, and for a just and honorable solution to the dilemma. The CCN will cautiously pursue 1997 as "the Year of God's Grace." Politicians may toy with the idea of an International Tribunal, or forcing the opposition parties and South Africa to deliver a "Volume Two" of "missing persons." As Bronkhorst has indicated in his analysis of similar problems elsewhere in the world (in Chile, Argentina, Peru, Philippines, Guatemala, etc.),[61] all conciliation processes (industrial or political) have four crucial elements that need to be addressed: *investigation* (through which the truth needs to be established); *mediation* (which needs grace, preparedness to reconcile, to apologize and to forgive); *adjudication* (which could mean legal action, the purpose of which is to let justice be done to victims); and *settlement* (which looks for redress, retribution and restoration of peace).[62]

A significant development recently has been the establishment, quite independently from the CCN and the BWS Movement, but also from party politics, of a Project for the Study of Violence and Reconciliation, the purpose of which is to establish the truth about atrocities committed by both SWAPO and South Africa, to have the stories of the victims recorded and told, to offer counselling for victims and their relatives, and to prepare sworn legal statements.[63]

For people interested in the role of religion and morality in society, this Namibian test-case has many interesting and vexing questions. Truth and justice are obviously of paramount importance. Forgiveness, seen in a Christian context at least, is not dependent on confession or apology, but of course the process of reconciliation is incomplete without both. A process of reconciliation cannot seek revenge and cannot attempt to keep open a can of worms forever. It also cannot tolerate easy solutions, such as "forgive and forget." It will look for a long-term solution, a permanent "healing of the wounds," but wounds cannot be healed if their existence is not acknowledged.

Namibia is confronted with a real test-case in which important religious and moral principles are strongly implicated: will SWAPO admit its human rights abuses and democratize itself for the benefit of the whole nation? Will South Africa and the opposition parties in Namibia "open up their books," contributing to a balanced approach to reconciliation? Will the churches regain their independent prophetic voice and lead the way as "the Servant of the Lord," carrying the burdens of a nation vicariously? Will the media and the diplomatic world react responsibly, fairly and justly? Will civil society organize itself, allowing independent initiatives to develop their unique contributions to the "common good"?

In this test-case a lot is at stake: perhaps nothing less than the future of a nation!

NOTES

1. This was especially true since the famous "Open Letter," addressed to Prime Minister John Voster, and signed by Bishop Auala and Pastor Gowaseb on behalf of the two (black) branches of the Lutheran Church (representing almost half the population of Namibia), on June 21, 1971. In this prophetic letter these leaders clearly spelled out the churches' concern for social justice, which henceforth brought the ecumenical churches in direct conflict with the colonial oppressors.

2. See also P. Trewhela, "Swapo and the Churches: An International

Scandal," in *Searchlight South Africa*, Vol. 2, No. 3 (1991): 65-88 for a similar assessment.

3. The detainee and missing persons issue is a result of SWAPO's unfortunate history, since the "Kongwa crisis" of the late 1960s, of detaining hundreds, even thousands, of its own members, accusing them of being dissidents, rebels, traitors and spies. Not only were these people detained and tortured in the most inhumane fashion, but many are still considered to be "missing persons," unaccounted for by SWAPO. After protracted investigations by the International Committee of the Red Cross into this issue, the ICRC report, issued after its search deadline of April 30, 1993, still considered 1605 out of 2161 tracing requests as unaccounted for by SWAPO, where the previous South African government still had to account for 34 persons. SWAPO's book, *Their Blood Waters Our Freedom*, released on Heroes Day (August 26) 1996, and containing lists of almost 8000 fallen heroes, unfortunately still does not provide a satisfactory answer to these grim statistics.

4. This is the overall drive of the analysis given in the authoritative publication of Leys and Saul on the legacy of Namibia's liberation struggle: that the same authoritarian leadership style of the "Old Guard" may be allowed to continue unabated, within the rhetoric of democracy (see e.g., C. Leys and J.S. Saul, *Namibia's Liberation Struggle: The Two-Edged Sword* [London: James Currey, 1995], pp. 1-8; 196-203).

5. "Epistle to the Namibians," quoted in P. Katjavivi (with Frostin and Mbuende), *Church and Liberation in Namibia* (London: Pluto Press, 1989), pp. 136-138. It is interesting to note how many prominent church leaders were speaking out against "neutrality" and "silence," cf. Rev. A. Maasdorp (a Namibian church leader who became a high official in the Lutheran World Federation): "In the matter of racialism, no one may ever be neutral or silent" (quoted in P. Katjavivi [with Frostin and Mbuende], *Church and Liberation in Namibia* [London: Pluto Press, 1989], p. 23).

6. See Trewhela, "Swapo and the Churches," *op. cit.*, p. 71.

7. Cf. LWF Documentation, *The Church and the Namibian Quest for Independence*, Nr. 22/23, July 1987 (edited by F. Maher), Geneve: WCC, pp. 75-79.

8. See Z. Kameeta, "South African Illegal Presence in Namibia and the Confessing Church," in G. Tötemeyer (with V. Kandetu and W. Werner), *Namibia in Perspective* (Windhoek: CCN, 1987), p. 209. In February 1982 the CCN issued another statement to the South African Prime Minister in Windhoek, challenging him to allow free and fair elections in Namibia.

9. See LWF Documentation, *The Church and the Namibian Quest, op. cit.*, pp. 80-82. The Statement also deplored the mass massacre at Kassinga, which took place in southern Angola on May 4, 1978, and again spoke out strongly against the continued use of torture and violence by South

Africa, ending with this significant sentence: "Reconciliation will only come to Namibia when true justice is accorded to the oppressed."

10. See Hunke in LWF Documentation, *The Church and the Namibian Quest, op. cit.*, pp. 35-45.

11. See Steenkamp in Leys and Saul, *Namibia's Liberation Struggle, op. cit.*, pp. 97ff.

11. *Ibid.*

12. See the many "Open Letters" to members of the Western Contact Group, the Christian Churches in Europe and North America, and the report of the WCC Washington Hearings on Namibia (May 2-4, 1988). For these documents, cf. Katjavivi, *Church and Liberation, op. cit.*, pp. 145-206.

13. See Winter's description of the harassment, including arson, in C. Winter, *The Breaking Process* (London: SCM, 1981), pp. 48-50.

14. Bonhoeffer, as quoted by Kameeta, "South African Illegal Presence," *op. cit.*, p. 212. Steenkamp (in Leys and Saul, *Namibia's Liberation Struggle, op. cit.*, p. 94) also presents a useful typification: There were three distinct facets of the church's role in opposition to the authoritarian regime: institutional, ideological and operational.

15. See Steenkamp in Leys and Saul, *Namibia's Liberation Struggle, op. cit.*, pp. 107-111; also Trewhela, "Swapo and the Churches," *op. cit.*, pp. 67-72.

16. See Kandetu's article on the work of the CCN, in Katjavivi, *Church and Liberation, op. cit.*, pp. 207-214.

17. S. Nambala, *History of the Church in Namibia*, edited by O.K. Olson, *The Lutheran Quarterly*, 1994, pp. 159, 169.

18. In Katjavivi, *Church and Liberation, op. cit.*, p. 190.

19. See Trewhela, "Swapo and the Churches," *op. cit.*, p. 65: "The complicity of the churches—their refusal to speak out, and the sanitary screen they provided to the torturers—is continued in this book, which serves to perpetuate the offence. Like the churches, the editors of the book are culpable. The book is a knowing deception, offered to readers at the moment when the truth could no longer be concealed."

20. See Katjavivi, *Church and Liberation, op. cit.*, p. 24 (taken from: *Violence in Southern Africa* [London: SCM, 1970], p. 73).

21. See Katjavivi, *Church and Liberation, op. cit.*, p. 25 (a quotation from the Statement by the Church Group at the International Conference for Solidarity with the People of Namibia, Paris, September 11-13, 1980).

22. After independence the real test would be exactly whether the churches would still be the voice of the voiceless, the thorn in the flesh of those who violate human rights, a prophetic opposition to any new tyranny that may emerge! If the churches fail to address the issue of justice and human rights within the legacy of the liberator, of SWAPO itself, they would be guilty of contributing to a cover-up of injustice, endorsing an authoritarian political tradition and a false basis for true reconciliation in Namibia, in spite of the sound Constitution and the rhetoric of

democracy, as endorsed by SWAPO. Cf. also Winter, *The Breaking Process*, *op. cit.*, p. 46.

23. Cf. the article on the work of the RRR Committee in *CCN Messenger*, August 1991, p. 16.

24. Cf. publications such as *CCN Messenger* (which was produced monthly beginning August 1991, unfortunately only for some months) and *CCN Documentation* (a series in which various high-profile CCN conferences and annual reports were highlighted).

25. See the Conference report: "Together in Jesus Christ, The Role of the Church in the Transformation of the Namibian Society," Windhoek, March 27-31, 1990, pp. 55-56.

26. Cf. the contributions in *Together in Jesus Christ* (Report of CCN Conference, March 27-31, 1990); "Proceedings of the CCN-Roundtable Consultation," September 25-27, 1990, Windhoek, pp. 20-32, as well as *CCN Messenger*, September and October 1991, the focus of which was "national reconciliation."

27. *CCN Documentation*, March 1991: "Focus on right-wing religion in Southern Africa."

28. Cf. the *CCN Documentation*, February 1994: "Towards Ministry with the Unemployed," a report of the October 1993 Conference, and: *Worshipping God as Africans*, 1995 (editor: C. Lombard).

29. If the recommendations of the Unemployment Conference, where the churches, trade unions and NGOs shared a common vision for challenging the government to create joint development ventures instead of buying expensive presidential jets, could be acted upon, the churches could have played a major role in consolidating donor interest in the real problems of the Namibian nation!

30. The report mentions the Prime Minister's Consultative Meeting with church leaders, held July 28-29, 1993, merely listing concerns that were discussed: alcoholism, child abuse, pornography, rape, and other socioeconomic problems facing Namibia—without acknowledging the crisis for the churches that they could offer very few initiatives to help solve these issues, or the bigger crisis that they could merely respond passively to a summons from the political authorities. (Proceedings of the Ninth Ordinary General Meeting of the CCN, July 12-14, 1994, pp. 30-45.)

31. For details of Groth's "revelations" in the seventies and eighties, cf. Trewhela, "Swapo and the Churches," *op. cit.*, and Steenkamp, in Leys and Saul, *Namibia's Liberation Struggle*, *op. cit.*

32. Steenkamp gives a useful summary of the "detainee crisis," the attempts by Erica and Attie Beukes, as employees of the CCN, to get the churches and ecumenical world to react effectively, and their summary dismissal from the CCN on account of their "very serious allegations, *inter alia*, in regard to the role of the Churches and its commitment to upholding basic human rights." (See Steenkamp, in Leys and Saul, *Namibia's*

Liberation Struggle, op. cit., pp. 104-107).

33. Cf. Steenkamp, in Leys and Saul, *Namibia's Liberation Struggle, op. cit.*, p. 107.

34. For background, see the analysis in *Namibia Peace Plan 435 or Society under Siege*, published by the NPP 435 Group early in 1987, as well as the strong resolutions of the Ai Gams Meeting (composed of all the pro 435 parties, including the churches), held in Windhoek, April 1986.

35. In the context of the international peace plan for Namibia, SWAPO was forced to release more than 200 detainees from its prisons (the "dungeons") of Lubango in Angola on April 19, 1989. The first reports of these persons' testimonies sent shock waves through pro-SWAPO circles, but it was the press conference of the first group of 153 on July 6, 1989 in Windhoek, where some of them showed their torture scars, that forced the churches, and other SWAPO allies, to break their silence publicly as well.

36. Steenkamp, in Leys and Saul, *Namibia's Liberation Struggle, op. cit.*, p. 107.

37. *Times of Namibia*, July 10, 1989.

38. The PCC was a political lobbying and conscientizing group, formed by ex-detainees, with the express purpose of revealing SWAPO atrocities and enforcing a public apology from SWAPO and a permanent solution to the detainee issue.

39. Ex-detainees, working together in the PCC, issued detailed statements and documents, giving grim details of torture, lists of missing persons, and names of torturers and high-ranking SWAPO officials who knew about or who were even actively engaged in torture practices. See e.g.: *A Report to the Namibian People*, 1989; *Appeal for the Release of Over 1,000 Namibians in Detentions in Zambia and Tanzania*, 1977; R.A. Kaakunga, Letter to the Director, SWAPO Directorate of Elections, July 13, 1989, on behalf of the Political Consultative Council (with a list of people who died in SWAPO prisons); Z.A. Mnakapa, "1986: the Tenth Anniversary of Death" (text of a document signed by Zen Mnakapa, January 7, 1987, with details of people who died at Mboroma prison, and the circumstances in other prisons in Zambia and Tanzania where scores of SWAPO dissidents were detained). See also D. Niddrie, "The Detentions," *Work in Progress*, September/October 1989: 21-23.

40. Interesting in this regard is the strong reaction by Bishop Dumeni (the successor of Bishop Auala, and currently President of the CCN) in *The Namibian* of October 16, 1989 to a letter by Rev. Salatiel Ailonga, challenging his view that the churches were silent. Dumeni stated that the Namibian churches and the LWF on occasion did speak to SWAPO and did book a measure of success through this approach. Going on to reject human rights abuses from whatever quarter, calling on anyone who may still have prisoners or detainees to release them, and rejecting torture unequivocally, he went on to say: "It is now time to confess the truth on

all sides, to ask and grant forgiveness, to put the past behind and to start anew. The future is very important. The people of Namibia have suffered tremendously over the years of colonialism and foreign occupation. It is now our task to build our nation on the firm foundation of peace, justice and respect for human rights. It is for this very reason that through the CCN and within my own church, we are now engaged in a process of trying to heal the wounds, for we regard this to be very important for the future of our country." The question however remains whether the churches could not have initiated this process of healing, of "telling the truth," of asking for forgiveness, by admitting openly that they did not speak out loudly enough (instead of silently addressing the issue with those ultimately responsible for the torture, disappearances and even murder of SWAPO cadres), when people cried out for help—people like Rev. Ailonga and Rev. Groth, and scores of Namibians in exile.

41. *The Namibian*, October 20, 1989 ("Siegfried Groth Taken to Task"). This reaction differs markedly from that of the Green Party in Germany who criticized SWAPO's statement of July 7, 1989, saying it "does not contain a single word of self-criticism," and asked for immediate action on four crucial points: that SWAPO provide reliable official information on whether—and if so, how many—prisoners were still being detained in SWAPO camps, and that these should immediately be released; that an independent commission of investigation be set up, as promised, without delay; that the responsible persons be identified and called to account as soon as possible (including the security chief, Jesus Hauala, whose continued employ as high ranking officer "would augur ill for SWAPO's willingness and ability to subject what has happened to a critical and impartial examination"); that the victims of torture and the members of their families be rehabilitated and given adequate compensation. (See *The Namibian*, August 21, 1989.)

42. P. Koep, "Coming to Terms with the Past," in *Namibia Brief*, No. 16, March 1992: 59-61. He states: "In retrospect, I believe this was the only real opportunity to have revealed the truth." The only alternative he sees would be a so-called Truth Commission in Namibia, similar to those established in Chile and Argentina (and now, more recently, also in South Africa): "The objective of such a commission would be to ascertain the truth about human rights abuses committed by Namibians on Namibians prior to independence, as well as abuses committed by South African Forces on Namibians, to expose the perpetrators to the public as well as to make known the atrocities committed by them. The ultimate aim would be to reveal the truth in order for it to act as a deterrent to society and to ensure that abuses of such nature never occur again. This process would serve primarily to educate, inform and to heal society."

43. See R.J. Enquist, "Politics of Reconciliation, Namibian Style," *Christian Century*, March 15, 1995, pp. 300-301.

44. S.J. Titus, "Church and State Relations in Namibia since Independence," (unpublished paper, 1996), pp. 1-6.

45. Steenkamp in Leys and Saul, *Namibia's Liberation Struggle, op. cit.*, pp. 111-112.

46. Trewhela, "Swapo and the Churches," *op. cit.*

47. *Namibische Passion. Tragik und Größe der namibischen Befreiungsbewegung.* The term "Passion" conveys both the Christian notion of suffering and the general sense of strong emotion.

48. BWS media release, February 29, 1996. Bishop Dumeni e.g. stated that the Groth book was "one-sided"; "not written on the assignment of the CCN"; "even written by an outsider" and was "disturbing the policy of reconciliation in the country." It soon transpired that selected church leaders were summoned for "talks" with the President, Mr. Sam Nujoma —the content of which is unknown.

49. This ignores the fact that Groth was banned from Namibia by South Africa for almost seventeen years exactly because of his involvement with SWAPO and Namibia's liberation struggle.

50. This came as quite a shock and surprise for many, since Namibians know that I was one of the few Namibian whites who travelled to Lusaka and Stockholm to discuss the implementation of UN Resolution 435 with the SWAPO leadership (including the President), and who, together with figures like Adv. Bryan O'Linn, and other professional people, launched NPP 435, a group that campaigned successfully, nationally and internationally, for the scrupulous implementation of the "Namibia Peace Plan 435."

51. In my "Open Letter to the President" of March 9, 1996, I explained the motives for BWS' pressure that the truth be revealed for the sake of true reconciliation, pointing out that SWAPO's policy of national reconciliation has up to now not provided for mechanisms to handle this issue. "I agree with you that we can be victorious as a nation, but I urge you to take the real process of reconciliation seriously; admitting first of all where things went wrong, confessing those mistakes in humility, restoring the honour of those affected and making good as far as possible...." "I urge you to have SWAPO participate in the CCN conference and to trust God and 'the way of truth' to help us clear this serious hurdle to real reconciliation. If we fail here, the tradition of fear and authoritarianism will simply continue in our beloved Namibia. Then all SWAPO's good work would have been in vain."

52. For selected documents reflecting the enormous national debate, see the two documents prepared by BWS: *BWS Statements and Clippings: February - April 1996* and *BWS Statements and Clippings: August - November 1996.*

53. See NSHR, *Namibia: Human Rights Report 1995*, released by the National Society for Human Rights, Windhoek, February 12, 1996; NSHR, *Breaking the Wall of Silence: Reaction to Bishop Dumeni's Remarks*, media release

by the National Society for Human Rights, Windhoek, February 28, 1996; NSHR, "SWAPO's Book of the Dead," statement released at a Media Conference by the National Society of Human Rights, Windhoek, September 1996.

54. See e.g. M. Braun, "Siegfried Groth: Namibische Passion," *Junge Kirche*, 4/96:251; R. Kössler, "Bricht die Mauer des Schweigens?" *Afrika Süd*, 2/96: 23-25; Ökumenisches Forum Rheinland, "Presseerklärung: Die 'Namibische Passion'—ein Buch verursacht Schaden in Namibia, in Deutschland und in der Kirchen," *Transparent*, 42/96:17-18; and H. Weiland, "Namibische Passion," *Anmerkungen zu einem Buch über die Menschen-rechtsverletzungen der SWAPO während des Befreiungskampfs, Afrika Süd*, 4/95:28-29.

55. Initially there were critical questions at the University of Namibia, where the Ecumenical Institute for Namibia (EIN), of which I am the Director, took responsibility for the translation and publication of the book in Afrikaans. Academic freedom seems to be restored after the EIN Board affirmed and explained its endorsement of the project as an approved and donor-funded EIN project.

56. Particularly influential was the in-depth article by David Miller in *The Lutheran*, an American-based church magazine with a circulation of a quarter million: "Tortured by the past: can Namibian Lutherans free themselves from their liberators?" (July, 1996).

57. See especially the media statements of the NSHR, dated September 4, 1996 (NSHR, "SWAPO's Book of the Dead," *op. cit.*), and calling the "Book of the Dead" a massive cover-up, and of the BWS, dated October 29, 1996, in which they called on SWAPO to apologize to the victims of their human rights abuses and to meet such victims under the auspices of neutral mediators. On October 1, 1996 the Prime Minister admitted that the SWAPO book contained mistakes, and also regretted that some innocent people might have been branded as spies.

58. See *The Namibian*, October 16, 1996.

59. See the full speech in the *Windhoek Observer*, October 12, 1996.

60. See his booklet (1996) and "The Role of Fear in Politics," in *The Namibian*, October 25, 1996.

61. D. Bronkhorst, *Truth and Reconciliation: Obstacles and Opportunities for Human Rights* (Amsterdam: Amnesty International, 1995), chapter 6, "The model of conciliation."

62. It is interesting to see how the four elements of Psalm 85:11 are all part and parcel of a truthful process of reconciliation (as depicted by experts from Amnesty International, such as Bronkhorst, *Truth and Reconciliation*, *op. cit.*): "Love and truthfulness meet together, justice and peace kiss each other."

63. The Board of Trustees consists of well-known, independently-minded Namibians.

The Role of Multi-Religious Education in the Transformation of South African Society

H. Christina Steyn

Faculty of Theology and Religious Studies
University of South Africa
Pretoria, South Africa

1. Introduction

In the aftermath of apartheid and the democratic elections our country finds itself faced with new problems and new challenges. It desperately needs to heal the hurts of the past and to create a society in which all South Africans can grow, prosper and lead dignified lives. Everything possible should be done to restore the dignity of the oppressed and the oppressors and to harmonize the relationships between the different groups in this land. Religion has a role to play in this process. This is, however, a laboriously slow process and the sooner we begin the sooner we will see results. If the racial, cultural and religious antagonism is not to be perpetuated we need to raise our children differently than in the past. We have an opportunity with Religious Education to give children the opportunity to grow into tolerant human beings who respect and appreciate all manifestations of the deepest dimensions of the human spirit.

At present there is a heated debate on the form that Religious Education (RE) should take in the new South Africa, if any at all. Some people argue that Religious Education fulfils no important function and should be eliminated from school curricula. Others are fighting for the survival of a Christocentric model, while still others plead for a multi-faith program to be introduced into schools.

In the past RE took mainly the form of Biblical Instruction or Biblical Studies, with a few exceptions for Indian schools where the subject "Right Living" was introduced. Biblical Instruction/Studies were focused on the Calvinist reform tradition with variations only in private church schools such as those of the Roman Catholic Church and Evangelical charismatic ACE (Accelerated Christian Education) schools.

2. Why Include RE in the School Curriculum?

"Religion" is a natural part of life. It is the highest and deepest and widest experience that a human being is capable of. All people who are interested in the meaning of life are religious and not only those who belong to any organized religion. Even critics of religion will agree that it forms an important part of the lives of the vast majority of people in South Africa. No one can be deemed properly educated if this dimension of human experience is not considered. Should religion therefore not be included in the school syllabus, a secular perspective is reinforced.

In a multicultural and multi-religious society such as ours the study of different religions can promote understanding and respect for one another and can prepare children to live in harmony and sophistication in our unique society. It can promote good community relations and foster acceptance and appreciation among people from different backgrounds.

Given the importance of religion in people's lives, how then will we teach religion at school?

3. Five Types of RE Courses

Each of the following five types of RE will be considered briefly:

- the "confessional/missionary" approach
- the "multiple single-faith" approach
- the "single-faith plus" approach
- the "neutral" approach
- the "understanding" approach.

3.1. The Confessional/Missionary Approach

This approach entails that children (of whatever religious tradition) will be instructed in a religion which will be held to be *the* religion—the only true religion. This is what was practiced in South Africa for many years with the official policy of Christian National Education, but the approach can, of course, be used with any other religion as its center. In South Africa many people accepted this without any objection, but many others, for various reasons, believed this to be an unhealthy way of teaching religion at school.

Examples of the aims of this approach include Kitshoff and Van Wyk who elaborate as follows:

> The aim for the devout teacher is then to help pupils, through belief in the Holy Trinity, to develop a balanced personality, so that they together with the Church through the centuries, will be able to affirm the Apostles' Creed with sincerity and conviction.[1]

And De Wet, Nel and De Wet advise teachers on the aims of the course "Biblical Instruction" for primary schools as follows:

> In acquiring this knowledge [of the Bible]...the effective pupil will be in a position to come to satisfactory decisions concerning his acceptance of and attitude towards Jesus Christ, the Bible and the church.

And

> Children should be led towards a Christian commitment.[2]

All this while also drawing the teacher's attention to the fact that there might be pupils of other religions in their classes.

It is now realized that in a multi-religious country such as South Africa this approach is no longer acceptable in state schools where pupils of many different religions (and of none) receive their education.

3.2. The "Multiple Single-Faith" Approach

With this approach children will study only their own religion. Provision will be made for parallel programs in the different religions for their adherents in the school. Proponents of this approach fear that children will be indoctrinated into a faith that is not their own and want to give children the opportunity to study their own religion at school. They are on the whole concerned that by introducing children to other religions, they will create confusion in the minds of the children. The variety of form and interpretation within one tradition will undoubtably also present problems and one can imagine that a Methodist parent might not trust a Roman Catholic teacher to present Christianity in a suitable manner to his or her child.

However, a study of only one's own tradition seems rather to be the duty of the parents and the specific religious institutions, than the school's. The very real danger inherent in this model is that of religious apartheid—the entrenchment of separation along religious lines. Children will never learn anything about the religions of people with whom they share the country. This type of ignorance will continue to breed mistrust and animosity towards others who are dehumanized and sometimes even demonized by people who claim absolute truth for themselves.

3.3. The "Single-Faith Plus" Approach

In this approach children will study their own religion, but as a concession to the plurality of religious traditions in the country, proponents are prepared to include some material on other religions. This will mean that other traditions will be taught from the perspective of one particular religion. This is an approach favored by many conservative Christians who will agree to the inclusion of other traditions if this can be taught in a Christian framework.

This seems a particularly insidious model, because under the guise of teaching multi-religious education (MRE), divisions and prejudices are entrenched. The division between "us" and "them" underscores differences and leaves no room for understanding or empathy.

3.4. The "Neutral" Approach

People who advocate the neutral approach realize that religion forms an integral part of most South Africans' lives and that there is a need to learn about different religions and worldviews. But in reaction to the confessional approach which they find unacceptable and even offensive, they offer an approach that rips the heart out of the subject. Bastide compares this approach to an education in music where the pupil learns about the lives of the great composers, about the different instruments and music scores, but without ever listening to music or making music.[4] In this approach youngsters will be given the "facts" about religion but will never understand the power that religious beliefs can wield in people's lives—it will always remain merely an assortment of strange facts.

3.5. The "Understanding" Approach

The fifth approach stands in opposition to all of the above. It does not strive to convert a child to a specific religion, but assumes that in a pluralistic society it is important to learn about other religions and also to go beyond the mere facts *about* religion.

Here the aim is to develop an understanding of religion, to empower children through disciplined imagination to appreciate the common humanity underlying different religions. Children are helped to empathize with others who differ from them in religious observance. Through their studies they gain some idea of what it means to be a devout Christian, or Jew or Muslim, etc., and to develop mutual understanding among different people of our land. Those who argue that this model promotes syncretism do not understand the intention and aims of the model, since syncretism certainly does not form part of what is aimed at—it is particularly the uniqueness of the different religions that is emphasized in this model.

4. The Aims of Multi-Religious Education

The explication of aims is of primary importance in MRE since this gives focus and lends direction to the teaching process. Without clearly defined aims it is impossible to develop syllabi and lessons.

In considering the question as to what teachers are aiming for in religious education in general, Gower states that by about the age of 14 the child should be "religiously literate."[5] This he defines as having sufficient confidence, knowledge, understanding and skills within the subject of religion to be able to respond appropriately when it is discussed and to communicate ideas relating to it.[6]

A few examples of MRE aims:

...to enable pupils to reflect upon and respond to the religious and spiritual beliefs, practices, insights and experiences that are expressed in humankind's search for meaning in life.[7]

...to help young people to achieve a knowledge and understanding of religious insights, beliefs and practices so that they are able to continue in or come to their own beliefs and respect the right of other people to hold beliefs different from their own.[8]

The school's responsibility is to provide conditions in which sensitive, informed understanding of varied viewpoints may grow, to help pupils towards discrimination so that they will not be a prey to all the blandishments that come their way.[9]

To help the pupils to develop skills in understanding religious ideas and concepts and in understanding the meaning and importance of religious practices for those who practice them.[10]

These aims fall into three broad categories: knowledge, skills and attitudes. It is therefore fair to state that the aim of MRE is *educational* in as much as the outcome that it strives for is to equip pupils with the knowledge, skills and attitudes that they need to live sensitively in a pluralistic society.

Knowledge and understanding go together and in order to attain this the child should be introduced to religious language and the meaning of key concepts from an early age. The information should, however, not be divorced from the child's experience and abilities. However, children do not remain children and they should be presented with progressively more complex material in order to grow in understanding.

Skills and attitudes do not sprout on their own when children are introduced to material on religion—they must be fostered and taught. Here the role of the teacher is of utmost importance.

The skills aimed at are *cognitive* (communication, listening, language, reading, writing, investigation, observation, enquiry, description, discovery, analysis, reasoning), *affective* (the ability to empathize, and to imaginatively identify with someone who believes differently from oneself), and *expressive* (art, drama, music and movement).

Attitudes that are aimed at in religious education will include: Attitudes to learning (curiosity about self and others and the world, the quest for meaning and purpose, open-mindedness), attitudes towards self (acceptance, personal value, self-esteem, integrity), *attitudes towards others* (acceptance, appreciation, tolerance, consideration), and *attitudes towards the world* (respect, wonder, awe, responsibility).

With these aims in mind it is necessary to decide how they are to be realized in school. One cannot reach these aims in one or two lessons—it is a process that should begin at primary level (even preprimary school) and continue all through the school years. At primary level the foundation can be laid for what we hope to achieve eventually with the children.

5. Child-Centered MRE

Many MRE curricula in Britain have been influenced by the developmental theories of Piaget[11] and Fowler.[12] These theories have been criticized, and while taking these criticisms into consideration, these theories are still a sufficiently useful guide to the development of children not to be discarded entirely.

According to Fowler's theory the thinking of pupils in the intuitive-projective stage (before age 7) is very concrete, unsystematic and fragmented. The introduction to religious diversity must take place through exploring the material basis of religion such as buildings and special clothing. The senior primary level (the mythic-literal stage according to Fowler) is a time of great intellectual quickening in which vast amounts of data can be analyzed and classified. However, these children are still limited to the concrete and find it difficult to work with abstract ideas. The content matter for MRE will therefore include the studying of the basic component phenomena of religion such as stories, founders, rituals and festivals. During this stage of their moral development youngsters acquire the ability to take the perspective of other people. They are able to understand and empathize with people who are different from themselves and they have a strong sense of fairness and justice. This phase with its growing social sensitivity offers a golden opportunity for careful exposure to the beliefs of others and should be used to foster respect and understanding in a pluralistic society. Children in this stage are intensely interested in correct "facts" and it is an ideal opportunity to prevent the development of caricatures of other religions, built on misinformation.

In the early phase of the synthetic-conventional stage (11-17 years) youngsters start to develop the ability to think abstractly and hypothetically. This is a time when they can be introduced to the disciplined study of different religious traditions. The later phase of this stage which coincides with the senior secondary level at school heralds the time when pupils seek to come to terms with their own identities and their relationship with others. They are becoming acutely aware of the flawed nature of existence and have to devise their own responses to the world. They are well-equipped to think about the deeper issues of life such as life and death, marriage and service to the world, truth, justice and so on. These are precisely the issues that religions are all about and the MRE class can become the place to discuss and debate these issues.

A minority of young adults in this stage may be moving into the next stage of religious development, although most people only reach it at 35-40 years, if they reach it at all. This is the stage when a person consciously constructs a coherent system of belief and faith. The teacher of MRE should be especially sensitive to the needs of such young people.

6. Moral Education and MRE

In the minds of many people religious education is equated with moral education. This is a false assumption. While there is overlap, these are two separate areas of study.

Many different combinations of ME and RE are found in the syllabi of different countries. There are those in which they are virtually synonymous, those in which they are complementary, those in which ME encompasses RE, others in which ME is a subsection of RE, and still others in which ME is seen as a benefit of RE.[13]

In the "understanding" approach to multi-religious education as proposed here, these are two distinct areas of study. However, the moral development of a child will be enhanced by the aims of MRE as stated above (more specifically the affective skills that are aimed at—e.g., empathy and imaginative identification with others).

There is vast disagreement between religions and even within religions on what constitutes moral behavior. When we consider issues such as abortion, the death penalty, the system of apartheid, or the production or use of nuclear arms this becomes apparent. There is, however, an area of morality that most people in our society will probably agree on. This consensus morality consists of two elements: *human solidarity* and *personal autonomy*. Human solidarity refers to our understanding of other people as in need of the same consideration that we would want for ourselves, and personal autonomy refers to the basic right of every human being to be him- or herself without being exploited.[14] Matters such as these can be dealt with in a MRE course for senior secondary students as one aspect or dimension of religion.

7. The Role of the Teacher in MRE

In teaching MRE sensitivity is everything. The attitude of the teacher cannot be overemphasized. Children are enormously influenced by the example of teachers they admire and respect. There is no mightier tool in MRE than the example of the teacher. If what we expect from the pupil is knowledge, understanding, empathy, imaginative identification, open-mindedness, tolerance etc., we cannot hope to achieve this if these qualities are not present in the teacher. There is no substitute for a caring, empathetic and well-prepared teacher. A teacher who respects each child whether from a Christian, Traditional African, Hindu, Muslim, Jewish, Buddhist, secular, or merely uncaring home, will convey this attitude to the children.

Teachers of MRE should not instruct pupils in any faith but assist them to understand and appreciate religion as a human response. One does not have to be religiously committed to teach religion in this way, although the committed teacher has much to offer. However, the religiously uncommitted teacher can be every bit as sensitive and appreciative of the role of religion in the lives of believers, and unbelief should not disqualify a teacher from teaching MRE. One does not expect teachers to hide their beliefs from students, but they should convey to pupils that their beliefs are not universally accepted.

Teachers need to be trained to guard against their own prejudice and bias. This is an acquired skill that teachers (having acquired it themselves) can transfer to their pupils. This entails that there will be no distinction between "us" and "others" in the classroom, even if the teacher and all the pupils are from the same religion. There are only human beings, all bound by their common humanity, despite their cultural and religious diversity.

The total lack of teachers trained for this task is certainly the major obstacle in the way of effective multi-religious education in this country today.

8. Conclusion

In 1992 the Institute for Comparative Religion in Southern Africa (ICRSA) brought out a report on the policy options for RE in public education. This report is still the best of its kind, but regrettably, at the end of 1996 these policy decisions have still not been taken.

Some progress has been made. From this year, all prospective teachers studying at the University of South Africa (Unisa) will have included in their study program one course in Religious Studies/ Religious Education, and at the Johannesburg College of Education, students follow a multi-religious program in their RE classes. Sterling research work is also being done at the University of Cape Town. Furthermore, the Institute for Theology and Religion and the Department of Religious Studies at Unisa will present a conference on multi-religious education in July 1997 which will hopefully give teachers some guidelines in the presentation of MRE at school.

A few resource books have been published[15] and there are many more in process. It is vitally important that these books be ready by the time the policy on RE is decided upon.

What is needed now is for the policy makers to take the necessary decisions to include the study of religion in the new syllabi in order to convey accurate information and encourage the development of harmonious relationships through attitudes of mutual tolerance and respect. Courses such as these can in the future result in more amiable and considerate social relations in our troubled country.

NOTES

1. M.C. Kitshoff and W.B. van Wyk, *Method of Religious Education and Biblical Studies* (Cape Town: Maskew Miller Longman, 1983), p. 7.
2. D.R. De Wet, Malan Nel and M.S. De Wet, *Teaching Biblical Instruction in the Primary School* (Orion, 1991), p. 11.
3. *Ibid.*, p. 3.
4. Derek Bastide (ed.), *Good Practice in Primary Religious Education 4-11* (London: The Farmer Press, 1992), p. 9.
5. Ralph R. Gower *et al.*, *Religious Education at the Primary Stage* (Oxford: Lion Educational, 1990), p. 139.
6. *Ibid.*, pp. 139-140.
7. Manchester Agreed Syllabuses.
8. ILEA: Inner London Education Authority.
9. Carol Mumford, *Young Children and Religion* (London: Edward Arnold, 1980), p. 26.
10. Ministry of Education: Malawi.
11. J.H. Flavell, *The Developmental Psychology of Jean Piaget* (Princeton, NJ: Van Nostrand, 1963).
12. James Fowler, *Stages of Faith* (San Francisco: Harper, 1981).
13. Institute for Comparative Religion in Southern Africa, *Religion in Public Education: Policy Options for a New South Africa* (Cape Town: ICRSA, 1992), pp. 92ff.
14. Gower, *op. cit.*, p. 97.
15. J.S. Krüger, G.J.A. Lubbe and H.C. Steyn, *The Human Search for Meaning:*

A Multireligious Introduction to the Religions of Humankind (Pretoria: Via Afrika, 1996); Janet Stonier, *et al.*, *Festivals and Celebrations: A New Approach to Religious Education for South African Primary Schools* (Kenwyn: Juta, 1996).

From Racial Oppression to Religious Oppression:

African Religion in the New South Africa

Nokuzola Mndende
Department of Religious Studies
University of Cape Town, South Africa

> Any form of liberation which does not address itself to the emancipation of the whole person should be seriously challenged for misrepresenting the concept of liberation. For no person can be free when part of that which gives you your humanity is in chains.[1]

When I received the invitation to present a paper I was not sure whether the members of the organization knew who they were inviting, or whether I was really the person they wanted to hear and involve in their project. The reason for that hesitation is because I come from a religious community that is regarded as non-existent—a group of people that is often perceived as non-progressive, living in the past, or even "crazy." I come from a community that is not vocal, no matter how loud the people's voices could be. The only way they can be heard, as far as the situation in South Africa is concerned, is if they are converted first—only then can they practice their religion freely, under the name of

Christianity. The religion I belong to, African Traditional Religion —to use the western and academic term for it—is either misrepresented, misunderstood, displaced, or distorted by people of other faiths.

I have mentioned that I am using a foreign term for this religion, for its own adherents call it *Ukholo lwemveli/lomdabu, Tumelo ya Bantsho,* or *Vhureleli ha sialala,* which simply means the indigenous religion of the black people of this country. For scholarly purposes I will use the well-known term, African Traditional Religion (ATR). African Traditional Religion, it seems, is always defined by people who have one foot in and one outside it, or by those who are totally outside and have no interest in understanding how those with both feet inside feel. As a result, followers of African Religion suffer from alienation and isolation in their praxis. I intend to discuss all these claims in detail.

The Bill of Rights

The Bill of Rights in the new Constitution of South Africa asserts that "everyone has the right to freedom of conscience, religion, thought, belief and opinion."[2] When the new Government recognized that South Africa is a multi-cultural and multi-religious country, the practitioners and believers within ATR were able to say: at last we are able to come out of the bush and be ourselves; we no longer have to pretend on paper that we belong to a recognized religion which, in the specific case of South Africa, most often means Christianity. For in the past, circumstances forced us to belong to a "church" even if we did not attend any church. Professor Oosthuizen noticed the "pretense" when he was doing his research in the Eastern Cape. He explains like this:

> Most black people accepted Christianity for secular reasons such as the supposed improvement in their social status, the education of their children, gaining entrance to white man's civilization, so that they might be better understood by the white man. Here again very few emphasized that they joined the Church because Christ is Savior and Redeemer.[3]

By simply filling in the forms, a person would be able, for example, to get into a school; obtain a testimonial from a minister which, along with the last school attended, was a prerequisite for a job; or even gain recognition as a full human being. A baptismal certificate, with one's "Christian" name on it, was more important than a birth certificate. It was, therefore, a matter of "joining" the Christian religion, even if one did not practice it or have faith in it.

The emphasis on the so-called "Christian" names is supported by the State President himself when he says, "My more familiar English or Christian name was not given to me until my first day at school."[4] The State President later explains further how the name "Nelson" was given to him as he says:

> On the first day of school my teacher, Miss Mdingane, gave us an English name and said that thenceforth that was the name we would answer to in school. This was the custom among Africans in those days and was undoubtedly due to the British bias of our education.[5]

The above statement clearly shows that the President himself was born and bred in African Traditional Religion; it is the western way of schooling that started to indoctrinate and gave him another identity as Nelson instead of Rholihlahla. As he clearly states that the name was given to him at school, it also becomes clear that his own people never called him by the foreign name so he had to play double standards, to be Nelson at school and Rholihlahla at home.

The president also tells of his father's religious beliefs who stood by his indigenous religion even if there were those who wanted to convert him.

> Despite the proselytizing of the Mbekela brothers, my father remained aloof from Christianity and instead reserved his own faith for the great spirit of the Xhosas, Qamata, the God of his fathers. My father was an unofficial priest, presided over ritual slaughtering of goats, birth, marriage, initiation ceremonies and funerals.[6]

However, African Religion not only includes those people who were forced by colonial and apartheid regimes to be baptized, but also a large number of people who have never baptized their children and were never baptized themselves. This is the group which amaXhosa call *amaqaba*, or the "red people," a group that practices its indigenous religion without any Christian influence.

But unfortunately, these people are also regarded by black Christians as heathen and conservative; it is believed that the only hope for them is conversion to Christianity, which is, in turn, considered synonymous with "religion" and "civilization." But when the new Government announced "freedom of religion," the adherents of African Traditional Religion asked for recognition as an independent religion with the same status as other religions, such as Islam, Judaism, Hinduism, Buddhism, Baha'i, etc.

In the context of the status quo of the past, there was no freedom of expression, religion and conscience for many people, and so some of them resorted to pretense while in reality practicing what they believed in. Most black Christians were, and are, Christians on Sunday, but ATR from Monday to Saturday. This group of people creates further problems for those who are exclusively ATR and present stumbling blocks for the liberation of ATR. While embracing Christianity, they still want to represent ATR because their consciences tell them they are still ATR. This is one of the reasons why it is thought that every black person practices both religions— Christianity and ATR—which is certainly not the true situation. Rev. Arnold Stofile, the ANC chief whip and now the Eastern Cape Premier, in his letter dated 10/16/96 responding to our cry about the marginalization of African Religion said, "Some of us have advocated for the recognition of traditional religions as early as 1972—long before this became fashionable for SA universities. So we understand fully well what you are talking about." The Reverend did not even give us time to discuss what we need so as to be part of a rainbow nation, and instead he closed his door by saying that he knows what we are talking about, and it's not something new.

Culture vs. Religion

The use of these two terms, "culture" and "religion," still needs further critical investigation. Among black Christians, these terms continue to carry traces of racism on the one hand, carried over from the missionaries, and traces of an internalized inferiority complex on the other. Hinduism, for example, is recognized as a religion in its own right; Judaism, too, is recognized as a religion in its own right. But African Traditional Religion is not recognized in the same way, for when someone is talking about ATR it is assumed that s/he is not referring to religion, but to culture. S/he can only be talking about religion if s/he incorporates Christianity or Islam. It is this attitude that amounts to religious oppression of practitioners of ATR by the mission religions—religions that claim to bring the good news and peace.

When the missionaries and colonizers studied the beliefs and practices of the black people, they did not see religion, only culture. They saw the black people living in a religious vacuum which needed to be filled by Christianity. Whatever the black people said about their own beliefs was and is perceived as culture if it is not Christian. Now that Islam has taken root in South Africa, South African Muslims, too, are pursuing their own missionary agenda: they go to the townships and give out food; they write down people's names and give them new Arabic names, such as Tahir, Ishmael, etc. All this because the black people have no religion, only culture, an attitude that causes them to feel guilty about their own roots, to despise themselves and to believe that they are nothing until they are converted. Because they believe that their culture is "primitive" and that Christianity and Islam are civilized and progressive religions, black converts start to mock their own people and insult them for being backward and ungodly—for they, the Christians and Muslims, have seen the light. African Religion, although it does not seek to convert others and respects other religions, is thus demonized. Such a situation will never bring peace in this country.

The new Government itself is now paying lip service to the recognition of African Traditional Religion in the country. However, although the government says that African Religion is part of the multifaith program, it in fact only refers to African religion that is represented by a Christian. Adherents of this religion, therefore, are understood to belong either to the Zionist Christian Church or to other Spiritual Churches. This explains why government leaders are happy to see ATR represented by a bishop of the African Spiritual Churches.

The office of the Deputy President, Mr. Thabo Mbeki, for example, released some statistics on the religious affiliations of the peoples of the new South Africa, statistics that appeared in the *Mail and Guardian*.[7]

Protestant	42.00%
Roman Catholic	9.00%
African Independent Churches	26.00%
Uncertain	17.00%
No Religion	2.50%
Muslim	2.00%
Hindu	1.74%
Jewish	.40%
Confucian	.02%
Buddhist	.01%
Other	.13%

This information, we should recall, was published during the post-apartheid, democratic period of our history. When looking at the numbers, we see that there is no category for ATR. Apparently, it is mistakenly assumed that all black people fall under the "77 percent Christian" category. Only religions that were imported into this country from elsewhere, such as Hinduism, Islam, Judaism, Buddhism, and Confucianism are given categories, because they are recognized as religions. To the adherents of African Religion, it seems strange that the office of the Deputy President of the New South Africa should release statistics based on the apartheid census. It seems equally strange that these statistics, with their oppressive implications, could be released by leaders who claim to be against any form of oppression.

Post-apartheid democracy has been understood and implemented in most spheres of life in this country, but with regard to religion there appears to be no difference between the apartheid and the post-apartheid periods. For government, perhaps, religion was not affected by apartheid and, for that matter, black people were heathens before the missionary religions came to South Africa. The *Mail and Guardian* article comments that South Africa is "deeply Christian." Does this mean submitting your name in order to get into school, or to get a job, or to be given a decent burial? Does conversion mean to obey the status quo, or does it mean a change of heart?

To return to the notion of "culture," it is difficult to understand its true meaning, since the term is often imposed by one group of people to define and categorize another. I agree with Nangoli's following definition of culture:

> Culture is a language or languages people speak, the way they behave, live, relate to one another, dress, worship their God, care for their own, marry for reproductive purposes, name or baptize their children, treat the elderly, bury their dead and generally the way that they carry on—a way that distinguishes them from other peoples of the world.[8]

From the above definition of culture Nangoli has shown that it is impossible to divorce culture from religion. The way people bury their dead, for instance, is deeply religious; the language they speak expresses their culture and how they talk to their God, in other words, their religion, etc.

Religious Freedom

Religious freedom in the New South Africa is biased if it promotes one religion (Christianity) at the expense of others. When adherents of African Religion practice their religion, they are accused of taking people back to heathenism; they are accused of holding people back from progress. Because of this attitude, those who claim rights for ATR are excluded and are not heard. For example, during December 2-4, 1990 in Cape Town, the World Conference on Religion and Peace (WRCP), South African Chapter, organized an Inter-faith Conference on Religion-State Relations. Christianity, Islam, Judaism, and Hinduism were all represented at this conference organized by an inter-faith body. But there was no representative of ATR. The indigenous religion of the country was excluded by an organization which claims to represent all religious groups. Professor Mazrui noticed this exclusion and he remarked as follows:

> But I must first, with all due respect and to some extent with some impertinence, point out a missing legacy perhaps in your own proceedings here at this meeting. If I am mistaken, somebody in the course of the evening will put me right. I get the impression that the conference did not try hard to ensure the representation of followers of African Indigenous religion, who do not belong to any imported universalistic religions. I hope that at the very least

papers or presentations have been commissioned to address this omnipresent religious legacy in Africa's experience: the indigenous beliefs, rituals and values.[9]

Mazrui, in fact, was not aware that what he thought was excluded was believed to be present, but present in the shape of the African Independent Churches, which was mistakenly regarded as African Traditional Religion.

Similarly, at a later date, the Secretary of the South African Chapter of the WRCP, Rev. Mayson, suggested the following:

> It seems to me—tell me if I'm wrong—that you are trying to promote African Traditional Religion as a separate faith, just another religion or denomination in the religious ecclesiastical market economy competition we have foisted upon us by the west....The task of ATR, it seems to me, is not to promote separate religious institutions, or to oppose existing ones, but to spread traditional insights and teaching which people can take and incorporate any way they like into their lives, families, society, or beliefs.... It is thus crucially important for Africa and Christianity that the Good News of Jesus be reminted in the crucible of African experience in our continent, not used to perpetuate European or Western dominance. It seems to me that this argument can be used both to validate ATR, and also to legitimize the "independent" or "indigenous" churches.[10]

Rev. Mayson was responding to my claim that African Religion is independent of Christianity. Rev. Mayson claims to know exactly what African Religion ought to be.

In a memorandum submitted to the State President by the delegation mandated by the National Committee of African Traditional Religion, we gave reasons to the president concerning why we feel that even the present government does not recognize our religion, but only pays lip service to it. We summarized our reasons as follows:

1. President Mandela, before his installation as the first black State President, visited almost all the religious communities present in the country. People were informed in advance that he would be visiting them. He met the Jews in their synagogue; Muslims in their mosque; and on the Sunday before his installation, Nelson

Mandela attended a church service in Johannesburg. At no stage was the same procedure followed with regard to the religious beliefs of his own people, who were oppressed for more than 300 years. That made us feel that we were still at the lowest level of the religious hierarchy.

2.   During the installation of the first black president in the country, something historic took place—the opening "devotions." This was planned ahead of time but, as usual, African Traditional Religion was deliberately excluded. Christianity, Islam, Judaism, Hinduism, and Buddhism were falsely recognized to be representing the religious diversity of South Africa, leaving behind a religion that is truly "African," a religion that had never been imported. No one among the black elite was interested in African Religion, giving the false impression that all blacks in the country are Christian. That also showed the world that before all these recognized religions came to South Africa, black people were "heathen," as the missionaries said. Or, perhaps our black elite are so ashamed of the religion that they practice it in secret.

3.   On August 6, 1994 Archbishop Tutu delivered a peace lecture and his topic was "Let's celebrate our diversity." The State President also made his response to the Archbishop. The diversity of the South African population was shown by referring to all the religions that came to the country: Christianity, Hinduism, Islam, Buddhism, Bahai, Confucianism, and Judaism. ATR people celebrated exclusion with shame, an experience that was especially painful given the post-apartheid era in which we thought our leaders would recognize the need to empower the religion that had been so severely oppressed. Furthermore, our leaders know how painful it is to be oppressed, so we never thought that they could become part of oppressive circumstances.

4.   During the constitutional debates on moral issues such as pornography, abortion and homosexuality, it was said that all religious communities would be consulted. Again, African Religion was represented by Bishop Ntongana of the African Spiritual Churches. When we made our point, we were once again regarded as irrational.

5.   When the Truth Commission was formed, it was publicly announced that all religions would be represented, but this only meant the addition of Judaism, Islam and Hinduism to Christianity.

There was no interest in finding someone for ATR, since it was assumed that any black can represent African Religion, no matter how Christian he or she is.

6. When the State President was campaigning for local elections in May 1996, he was asked by some Muslims in the Western Cape to respond on the question of religion in South Africa. He said, "South Africa is not a Christian country, it is also a Muslim country, a Jewish country and a Hindu country." He said nothing about the beliefs and practices of the indigenous people, his own people.

7. When allocating air time to religious broadcasting, the South African Broadcasting Corporation gave Christianity 70 percent, while Islam, Hinduism, Judaism, and African Religion were given 5 percent each, with the remainder given for free allocation to interfaith dialogues and festivals. When asked about the criteria for time allocation, the SABC answered that the religions other than Christianity were *minority* religions in the country. We felt betrayed and believe that the state is not being democratic on this issue. Our question is this: Judaism is the majority religion in Israel, Islam in Arab countries, and Hinduism in India; but if African Religion is a minority religion in its own country of birth, where, then, is it a majority religion? We see this process as a colonization of the mind, a serious matter, since it is perpetrated by its own people and by more than one religion. We also wondered if the same could happen in those other countries—for example, just as African Religion has been designated 5 percent in South Africa, could Judaism be 5 percent in Israel, or Hinduism 5 percent in India, or Islam 5 percent in an Arabic country? It would never happen!

All the above points indicate that although South Africa has gained independence, racism is now clothed in religious attire. The struggle still continues, for the ATR people are still in chains. Moreover, we are still harassed, most especially by the "book religions" and those with a missionary agenda, making black people victims of manipulation.

The present government is nothing else but Christianity at prayer. In the past the Department of Education was based on the Christian National Education where Christianity with its western imperialism was imposed on the African people. The new government has just painted the same proselytizing style black. The minister of education, Professor Bhengu, is an ordained Lutheran priest; his deputy, Father Smangaliso Mkhatshwa, is an ordained Catholic priest. What then will be the change as far as the African Traditional Religion is concerned? As a result, all religions in the curriculum committee are represented except African Traditional Religion. The Truth Commission has Archbishop Tutu as the chairperson. The chairperson of the Truth Commission in the Eastern Cape is Rev. Bongani Finca, and in KwaZulu-Natal it is Bishop Mgojo. The Human Rights Commission's chairperson, Rev. Dr. Barney Pityana, still does not believe that there are Africans who can practice African Religion without Christianity. In such a situation, how can we speak of human rights when my right to believe and my freedom to practice my religion is still controlled and despised?

When looking at all these events, we begin to ask ourselves how this situation differs from P. W. Botha's reforms of his racial apartheid policy. P. W. Botha, when making what he claimed to be the reforms of racial apartheid, formed the tricameral government, gave preference to Indians and Coloreds and included them in his parliament, but left out the people who were most affected by apartheid, the Africans. As a result even the education system of Indians and coloreds remained "superior" to that of the Africans.

The same is happening now in the new government in its treatment of religion. The new government has developed a tricameral religious government, that is the inclusion of Hinduism and Islam to Christianity. The indigenous religious beliefs are left out as P. W. Botha did. The destruction done by the colonialists is made worse by the Christian black elite who not only make decisions about themselves but decide about the beliefs of the grassroots people who are made voiceless by the very people who used to despise oppression.

Possible Solutions to the Problem

I think it is important for the government of National Unity to listen to the adherents of ATR and to give them the recognition they deserve. Recognition of ATR does not mean denial of other blacks being African; we recognize that they have the right to practice Christianity within an African context. But they speak of "inculturating" ATR into Christianity, when they should recognize that there are black people who are not Christians, who would like to speak for themselves, and who equally have a right not to be Christian.

Secondly, there should be a redefinition of missionary work and conversion by the religions concerned. Conversion should, I think, be accompanied by action if it is not to be a deceit. No one can claim, just based on numbers, that South Africa is deeply Christian. We must bear in mind that a large number of black people *babha-lisa ecaweni* (submitted their names to the church), not because they believe in Christ but because of the circumstances I mentioned earlier. I have deliberately used the term "submit" because some just send in their names and pay for tickets so that they can be buried, for it is regarded by some Christians as a mockery if one dies without being a Christian. So in this context one can become a Christian by submitting a name without attending church or practicing the religion. In this case, there is no difference between Christianity and any social organization. Christianity should not be made into a "paper religion" but should be a commitment to Christ. If conversion is used as a synonym for "joining," like an organization, then there will always be religious struggles. Conversion to Christianity, I suggest, should not be like campaigning for a political organization, whereby representatives preach the policies of the party and promise the people housing and jobs. Then, if those needs are not fulfilled people lose hope and withdraw, because most of them joined only for their physical needs and not for spiritual needs. No religion should define another, as that creates a religious battlefield, a battlefield that would exclude adherents of ATR from the "rainbowness" of this country. To define African Religion from a Christian perspective violates the rights of its followers to have complete freedom of religion; when a particular way of seeing the truth is imposed on others, it violates their freedom to seek the truth.

Religious freedom is the cornerstone of the rights of each individual and it must be respected if the government is to be a truly non-racial and democratic one. And last, but not least, I would argue that the use of the census to assess the religious affiliations of the people is an inaccurate and false representation of the religious diversity of South Africa.

NOTES

1. R. Jordaan, "The Emergence of Black Feminist Theology in South Africa," in D. Ackermann, Draper, and Mashinini (eds.), *Women Hold Up Half the Sky* (Pietermaritzburg: Kendal and Strachan, 1991), p. 125.
2. Bill of Rights in the new Constitution of South Africa (1996), p. 8.
3. G.C. Oosthuizen, "Interaction between Christianity and Traditional Religion," in *The Ciskei—A Bantu Homeland, A General Survey* (Fort Hare: Fort Hare University Press, 1971), p. 128.
4. N. Mandela, *Long Walk to Freedom* (South Africa: Macdonald Purnell, 1994), p. 1.
5. *Ibid.*, p. 13.
6. *Ibid.*, p. 12.
7. *Wail and Guardian*, 9-15 February 1996: 3.
8. M. Nangoli, *No More Lies about Africa* (U.S.A.: Heritage Publishers, 1986), p. 10.
9. A. Mazrui, "Africa's Pro-Democratic Movement: Indigenous, Islamic and Christian Tendencies," in Klippies Kritzinger, *National Inter-Faith Conference on Religion-State Relations* (Pretoria: Printype, 1991), p. 3.
10. Cedric Mayson - Secretary WCRP, Letter, 16 June 1995.

Indigenous Christianity and the Future of the Church in South Africa

Gerhardus C. Oosthuizen

Professor of Religious Studies
University of Durban-Westville
Durban, South Africa

Introduction: Who Are the AICs?

The value of other people's perspectives can be destroyed by ignorance, and the African Independent/Indigenous Church (AIC) movement has been ignored throughout most of the twentieth century, despite receiving much attention during the period from 1890 to 1920. Yet the AIC movement has grown into the most dynamic church movement in South Africa, proliferating among Black South Africans, attracting African traditional religionists, and drawing into its fold many previous congregants of the "mainline" churches. This is despite having no special missionizing program. It would appear rather that "mainline" church members and traditional religionists flock to them for what they are and what they do.

Who are the African Independent/Indigenous Churches (AICs)? To answer this, it is important to distinguish between the "independent" and the "indigenous" strands of the AIC movement. Those AICs which "split-off" from the "mainline" mission churches are referred to as "independent" churches, whereas churches which were indigenously self-initiated are "indigenous." The following section will outline the history of the independent and indigenous churches in South Africa.

A Brief History of the AIC Movement in South Africa

AICs may be divided broadly into three categories:

- the Ethiopian churches
- the Zionist churches
- the Apostolic churches

An important fourth form of AIC is represented by the Nazarite Baptist Church, which cannot easily be classified under any of these three headings, though it shares much in common with some churches in all three types.

It will be seen that the independent churches have their origins in the missionary activities of non-mainstream American religious movements in the late nineteenth century in South Africa, but that in the case of the Apostolic and Zionist churches, these elements have been assimilated into authentically indigenous forms of religious expression, so that today's South African AICs can truly be said to be South African churches, not merely the off-shoots of American religious movements.

Moreover, the first fully-established Independent Church in South Africa was not influenced at all by American religious movements, but was authentically South African, and closely linked to the birth of South African black national liberation movements. The Thembu National Church came into existence in 1884 when Nehemiah Tile, a Thembu and a probationer in the Wesleyan Mission, led a protest movement against the annexation of the Transkei to the British Cape Colony. Tile's actions form part of a tradition of political activism within the Thembu Chiefdom which has produced politically active figures as diverse as Transkei bantustan leaders Kaiser and George Matanzima and present South

African State President Nelson Mandela. Tile, who was seen to be a potentially influential figure (he was a close advisor of the Thembu paramount chief) was criticized for politicizing his faith, and in reaction he left the Wesleyan Mission and founded the Thembu National Church.[1] As Kamphausen argues, dissatisfaction with colonial rule at that time manifested not only as political activity but also religious activity.[2]

Unlike the Thembu National Church, so closely linked to one ethnic group, the independent *Ethiopian* movement, as it became known after the 1890s, was a reaction to a general dissatisfaction with the inequality that existed between black and white clergy. These churches were inspired by Ethiopian-type churches in the USA at the turn of this century, especially the Africa Methodist Episcopal Church.[3] The significance of Ethiopia as a symbol of freedom in Africa needs comment. Ethiopia alone on the continent of Africa had at this time never succumbed to foreign rule; it therefore had been the symbol of black liberation during the struggle against slavery in the USA, inspired by a passage in Psalm 68:

Let Ethiopia hasten to stretch out her hands to God. (Ps. 68:31)

This was read as a prophecy that, as Ethiopia had escaped colonialism by "stretching her hands out to God," so too could Africans escape white domination, both in the USA and in Africa, and both in terms of secular life and in terms of internal church hierarchies, by seeking to serve God.

The extent of the discontent within the white-dominated Missionary Churches is illustrated by the letter which Mangena Maake Mokone, who later took the name of Moses, wrote on October 24, 1892 to Mr. Weavind, his Wesleyan Missionary Superintendent:

Dear Sir

I hereby give you notice that at the end of this month I will leave the Wesleyan Church ministry and serve God in my own way. It is no use to stop me for I won't change. If you like, I can pack up all I've got and leave tomorrow morning before breakfast.

Your grumbling servant,
Mangena Maake Mokone[4]

The tone of this letter indicates quite clearly a lack of contentment which was widespread among black clergy in the Mission Churches, and indicates how decisive was the step which Mokone had taken. Soon after this letter, "Moses" Mokone established the Ethiopian Church, which would play a significant role in its reaction against white ecclesiastical domination and white overrule.

Within a few years, several Ethiopian denominations had been established in South Africa: one of the major leaders in the Ethiopian Church movement at the time was James Mata Dwane, who had been in contact with the Abyssinian King Menditi at the end of the nineteenth century. In 1912 Ethiopian church leaders were actively involved in the formation of the South African Native National Congress, which would later become (in 1925) the African National Congress.

According to Sundkler, the Italo-Abyssinian war of 1935 had the effect of stimulating the growth of Ethiopian movements in South Africa.[5] The Ethiopia Star Church of God, the Melchizedek Ethiopian Catholic Church, the Abyssinian Baptist Church, and the Ethiopian Church of Abyssinia among others all date from this period. Some of these churches incorporate the name Cush into their titles—a reference to one of the sons of Ham in the Old Testament, who is often identified with Ethiopia.

In spite of its close links with the movement towards black political liberation, the Ethiopian churches have remained the smallest grouping within the AIC movement generally, possibly because they are ecclesiastically closest to the "mainline" churches. In contrast, the Zionist and Apostolic movements have been more assimilative of traditional African culture and religion.

The largest and most influential group of independent churches in South Africa are those in the *Zionist* movement, which resulted from contacts with the Christian Catholic Church founded by John Alexander Dowie on February 22, 1896 at Zion City (not far from Chicago). Dowie, a Scotsman who had been brought up in Australia, repudiated scientific medicine and advocated faith healing through a periodical which was published in Zion City, *Leaves of Healing*. The evidence of this publication suggests that within a year of the establishment of Zion City, the Christian Catholic Church in Zion had established a South African affiliate under an ex-minister of the Congregational Union of South Africa, Rev. J. Buchler.[6]

Buchler was responsible for the initial propagation of the faith among Zulu- and Swazi-speaking South Africans in the area around Wakkerstroom. After Buchler resigned in 1900, his task was continued by Pieter le Roux and Edgar Mahon. In 1904 Emma Dempcy Bryant, an elder in the American branch of the church, arrived in South Africa with her husband from Zion City; she took a particular interest in the black South African church.

There were initially close links between the Zionist churches and the third type of independent church, the so-called *Apostolic* movement. The Apostolic Faith Mission (AFM) was established in South Africa by John Lake and Thomas Hezmalhalch of the Apostolic Faith Church in the USA, who arrived in South Africa in 1908. Lake and Hezmalhalch brought with them the emphasis on glossolalia or "speaking in tongues." This explicitly Pentecostal form of Christianity had its roots in the account in the Acts of the Apostles of how this gift was visited on the Apostles on Pentecost when the Holy Spirit descended on them; furthermore, it became a means whereby early Christians were encouraged to discern truth from false prophecy: "Anyone who does not speak in tongues is not baptized with the Holy Spirit" (Acts 2:4). Modern-day Pentecostalism can probably be traced back to the establishment in Los Angeles of the Azusa Street Mission by W. J. Seymour, an African-American pastor.

Following his own experience of glossolalia, Pieter le Roux joined the AFM in 1908, and thereafter placed a substantial emphasis upon such external signs of the outpouring of the Holy Spirit as glossolalia. Though le Roux continued with the AFM, a number of his evangelists and assistants went on to establish their own new churches, many of which placed an emphasis upon Pentecostalism. The word "Zion" appears in eighty percent of AIC names; most of those influenced by the AFM added "Zion" to their names, as well as "of South Africa." Those who do not do so indicate thereby that they wish not to be as strongly associated with indigenous cultural expressions and beliefs as that section of Zionism which is so indigenized that some significant elements of Christianity may have been lost.

An extremely significant indigenous development occurred when Isaiah Shembe, a visionary and prophet, founded the *iBala lama-Nazaretha*, or Nazarite Baptist Church (popularly called the

Shembe Church) in 1911. Shembe was a close friend of John Dube, founder of the South African Native National Congress, and the influence upon one another was mutual. Shembe's doctrine was that racial and political oppression could be ended by reversion to Mosaic law. He promoted among his followers an independence from white domination through the establishment of self-sufficient communities. Integral to this was a respect for traditional Zulu customs and beliefs. The *iBala lamaNazaretha* is today the most popular AIC among Zulu-speaking South Africans, but members are to be found among other ethnic groups as well. Isaiah Shembe died in 1935, since which time the church has been led by his descendants: in 1976 one of Isaiah's grandsons led a schismatic group away from the main body of the Nazarite Baptist Church.

The Positive Influences of Traditional Culture and Religion on the AICs

Theologies produced and nourished in a western intellectual culture may not be relevant to African experience. Much western theology smothered what is positive in traditional African cultures. While western theology remains the intellectual foundation of the western-oriented churches, it may be blind towards basic issues of immediate relevance to African people. Yet utility is an important aspect of religion, particularly African traditional religion. It is not the structure of a religion which makes a lasting impact, but its essence; yet not only the theology of the western-oriented churches in Africa is becoming progressively more suspect, but also the structures.[7]

This in part helps explain why there are approximately six thousand denominations in the AIC movement. Fellowship and mutual support, caring and sharing, as understood in the traditional African context, do not find much expression in the modern western churches. Yet relationship is very, even desperately, important in Africa where the self is composite and not unitary, open to its surrounding environment, not closed in upon itself.[8]

Few of these six thousand-odd denominations assemble in a church; most AIC adherents gather in houses, shacks, shelters made from motorcar boxes, or in open spaces in the cities and towns. The type of venue is not important for the AICs, as long as there is fellowship, mutual discussion of problems, healing procedures which give them spiritual and physical refreshment and empowerment. Here the spirit of the traditional extended family finds expression in the ecclesiastical context, as well as the basic aspects of traditional culture and religion, excluded by more western-oriented churches.

The western ideological system and scholarship has also underevaluated African cultural heritages. Things African are seen as lacking any significance; African thinking is "pre-logical," i.e., under-evolved, because it does not fit the secular intellectualist approach. The former is seen as "primitive" and "traditional," the latter as "civilized" and "modern." Since this attitude has found sympathy in the western-orientated churches, it is not surprising that many African Christians in the "mainline" churches attend healing sessions of the AICs, and are reappraising the traditional approaches.

The New Dualism: AICs Bringing Two Worlds Together

The juxtaposition of the world of modern industrialism with the known world of traditional society has led to a "new dualism" which "causes a kind of mental and ethical schizophrenia in some spheres of conduct."[9] In the AICs, these two worlds are brought together in a new assessment of African spirituality and thinking on the holistic nature of religion. This is overdue in the African situation of rapid social change.

The AICs are protective of what they consider to be basic aspects of their indigenous culture. The onslaught against the balanced wisdom of centuries is counteracted calmly and strongly. From this background, new realities are faced in a balanced manner. Social, psychological, religious, political and cultural aspects are interwoven with the religious and the secular. Party politics, which implies struggle, disharmony and animosity, is avoided because the holistic self-help approach has proven more effective. Bill Keller's article in the *New York Times Magazine* (April 17, 1994) on the AICs has the meaningful superscription: "The Zion Church's millions work hard, abhor violence and respect authority. They are more likely than revolutionaries to shape the future. A surprising silent majority in South Africa."

This holistic approach encourages a Christianity and politics which emphasizes unity in doctrine and life. The loss of membership in some "mainline" churches could *inter alia* be ascribed to their support of apartheid; the great loss of membership in some churches is due in part to a climate of violence caused by some church activities, bolstered by large sums of money coming mainly from abroad.[10] Some have argued that churches with funds from abroad were misled in instigating "a culture of revolution." Whether this is true or not, most "mainline" churches have lost adherents at an alarming rate between 1980 and 1990. A large percentage of these were the youth; at the same time, surveys show that of all churches the AICs have the largest number of youth.

AIC Christianity versus Western Individualism

There is a level in African Traditional Religion (ATR) which runs deeper than westernized empirical Christianity. Certain features of ATRs not only survive but are vital to the dynamic growth of AICs. The most prominent of these are a strong sense of fellowship, of sharing and caring, and of not being individualized when it comes to mutual assistance. In the "mainline" churches where special committees have to be established to assist the poor, often on a selective basis, these committees often function poorly. This individualizing of the human being is a negative and un-Christian development which is not allowed in traditional African Christianity. Intellectual rationalizations of religion, and philosophical and theological fashions, do not endure, but deep spiritual structures do, alongside certain "axiomatic themes"; this is what the AICs convey.

In the ATRs, reality is human relationships; and relationship means "more power and transcendence, for power flows, through relationship."[11] This is the basis of family relationships within the context of the extended family. The impact of this can be seen in the tremendous conversions from mainline churches to the AICs. In 1950, 75-80 percent of all black South African Christians were members of "mainline" churches, as opposed to 12-14 percent belonging to the AICs. By 1980 the respective percentages were 52 percent and 27 percent; and by 1991, 41 percent and 36 percent. By early next century, most black South African Christians will belong to AICs.

Adapted forms of African traditional healing is a prominent feature in the AICs; it even draws large numbers of "mainline" church adherents. They find great benefits from it and *inter alia* save themselves the expensive costs of western medicine. The healing process is humanized; a deep relationship is established with the patient, who is never a mere object to be cured.[12]

The AICs are changing the theological and institutional stance of the church in Africa. Critical thinking has already taken place on the ecclesiastical, theological, liturgical and institutional levels. Indigenous values and socio-moral injunctions based on African cultural and religious inheritances have been underestimated and misrepresented. The collapse of values, especially in urban areas, cannot merely be solved by economic means. African traditional moral systems have human interests at heart; as Sogolo rightly states, "an action was judged right or wrong depending on the extent to which it promoted well-being, mutual understanding and social harmony."[13] African moral thinking needs to be elucidated and clearly contrasted with the misconceptions that exist in modern westernized societies.

African religion was distorted by the missionary-oriented evaluation of African thinking. The average missionary and anthropological literature presented African religion in a negative manner: as overruled by, or "infested" with, beliefs in magic, fetishes, spirits, ancestors, etc. There is more depth in African religion than this *prima facie* judgment indicates. By accepting Christianity, crises of identity were often experienced—crises still apparent among black members of many "mainline" churches These are due to the fact that many of their members aspire to the benefits of traditional religion, for example, spontaneity in liturgy, healing procedures, emphases on sharing and caring, and thorough and concerned discussion of problems during worship. The benefits of traditional mutuality are deeply felt.

Because they have overcome these crises, the AICs are of great help to those from the "mainline" churches who seek their help. They have solved the dualism between empirical western-oriented Christianity and African traditional culture and religion. AICs manage this dualism on their own without becoming "schizo-phrenic." A mental and spiritual decolonization process is important, in which a traditional cultural orientation puts the new South Africa on a more secure footing than is provided by a superficial and shallow secularism.

The dualism introduced into South Africa and elsewhere by western-oriented Christianity has been effectively handled in the AICs. Here the reconstructive mission of the church has begun: the fundamental principle of traditional African religion has been analyzed and interpreted in the Christian context. The emphasis is on being part of the cosmic web which holds all things and beings together. Here life flows through fellowship. Furthermore, the more intense and numerous are one's established relationships, the more one's own spirituality is enhanced: this intensity is reflected in the style of services and communication. "Secular concerns," in the ATRs and AICs, are appropriate spiritual concerns. It is thus important to enter into networks of solidarity, which explains the numerous AIC mini-congregations which act as fully-fledged denominations, especially in African-oriented urban and informal settlement areas.

Social Conflict and Reconciliation

Reconciliation is a continuous activity in the AICs. In the AICs, more attention is given to evil forces than to Satan. These forces destroy harmony in a context where societal harmony is a primary concern. Many of these evil forces are, however, projected socio-political problems; this explains the avoidance by AICs of political party contestation. To remove the evil effects of such forces, exorcism, the most prominent ritual of AICs, is applied.

AIC methods are considered most effective by adherents of the "mainline" churches who continuously seek exorcism and healing. The cosmic order and not merely the individual benefits from such procedures. This explains the AICs' tremendous emphasis on healing, and why many "mainline" adherents attend their night healing sessions.[14]

Traditional Healing Procedures

ATRs give attention to cultural diseases which western-trained doctors and psychiatrists are unable to handle. Many activities of the traditional healer are psycho-therapeutic, provided with warmth, empathy and integrity, which bring more comfort to the patient than the cold, clinical, often impersonal western approach.[15] This approach is characteristic also of AIC healers. In the AICs, as in the ATRs, disease is not just a physical or mental condition but also a religious matter.[16] Sickness implies an imbalance between the metaphysical and the human world disturbing the flow of life force (numinous power). Traditional healers effectively treat (as do the prophets/prayer healers in the AICs) therapy-resistant cases. In this way effective traditional and prophet/prayer healers in the AICs become primarily health workers. Medicine and methods used in the treatment of patients should be brought more within the context of the African world-view for the sake of those who adhere to it. Prayer healers and prophets, by creating harmonious relationships, are also healers of society. This cannot often be said of the western-trained psychotherapist.

Religion remains of major significance in healing procedures among Africans. A large section of Africans still seek the traditional medical approach.[17] Cooperation between traditional healers and western-trained professionals becomes increasingly more acceptable in Africa.[18] The impact of the AICs is due to their holistic stance towards healing, including healing of human relationships on the individual and social levels, apart from psychosomatic issues. To their adherents the AICs are churches in the true sense of the word; they are hospitals and social welfare institutions.[19]

AICs Against Secular Depersonalization

Ideologies come and go but not before they do much harm. Colonialism, although associated with racial separation in South Africa, never made an ideology of apartheid; this happened only after 1948, leading to disempowerment and its consequences, anomie and poverty. The partial collapse of the rural areas, especially the under-industrialized homelands, led to massive migration to urban areas, with most people settling in informal areas with very little hope of employment and decent living conditions. The "mainline" churches have very little hope of being of real help to these millions of people. It is in this situation that the AICs, with their numerous small-house denominations, provide reception networks for the newly urbanized poor.

To use party politics as a main criticism of the AICs' approach to social issues is a simplistic and unfair analysis of a desperate situation.[20] The South African "mainline" churches are to a large extent strangers to the suffering at the grassroots level. It is here where the AICs are involved in a desperate situation, without any funds; here the poor help the poor, basic to traditional African humanity and lost to much of westernized Christianity.[21]

The AICs carry forward the humanity of the traditional African society into the informal and formal urban areas. Here they spontaneously hold onto the model of family relations "to structure a caring enclave in the impersonal urban world."[22] Through employing a more vibrant form of worship in which healing, music, and hand-clapping bring back the traditional atmosphere of the rural areas, AICs "in effect adopted into an urban family idiom"[23] the alienated urban poor. In this way mission activities take place without any mission programs or special mission funds. Where the "mainline" churches spend millions on mission activities (proclamation of the word, healing via hospitals, etc.) the AICs exist simply as dynamic church family units. People flock to them for a feeling of what true humanity implies and what it does.

Transformation in the AICs

The AICs provide a sense of continuity between the traditional and the modern; the success of this process depends on flexibility. In the present rapidly-changing South Africa, the focus is on the women and the youth. Women have key roles in the AICs: two-thirds of all healers in the AICs are women, which makes them a significant force in the AIC movement. Women are also influential in small businesses, in various fund-raising activities such as in sewing, cake baking, etc. Women are drawn into the formal and informal economic sectors. Many act as heads of households; men are often away seeking employment, or the women are widowed, divorced, abandoned or separated. Often women heads of households come from various rural areas—in one sample of seventy women household heads, fifty-five came from different parts of the country. Networking is thus an important aspect of their survival, and that of their children, in the informal settlements. It is here, in situations where the "mainline" church structures are ineffective, that the AIC support system is of special value.

The role of the youth is also changing. Within the AICs, youth have their own sphere of activity. The youth tend to be more literate and thus more educated than their parents, in spite of tremendous crises in their education which left most of them under-educated. Youth played an important role in the anti-apartheid struggle since 1976. School boycotts and other manifestations of youth activism have brought about among the youth a higher degree of awareness and organization. They were pressured to take sides in the political struggle instead of trying to avoid it.[24] Many of the youth have remained with the AICs despite these churches being described as apolitical. Rather than being a "silent majority," the AICs are South Africa's silent source of power.

They have never been irrelevant—the impression given by some of the unresearched, superficial writings. "While the AICs have turned away from public causes, they have been strongly involved on their own ground at the coalface of urban poverty."[25] They have replicated and preserved the equality and mutualism of the traditional extended family system in the peri-urban and urban context, along with other advantageous social practices of an earlier rural generation. Here lies the secret of their success with the traditional religionists who flock to the cities. The westernized, over-institutionalized and over-intellectualized churches struggle to make an impact in this context. Christianity started as a religion of the downtrodden, the underprivileged, the outcast. The AICs continue this tradition in the African context.

To their youth the AICs offer a humanistic vision of a strong, dedicated society based on self-reliance, as well as a structured relation to what is considered to be the source of inner strength and stability. The "lost generation" of youth pose to the AICs a challenge of considerable importance. Their small communities are indeed the best urban institutions to mediate the shock of transition from rural conditions to informal, semi-urban and urban life—a singular advantage they have over the mainline churches.

The AICs in Mediating Urbanization

The rapid growth of AIC adherents and the numbers of AIC denominations after the mid-1970s, at a time when influx from rural and semi-rural areas reached tremendous proportions, suggests a close relationship between AIC growth and urbanization. The rural-born component of the Durban Functional Region's informal population is about seventy percent;[26] figures are probably comparable for other urban areas. In this context the grass-roots structures of the AICs, their ultimate family relationships, their intense stress on mutual aid, their practical help in seeking or obtaining work, their contacts with skills trainers have given them a special place in the South Africa context. They replicate the rural extended family.

Local government institutions at the grassroots to assist in the settlement process hardly exist, while few non-government organizations assist families in the urbanization process. Research suggests that the AICs are the only popular institutions mediating the urban settlement process for inmigrant households.[27] The AICs are in structure voluntary organizations, institutions of the poor; in the spirit of the traditional African relationships, they are prepared to assist any person in need. They constitute networks of the people which, because of their mobility and omnipresence, are deeply involved with the lot of the poor. They offer "a portable community" and "unite the disadvantaged in stable alliances... quick and reliable networks in unfamiliar areas."[28] Strangers who enter as members of local AICs have immediate contact "assembled round an ideology of mutual support, which operates in a Christian framework directly related to poverty."[29] In a situation of considerable urban anonymity, the AICs offer emotional and spiritual help.

Marginalization of the "Mainline" Churches

The dynamics in the AICs in South Africa—and in Africa—are deeply related to the depth of traditional African spirituality, with its emphasis on relationships of sharing and caring in a holistic sense, and of genuine fellowships. This will direct the future church in Africa. The deep structures of African spirituality and worldview will not be destroyed but it's influence will continue to be felt. This is particularly true in an era of emphasis on socio-economic development. The AICs, through money-saving clubs (*stokvels*), small businesses, and skills-training, have much to offer their prospective congregants.

The traditional religious approach has made worship in the indigenous church more existential and holistic. Religious activities are not lifeless exercises but rather dynamically related to one's "neighbor." The ATRs tell the "mainline" churches that if they continue to act as they do, they will continue to be ignored by Africans. In South Africa, nearly twenty percent of black South Africans still adhere to the African Traditional Religions while in most of Africa the percentage is higher, much higher. They will become more and more associated with the AICs.

This is abundantly clear in South Africa where the "mainline" churches spend millions of rand on missionizing activities which have little consequence. Meanwhile the AICs receive converts from both the ATRs as well as the "mainline" churches. AICs overcome the problem of ethnicity: AICs are examples of inter-ethnic and intra-ethnic harmony. In a society where the major lines of cleavage have often been ethnic, this strong inter-ethnic fellowship orientation is an important development, and will benefit greatly the peaceful development of this multi-ethnic country.

NOTES

1. C. Saunders, *Tile and the Thembu Church: Politics and Independency on the Cape Eastern Frontiers in the Late Nineteenth Century* (Cape Town: The Abe Bailey Institute of International Studies, Reprint No. 3, 1971).
2. E. Kamphausen, *Anfäge der Kirchlichen Unhabhängigkeits—bewegung in Südafrika: Geschichte und Theologie der Äthiopischen Bewegung, 1872-1912* (Frankfurt: 1976), pp. 93-109.

3. *Ibid.*
4. *Ibid.*, p. 514.
5. B.G.M. Sundkler, *Bantu Prophets in South Africa* (London: Oxford University Press, 1961), p. 56.
6. Mahon, "The formation of the Christian Catholic Church in Zion and its Earliest Contacts with South Afirica," in C.G. Oosthuizen (ed), *Religion Alive: Studies in the New Movements and Indigenous Churches in Southern Africa* (Cape Town: Hodder and Stoughton, 1986), pp. 172-173.
7. P.P. Ekeh, *Colonialism and Social Structure* (Ibadan: Ibadan University Press, 1983).
8. J. Beattie, "Review article: Representations of the Self in Traditional Africa," in *Africa* 50/3 (1980):313-20.
9. K. Wiredu, Philosophy and African Culture (Cambridge: Cambridge Uiversity Press, 1980), p. 23.
10. R. Tingle, *Revolution or Reconciliation? The Struggle of the Church in South Africa* (Cape Town: The Christian's Study Centre, 1992).
11. E.M. Zuesse, "Perseverance and Transmutation in African Traditional Religions," in J.K. Olupona (ed), *African Traditional Religions in Contemporary Society* (New York: Paragon House, 1991), p. 173.
12. I.S. Mkhwanazi, *An Investigation of the Therapeutic Methods of Zulu Diviners* (Pretoria: MA Thesis, University of South Africa, 1986); M. West, *Bishops and Prophets in a Black City: African Independent Churches in Soweto/Johannesburg* (Cape Town: David Philip, 1975).
13. G. Sogolo, "The Task of African Philosophy in a Changing World," paper read at the University of Zululand, May 23, 1994.
14. G.C. Oosthuizen, "Interpretation of Demonic Powers in South African Independent Churches," in *Missiology*, Vol. XVI.1 (January 1988): 3-22.
15. H. Ngubane, *Body and Mind in Zulu Medicine* (London: Academic Press, 1977), p. 28.
16. J. Mbiti, *Introduction to African Religion* (London: Heinemann, 1975), p. 134.
17. R.W.S. Cheetham and J.A. Griffiths, "The Traditional Healer/Diviner as Psychotherapist," in *South African Medical Journal*, 62 (1978); S.D. Edwards, "Attitudes to Disease and Healing in a South African Context," in G.C. Oosthuizen (ed), *Religion Alive: Studies in the New Movements and Indigenous Churches in Southern Africa* (Cape Town: Hodder and Stoughton, 1986); D. Farrand, "Choice and Perception of Healers among Black Psychiatric Patients," in G.C. Oosthuizen (ed.), *Religion Alive: Studies in the New Movements and Indigenous Churches in Southern Africa* (Cape Town: Hodder and Stoughton, 1986); M.V. Bührmann, *Living in Two Worlds: Communication Between White Healer and Her Black Counterparts* (Cape Town: Human and Rousseau, 1984).
18. R.D. Schweitzer, "Indigenous Therapy in Southern Africa," in *Bulletin of the British Psychological Society*, 1978.

19. M. Stovall, *Indigenous Churches in Southern Africa* (Bloomington: University of Indiana Press, 1976), p. 20.
20. C. Cross, G.C. Oosthuizen, S. Bekker and J. Evans, *Rise up and Walk: Development and the African Independent/Indigenous Churches in Durban* (Durban: Report by Rural Urban Studies Unit and NERMIC, 1992).
21. P.M. Zulu and G.C. Oosthuizen, "Religion and World Outlook," in G.C. Oosthuizen and I. Hexham (eds), *Afro-Christian Religion at the Grassroots in Southern Africa* (Lewiston: The Edwin Mellen Press, 1991), p. 13.
22. C. Cross, G.C.Oosthuizen and C. Clark, *Out of the Wind: The African Independent Churches and Youth Urbanization in Metropolitan Natal* (Durban: Unpublished Report, Centre for Social and Development Studies, University of Natal, 1993), p. 31.
23. *Ibid.*
24. M. Mohr, *Negotiating the Boundary: The Response of Kwamashu Zionists to a Volatile Potitical Climate* (Durban: Ph.D. Thesis, University of Natal, 1993).
25. Cross, Oosthuizen and Clark, *op. cit.*, pp. 31-35.
26. *Ibid.*, p. 5.
27. *Ibid.*
28. *Ibid.*, pp. 41-42.
29. *Ibid.*, p. 42.

The Role of Religion in the Transformation of Southern African Societies:

A South African Jewish Perspective

Jocelyn Louise Hellig
Department of Religious Studies
University of the Witwatersrand, South Africa

Introduction

The question of the role of religion in the transformation of Southern Africa is a very broad and complex one. For this reason, I shall confine my remarks to transformation of South Africa whose present conditions are inextricable from its history of apartheid. It is well known that religion played an important part in the formation and dismantling of apartheid and that religion has resources for promoting a variety of motivations for good or ill. But religion does not operate in a vacuum. Apartheid, in essence, was an affirmative action program for indigent white Afrikaners. Religion was used as its legitimation, but its real motivation was socioeconomic. In fact, apartheid was a long time in the making. South Africa's predominantly Christian culture, as Martin Prozesky has pointed out, had developed a system of hierarchical exclusion by creating a social pyramid in which the white Christian elite was at the apex and the black majority was at the base. Christianity established itself as the majority religion in South Africa and by the time that the various religious minorities had arrived in the country, the ingredients for apartheid were already in place. All that was needed was something to cement these ingredients into an edifice of state and this came in the form of the vast wealth that was to ensue from the discovery of diamonds and gold towards the end of the nineteenth century. Economic considerations thus "massively intensified the drive towards total conquest and the consequent total economic subservience of all people outside that white, overwhelmingly Christian elite."[1] It thus becomes difficult to isolate what role religion, per se, has played in setting up apartheid and what it can contribute to the transformation of South Africa.

Before attempting to isolate religion's role in South Africa, I shall give consideration to the nature of the transformation that the country requires. I shall then give a brief indication of the way in which religion shaped the broad South African reality. The main body of the paper will be devoted to reflections on how my own community, the Jewish community, can best contribute to the reconstruction and development of South Africa. In this last section two issues which require attention are: the need to foster among South African Jews a new, all-inclusive South African identity and the need to mine Judaism's ethical insights in order to motivate action.

The Nature of the Transformation

South Africa has entered what a recent cover story in *Time Magazine* so aptly describes as the "post-miracle phase."[2] With its democratic election in April 1994, South Africa took its first giant step towards transformation. Oppressive government by a minority gave way to democratic government in which all parties are represented. The elections were preceded by negotiations through which the white minority handed power over to the black majority. The easy transformation to a fledgling democracy was seen by many, the world over, as a miracle. But now that the heady days following the elections are long past, South Africans have to face the sober reality that the major work of transformation still has to be done. The inequities of the past have to be repaired so that their legacy does not continue to operate in the lives of South Africans. The process will be a long one and will involve not only material factors but a transformation of people's thinking patterns.

Much of the groundwork has already been laid, but great hurdles still need to be crossed. The South African Constitution has recently been ratified, giving equality to all South Africa's citizens and affirming religious freedom. The Truth and Reconciliation Commission is in process. As a confrontation with South Africa's brutal apartheid past, it is allowing both perpetrators and victims of apartheid's gross violations of human rights to come to terms with the past in order to build the future. Affirmative action is providing employment opportunities for those who were grossly disadvantaged by the old system of white privilege. But despite all these measures, South Africa does not look all that different from the way it looked before the elections. Steven Friedman pointed out in 1991 that "South Africa has one of the most unequal income distributions in the world; virtually all the rich are white and almost all the poor are black."[3] Little has changed in this regard. Underlining it today, however, is rampant crime, a factor which is threatening the very bases of South Africa's democracy. Clearly, meaningful transformation needs a vital and growing economy which will go hand in hand with the supply of education, housing, health care and a host of basic necessities which have been denied to South Africa's black majority.

As *Time Magazine* pointed out, the most pressing reality in South Africa today is sheer economic survival. Four decades of international disinvestment, coupled with political and economic mismanagement by the pro-apartheid National Party, have left South Africa ill-prepared for the challenge. Facing 40 percent unemployment, suffering a budget deficit amounting to 5 percent of its $118 billion gross domestic product, and having to compete for business in the international marketplace with countries such as Brazil, Chile, Indonesia and South Korea, whose economies are rapidly growing, South Africa has a formidable task.[4]

The transformation process therefore has to be twofold. It has to address the material needs of South Africans, but it also has to transform people's ideas and sense of identity, their very experience of what it means to be South African. This is where religion plays a vital role. In fact, realizing the importance of religion in influencing motivation and in identity-formation, the Editorial Board of *Jewish Affairs*, the cultural journal of the South African Jewish Board of Deputies, decided to devote an issue to the subject of "Religion and Change." I was privileged to be the guest editor for that issue. Much of the material in this paper has, therefore, already come under my purview.[5]

The South African Jewish Community in Context

One cannot examine the Jewish community in isolation from other religious communities or from the broader context of South African society. Nor, as indicated above, can one separate religion and religious communities from social, economic and political developments. The Jewish community, as were other South African religious minorities, was deeply affected by apartheid. In fact, the Jewish community of South Africa resembles other New World Jewish communities but for one reality, apartheid. Jews were the only white, and indeed, smallest religious minority in a country which enforced a system of legalized racial discrimination. As whites, they were beneficiaries of the system in that they shared the privileges of the whites in South Africa's white parliamentary "democracy."

Jews were molded into the structure which had been set up by South Africa's white Christian elite. While all religious minorities were regarded as alien, Jews were seen as the least alien and therefore were fairly high on the social pyramid. It must be said, however, that Jews suffered more indignities than any other white ethnic group in the country, primarily in the form of discriminatory immigration legislation. Their role in society was determined by their position in the social, political and economic hierarchy.

The interrelatedness of these factors is well illustrated by Martin Prozesky who points out the economic impetus to white settlement in South Africa. The rise of merchant capitalism was followed by wave after wave of European invasion and conquest of Africa. The effect of these incursions was the devastation of the culture of the native peoples. The ships that came from Europe were commissioned neither for religious nor initially for military purposes, but for commerce. What is often overlooked, however, is that the devastation of African culture was the work of people from a world exposed to Christianity for nearly fifteen hundred years,[6] though it was not necessarily Christianity per se that caused the damage. Whether Christianity was so ethically weak that it could not prevent the process, or whether the moral restraints provided by Christianity ensured that the devastation was not worse are questions that still need answering.[7] In spite of strong missionary activity and the fact that blacks embraced Christianity, South African Christianity was unable to generate a politics of inclusion. Black Christians were not accepted as equals. No longer African in the traditional sense, nor European, a new identity had to be created.

This is where Christianity, ironically, stepped in. It was to play a major role in the defeat of apartheid. African Independent Churches, the appropriation of Christianity on African terms, played a role in the formulation of a politics of inclusion. The much maligned African Traditional Religion must also have contributed its part.[8]

The same dynamic, as Gerrie Lubbe points out, can be observed in the development of South African Calvinism. White Afrikaner Calvinism produced a justification for division of people and races. As ethnic division was seen as God's will and plan for the world, diversity had to be protected by legislation. By 1948, when the Nationalist Party came to power, the theological justification for apartheid was a reality and its political application was a formality. What is remarkable, however, is that it was within this same tradition that the resources were found for a new understanding of salvation which can play an important part in liberating white Afrikaners themselves. In the hands of black Calvinists the same religious tradition yielded an entirely different understanding of God's plan for the world: "God used white Calvinists to bring the Good News of Salvation in Jesus Christ to their black brothers and sisters. Now He is using black Calvinists to bring liberation to their white brothers and sisters. It is to be hoped that, together, black and white will come to experience fully the essence of being human."[9]

This is the context in which the South African Jewish community was molded and to which it has had to respond. In South Africa, a country riven by racial discrimination, even religions are divided by race. Apart from the majority Christian community, whose members cut across all racial groups, religious minorities are made up of separate racial groups. Muslims are Indian, "Coloured" or black; Hindus are Indian; and Jews are white. People of different races were forced by the Group Areas Act to live miles apart from one another. This resulted in insularity which, from the positive side, fostered the maintenance of group identity (which, as indicated below, may not be the deepest and strongest identity, particularly with regard to South African Jews) but which on the negative side, resulted in isolation, ignorance and suspicion. This has markedly affected the way people of different religions interacted. It has also influenced perception of other religious groups because it had a bearing on the contribution the various religious traditions made to the elimination of apartheid.

The Jewish community was constrained by its historic circumstances. Communally, the Jewish response to apartheid was timid but, on the individual level, Jews were in the forefront of the antiapartheid struggle. This communal timidity was, according to Gideon Shimoni, a characteristic strategy for minority group survival.[10] The rise to power by the then antisemitic Nationalist Party in 1948 was greeted with immense trepidation by the Jewish community. The Nationalist Party had spearheaded the discriminatory immigration legislation that effectively ended Jewish immigration from Europe at a time when European Jews most needed refuge from Nazism. Antisemitism had, by the thirties, become a central plank of Afrikaner nationalism. Only three years after the end of World War II and the slaughter of one third of the world's Jews, the inception of nationalist government coincided with the rebirth of the State of Israel. The significance of the Jewish return to sovereignty, in the light of the complete political powerlessness that culminated in the Holocaust, can never be ignored. This must be emphasized along with South African Jewry's legacy of pro-Zionism from its Lithuanian forebears.

After its victory, the Nationalist Party consciously abandoned anti-semitism and, as an attempt to woo all sectors of the white population in the face of its mounting "race problem," entered a process of Afrikaner-Jewish rapprochement which was facilitated by genuine Afrikaner sympathy for the fledgling State of Israel. Caught on the horns of a dilemma, the South African Jewish Board of Deputies, the official spokesbody for the community and its protector with regard to civil and religious rights, was keen to foster this rapprochement and was anxious not to do anything that would undermine it. This resulted in a policy of communal non-involvement in politics. Jews were to make political decisions individually without communal pressure. This strategy was also motivated by the conviction that Jews were so small a community that they could not make a difference.[11]

The South African Jewish Community and Transformation

The South African Jewish community is ranked tenth in size of all Jewish communities in the world.[12] Estimated at about 100 thousand, it is a small and well-organized community whose most characteristic feature is its pro-Zionism. As Gideon Shimoni points out, in "the comparative perspective of the English-speaking countries there is no more distinctive feature of South African Jewry than its overwhelmingly Zionist character."[13] Like Jews of other Western countries of immigration, South African Jews have exhibited rapid upward economic, educational and occupational mobility. They have, for several decades, been better educated and enjoyed higher occupational status than any other white group in the country.[14] They constitute a visibly successful minority of whites.

This is pertinent in the light of President Mandela's plea for the Jewish community to make its contribution to the reconstruction of South Africa. In his keynote address to the Jewish community at the 37th South African Jewish Board of Deputies National Congress he said:

> Yours is a community that has a deserved reputation for being well educated and for the skills it possesses—professional, commercial and industrial. I believe those skills can and should be used both to help the development of the country and to mount programmes, using your own knowledge and skills, to contribute to the development of those who have been denied fair opportunities.... I believe that cooperation, commitment and imagination could ensure that more programmes for larger numbers of people can be established. The Jewish community must find a role for itself in such activity.

   Steven Friedman has suggested that there is less justification
than ever before—if indeed there is any justification at all—for the
South African Jewish community to remain aloof from events
around it. Though it has little political influence, the Jewish community has disproportionate resources and skills which it can share
in order to reduce material inequalities and help bring about a
successful democracy.[15]

   The Jewish community's particular expression of Judaism is also
pertinent to the question of transformation. Religiously conservative, the community shows a high level of affiliation with the
synagogue as the primary religious institution. About 85 percent
of those affiliated with a synagogue belong to Orthodox synagogues while about 10 - 15 percent belong to Reform (known in
South Africa as "Progressive") temples. There is virtually no official
Jewish conservative movement in South Africa,[16] yet religious conservatism is a characteristic of the community. The smallness of
reform Judaism in South Africa is associated with the way orthodoxy in South Africa is perceived and practiced. The existence of
a large body of Jews who are affiliated with an orthodox synagogue, but who do not live a Torah lifestyle and feel comfortable
picking and choosing which mitzvot to observe and which to
neglect, makes South African Jews' expression of Judaism unique.
It is not that such non-observant orthodox Jews do not exist elsewhere, but the fact that there is such a preponderance of them that
makes the South African situation different. These Jews are fully
aware of the demands of orthodoxy and the fact that their lifestyle
is closer to reform Judaism, but they are unwilling to change their
affiliation to a reform temple. Jewish orthodoxy in South Africa is
thus "more a widely accepted form of identification than it is a
matter of disciplined observance."[17]

   This type of orthodoxy, as Isadore Rubinstein suggests, is
associated with a shallow and non-challenging sense of Jewish identity,[18] a type of identity that may be typical of groups within the
South African context. Of importance for this paper is that this
kind of development does not take place in a vacuum. Unobservant
orthodoxy in South Africa is, on the one hand, a legacy from the
traditional piety of South African Jewry's Litvak forebears and, on
the other, a reflection of the conservative Calvinist context in which
the South African Jewish community grew. There has, up till now,

been no overarching South African identity.[19] As there was never a "melting pot" in South Africa, Jews, like other religious or ethnic groups, felt no need to obliterate immigrant cultural patterns. All South Africans have belonged to ethnic sub-groups, a separation and sense of identification which apartheid reinforced. This, as far as Judaism is concerned, tended to reduce pressure to conform to society at large and minimized the tendency to drift away from the Jewish community and Jewish self-identification.[20] But this identification, according to Rubinstein, has been shallow. Rather than being accompanied by religious examination and intellectual ferment, it displays desire for survival as a communal entity. Thus, the South African Jewish community has not seen the identity crises characteristic of other Western Jewish communities. Assimilation and intermarriage among South African Jews have been low while Jewish religious affiliation remains high. The strength of the South African Jewish community has lain more in structure and consensus than in ideological challenge.[21] As an historically homogeneous community, it exhibits a profound pressure to conform and exerts pressure for accommodation and civility. It has traditionally addressed ideological conflict with administrative solutions and conciliatory approaches in order to emphasize communal unity. This has inhibited the flourishing of creative Jewish thought in South Africa.[22] These trends were reinforced by South African Calvinism which itself discouraged change, heterodoxy and intellectual ferment.[23] Within this context, the small growth of reform Judaism and its moderate expression in South Africa become comprehensible. So does non-observant orthodoxy, particularly in that religious affiliation is dependent rather on family traditions than on ideological convictions.

An essential part of the transformation process will be for religious communities to see themselves as an integral part of the broader South African structure and to educate their children into developing a comprehensive South African identity. This should apply not only to Jews, but to the members of all minority religious groups. I suspect that other religious groups did not escape this unquestioning approach. This may be observed, for example, in the way the Muslim and Jewish communities unthinkingly take sides in the Arab-Israeli conflict, seldom allowing the complexities of the issue to enter the argument.

Transformation and Jewish Ethics

When analyzing the contribution religion can make to reconstruction of South African society, the most obvious source is the
ethical tradition that each religion espouses. These are too well
known to merit description here. I would therefore like to turn
immediately to aspects of the Jewish ethical vision, bearing in mind
that it, like other ethical systems, is embedded in a particular
worldview.

Undergirding the ethical values of Judaism is the belief that
God had intervened on behalf of the Jewish people—a group of
unworthy slaves suffering oppression in the land of Egypt—and
taken them to a promised land. They thus saw themselves as chosen. Their indebtedness to God had to be shown in their obedience
to the covenant which he entered into with them. Primary to their
memory of this historic event was their experience as strangers.
They were henceforth to emulate their God in extending mercy to
others: "The stranger who sojourns with you shall be to you as the
native among you, and you shall love him as yourself; for you were
strangers in the land of Egypt" (Lev. 19:34).

The use of the term "stranger" can only be appreciated when
one understands that the Jewish doctrine of chosenness is not one
of special privilege, but one of specific obligation. Being Jewish
means belonging to a set of people who have a shared memory and
who express their obligation to God by living a religiously ordained
lifestyle which can only be fully observed in a community context.
Jews alone are bound by obligation to keep the details of the
Torah. There is thus a distinct tension in Judaism between the
particular and the universal. God is creator and the God of the
universe, but he is also a God who chose the Jews for some mys-
terious mission in the world. Jews, while bound into a community,
are not free to dismiss the world outside of it. In addition to
maintaining Jewish life and identity, Jews are obligated to extend
concern to the world.[24]

This idea is an integral part of the Jewish understanding of God
as the God who acts in history. With the Exodus from Egypt as
their primary revelation, Jews understand their whole history in
terms of redemption and exile. It is God who makes history, not
humanity. God, who rewards obedience to the Torah and punishes

disobedience through exile, will bring about the ultimate redemption of history. Jews see themselves as his co-workers in perfecting history. This notion took on a particularly forceful emphasis with the development of the mystic tradition in Judaism and the doctrine of "*tikkun*" or the mending of the world. Due to a cosmic catastrophe at the time of creation, divine sparks descended to earth encased in matter. The task of the Jew is to act in such ways that the divine sparks are returned to their source. It is thus significant that a current reconstruction and development program coordinated by the South African Jewish Board of Deputies is called "Tikkun."[25] Fragmentation and disruption, it is believed, are there to be overcome and it is the duty of the Jew to assist in such a healing process.

The material world has never been irrelevant to Judaism. Nor have non-possession or denial of the world been Jewish virtues. On the contrary, Judaism enjoins the Jew to embrace the world, to enjoy its bounty to the full, but subject all actions to holy discipline. Jews are expected to elevate every act to holiness by maintaining an awareness of the God-given nature of all things.

It is in line with this view of the material world that one of the Jewish prophetic ideals is: "Each man shall dwell under his own vine, under his own fig-tree, undisturbed" (Micah 4:4). It is not surprising that a people who has suffered centuries of homelessness and persecution should conceive of peace in terms of quiet, simple and self-sufficient domestic life. In the light of their own historic experience and the importance of a sense of place and stability, this should act as a motivating factor for the Jewish community to extend its efforts on behalf of those who in the apartheid situation were rendered poverty-stricken and homeless. It is also with this view in mind that Judaism distinguishes eight degrees of charity. The highest is that type of giving that results in the self-sufficiency of the recipient.

Interfaith Dialogue

Related to the issues of identity formation and a sense of freedom in which to make a meaningful contribution is the question of inter-group relations, with specific reference to interfaith dialogue. As a result of residential segregation, religious communities in

South Africa know little about one another. So although religious
and ethnic diversity is celebrated in South Africa and Archbishop
Desmond Tutu's metaphor "the rainbow nation of God" is widely
used, there is a considerable amount of inter-religious conflict
which exists side by side with the fact that there is a new-found
interest in religion in South Africa and, for the first time, religious
minorities feel at home.

There is, as Charles Villa-Vicencio has remarked, an enormous
incentive in South Africa for people to learn to live together
religiously.[26] In a country seeking unity without uniformity in the
face of a past marred by exclusion, something new has to be found
to transcend difference without collapsing the many into the one.
All religions, he points out, have resources for openness, inclusiv-
ism and universalism. These clearly need to be explored in order
to create a new society.

As far as Judaism is concerned, these resources will be found in
the tension between Judaism's particularism and its universality.
Judaism's reluctance to seek converts stands side by side with its
universal thrust. The Seven Noahide Laws and their implications
need to be explored in an interfaith context. Most urgently,
however, is dialogue with the Muslim community, Muslim-Jewish
relations in South Africa being extremely tense. Despite efforts by
the Jewish community to cooperate with other religious communities in the transformation of South Africa, the relations with the
Muslim community remain strained. This is exacerbated by the fact
that the Jewish community is white as well as by the strongly
Zionist character of South African Jewry. Efforts need to be made
to foster dialogue and to deal with those issues that divide these
two communities. This was a lot easier when the Middle East Peace
Process was in progress. Its current apparently moribund status is
a cause for deep concern among most of South Africa's Jews.

South African Muslims' identification with the Arab world and
South African Jewry's support of Zionism both tend to be un-
critical. The South African Muslims understandably identify with
the plight of the Palestinians while South African Jews are justifi-
ably dedicated to the preservation of Israel. The safety and security
of Israel are not negotiable because Israel offers Jews political sovereignty in the face of the Holocaust, which is an example of what
can happen to a people totally bereft of power. Without questioning

the Jews' right to a homeland, one can question precisely how the Jewish state should relate to its Arab neighbors and maintain itself.

In this regard, it is important not to view the entire spectrum of Jewish history through the prism of the Holocaust. To do so, as David Biale points out, not only distorts Jewish history as being characterized by total powerlessness and passivity, but limits current responses to Israel's contemporary realities. It is all a matter of context. One of the problems is that a process of myth-making, accompanied by mutual demonization, has taken place on both sides of the Arab-Israeli conflict. This process is reflected in South Africa. Israel, by regarding the Holocaust as the sole spectrum through which diaspora history should be viewed, has, according to Biale, developed an "ideology of survival." A legacy of powerlessness is thus seen to justify the exercise of power. While militarily powerful, Israel perceives itself as extremely vulnerable. Israel's enemies perceive a mirror image, typically seeing themselves as impotent and Israel as omnipotent. Thus, there is a symmetry between the views of Jews and Arabs: each suffers from the same disjunction between images of itself and the other. It is out of such illusory perceptions of oneself and one's enemies that political conflicts become mythologized and their resolution grows increasingly remote.[27]

It is clear that the way in which communities perceive both themselves and others is of importance with regard to interfaith conflict. Thus, the nature of religious education becomes important. Chief Rabbi Harris, for example, calls for an emphasis on the richness and diversity of Jewish history and, while recognizing its undoubted importance, opposes the almost cult-like status that the Holocaust is given in South African Jewish education.[28] This type of reassessment needs to be taken by all communities.

Religious groups have to look to the truths that bind them rather than to those factors that divide them. South Africans of all religions have to communicate across the religious and racial divides not in order to blur differences, but in order to accept diversity and accord other religions respect. Respect can be based only on knowledge and understanding of the other.

Conclusion

Reconstruction of South Africa can only be sustained in an atmosphere of trust and security. Genuine altruism and care for those outside of one's own religious or racial group will become viable when a new identification of what it means to be a South African is forged. Communities, in the meantime, have to plumb the ethical insights of their particular religious traditions in order to promote action. Work in this period of transition is, of necessity, patch work. Communities have to overcome their separateness and come to the realization that individual South Africans share a common destiny. It is to be hoped that with sound education of our young, in an environment of democracy and freedom, South Africans of all colors and creeds will come to a new vision that, in itself, will inspire action.

NOTES

1. M. Prozesky, "Religion and Society during and after Apartheid," *Jewish Affairs*, vol. 50, no. 3, Spring 1995, p. 18.
2. *Time Magazine*, September 16, 1996, pp. 48-67.
3. S. Friedman, "South Africa in Transition: Implications for Jewry," *Jewish Affairs*, March/April 1991, p. 7.
4. *Time Magazine*, *op. cit.*, p. 49.
5. *Jewish Affairs*, vol. 50, no. 3, Spring 1996.
6. Prozesky, *op. cit.*, p. 15.
7. *Ibid.*, p. 16.
8. These are among areas which, as Prozesky noted, need research.
9. G. Lubbe, "Liberating Calvinists in South Africa," *Jewish Affairs*, Spring 1995, p. 26.
10. G. Shimoni, "South African Jews and the Apartheid Crisis," in D. Singer and R. Seldin (eds.), *American Jewish Year Book 1988* (Philadelphia: The Jewish Publication Society, 1988), p. 27.
11. The late Chief Rabbi Casper commented: "We don't see ourselves as wielding great power in this country and therefore we keep a low profile.... If we haven't spoken out more strongly, it is partly due to the fact that we realise our ineffectiveness." In T. Hoffman and A. Fischer, *The Jews of South Africa: What Future?* (Johannesburg, Southern Books, 1988), pp. 319f.
12. S. Della Pergola, "Where Are We Going? Demographic Trends in World Jewish Population," *Jewish Affairs*, Spring 1995, p. 47.

13. G. Shimoni, *op. cit.*, p. 5.
14. A. Dubb, *The Jewish Population of South Africa: The 1991 Sociodemographic Survey* (Cape Town: Jewish Studies and Research, Kaplan Centre, 1994), p. 60.
15. Friedman, *op. cit.*, p. 15.
16. Although the Shalom Independent Congregation, under the leadership of Rabbi Ady Assabi, is affiliated to the World Council of Conservative/Masorti Synagogues, it regards itself as independent of any of the major movements of Judaism.
17. S. Ashheim, "The Communal Organisation of South African Jewry," *Jewish Journal of Sociology*, XII (2), December 1970, p. 218.
18. I. Rubinstein, "Jewish Education in a Changing South Africa," *Jewish Affairs*, Spring 1995, pp. 53-59.
19. See Rubinstein, *op. cit.*, pp. 53f and Shimoni, *op. cit.*, p. 6.
20. Dubb and Della Pergola, 1988, cited in Rubinstein, *op. cit.*, p. 54.
21. Rubinstein, *op. cit.*, p. 54.
22. In South Africa there is little innovative Jewish thinking and there are no Jewish theologians of world stature.
23. *Ibid.*
24. As part of the Jewish contribution to the reconstruction of South Africa, an organization called Tikkun has been established. Its first publication is a booklet compiled by Chief Rabbi Cyril Harris, "Jewish Obligation to the Non-Jew," Tikkun Publications: no. 1, 1996.
25. Tikkun's mission statement is: "As the Jewish community, we seek to make a meaningful difference to the upliftment of disadvantaged people in South Africa."
    Tikkun's aims are:
    • to act as a co-ordinating body of Jewish communal organization initiatives in respect of upliftment of the disadvantaged towards nation building;
    • to highlight and enhance the historical role played by Jewish community outreach projects, as well as facilitate the expansion and partnership between projects and communities;
    • to harness Jewish community resources as well as encourage individuals to volunteer their skills and expertise.
26. See C. Villa-Vicencio, "Learning to Live Together Religiously: A Christian Perspective," *Jewish Affairs*, Spring 1995, pp. 31-36.
27. D. Biale, *Power and Powerlessness in Jewish History* (New York: Schocken Books, 1987), p. 164.
28. C.K. Harris, "The Elusive Balance: The Jewish Day School Predicament," *Jewish Affairs*, Spring 1995, p. 51.

A Hindu Perspective on the Transformation of Southern African Society

Thillayvel Naidoo
Department of Religious Studies
University of Durban-Westville
Durban, South Africa

The Inter-Religious Enterprise

This discussion takes its theme from a Hindu maxim which says if there is only one God, there is only one community of humanity.[1] Hindu teachers go on to say that one planet earth can have room for only one human family. This means that the diversity we perceive in our human and cultural composition has been seriously misinterpreted. Nations need the will to interpret their positions as members of the family of nations and religions.

Theocracies will have difficulty to accomodate a variety of religious perceptions within a single political structure, the state. Also such nations accentuate their differences both as nations and as religious systems. Such differences invariably draw attention to religious uniqueness and claims that special revelations underlie their religious systems. Challenges to claims of uniqueness are seldom tolerated, and nations based on theocracies very often exclude themselves from the family of nations because the claims to religious revelation make no allowance for a plurality of religions in society. Claims to uniqueness of revelation inevitably engender tensions. Some religions have difficulty seeing themselves as members of the family of religions because of their exclusivity. This often overflows into the socio-political arena. This was true for some churches as well. The Dutch Reformed Church, for example, felt honored to claim that it and not the governing nationalist party produced the blueprint for apartheid.[2]

In South Africa, few, if any, are ever willing to suggest that the multi-racial composition that is our nation should be recognized as a single human family.

The theme of unity that is sometimes alluded to in political discussion is crucial to our survival as a nation because it is the basis upon which our social responsibility is built. The greatest fear one harbors is that while social and economic objectives clearly delineate our combined responsibilities, the achievement of those objectives is stifled because our religions don't provide guidelines that could bring those objectives to the nation as a whole. I hesitate, therefore, to suggest that religions in South Africa have the potential to bring peace and stability to our national life. I am inclined, in fact, to suggest that some of the roots of our chaos have their birth in our religious differences.

Perhaps the most crucial question for religious communities is where does the chaos we see around us really begin? If one accepts the Hindu maxim that we are really one community of humanity as children of one God, then religious, cultural and racial differences must be superficial ones. Hindu scripture suggests that because the earth is one, nations must be one family.[3]

Religions appear to have great difficulty seeing themselves as a family. The family of nations then has to endure the further difficulty of formulating an ideal political system within the framework of a greatly divided human community. Our religious differences accentuate cultural differences, which in turn spawn political, economic, social and, of course, racial differences.

Individual citizens, like comunities of people, have difficulty identifying with national objectives. Young people may be forgiven for having difficulty identifying with the whole because South Africans often fail to see themselves as citizens of a country, a racial, cultural or political group, or a religious community. But this should not be a serious difficulty. The dilemma is not overly complex. Both the nation and the religious community should constitute the basis of a national family. This suggests that religious insights should guide people on how conflicts can be avoided in the context of national and cultural allegiances.

Pluralism is always a challenge. In India and other parts of the world it poses a challenge for cultural unity. One unfortunate feature of religion in South Africa and elsewhere, however, is its self-serving and divisive tendencies. We often hear that outside this or that tradition God's love is unknown. Proselytizing faiths often claim exclusive rights to salvation. Such religious propaganda has the inevitable result of engendering antagonisms and achieving very little else. Proselytizing faiths often spread their gospels on the basis of a disrespect for other faiths.

Universal Principles

Religion has been entrusted with the task of remaking the human conscience.[4] Religion says that we must look at ourselves for the purpose of transformation. Transformation implies cleansing the mind of all iniquity. Only when the base instincts are expelled can humans raise themselves to higher levels of moral excellence. The scientific nature of our present times no longer takes kindly to dogma or supernaturalism.[5] Even history is often written with partisan bias. Communities seldom attach much meaning to events outside the history of their own communities.

The greatest challenges that religions in South Africa will face in the twenty-first century will be to address human reason and understanding more intensively, beyond the narrow confines of parochial claims. The modern person asks, Do religions speak with any real authority? Do they appeal to the widest segments of human society and give evidence of being able to appeal more intelligently to human reason? Religions cannot continually confine their appeals to the emotive stockades of parochial palliatives.

The future of religion lies in universality.[6] The demands of the twenty-first century will be that the religions of mankind must enunciate with considerable evidence that their teachings are addressed to one comnnon humanity. One common humanity needs a religious view that is nurtured in universality beyond the borders of the parochiality that engenders ethnicity and racism. The religious consciousness suspects that some religious principles extend beyond the confines of religious traditions narrowly understood.

This is not to denigrate any existing religion. South Africa is proving itself to be a very fertile field in which many of the world's religions now flourish. And in many spheres some remarkable feelings of goodwill are being engendered. But the religions are also notorious for one rather serious failing—engendering the idea that some religions are exclusive pathways to God and that the moral and ethical values they propagate are morals of an exclusive brand. There is now a plethora of electronic and print media messages that appeal every day to South Africans to observe their moral responsibilities. One notices, however, that while the appeals are made for moral growth, they nearly always imply that the moral growth they call for can only be achieved by following one particular faith and that outside of that faith no moral discipline is possible. What South Africans have to learn is that moral discipline is a fact of universal import and no one religion holds exclusive rights to ethical prescriptions. Thus, when the universal message of our religious traditions become more sharply focused, we need to take a more comprehensive view of the religions of the country and their relevance for all its peoples.

The general elections of 1994 promised us a free, open, transparent and racially tolerant democracy. As far as we are aware, this was sought due to considerable agreement among our Constitution makers that democratic values would form our basic norms not for religious reasons but for purely secular ones. These included some important objectives, such as the elimination of poverty, the provision of homes to all citizens, health care for all and, of course, education for all. Many religious institutions of note were reasonably happy with these objectives. They needed to be reminded, however, that these achievements did not result from any strong part played by them in the years that apartheid prevailed. In fact it is the violence and corruption spawned in that era that still survives today as endemic features of South African society.[7]

It is important for religious institutions to ensure that our Parliament adheres strictly to a moral code enshrined in our new Constitution. The old Parliament had little interest in moral principles. The present Parliament demands that the nation become sensitive to ways in which laws are executed. Never again should they infringe on ethical principles, no matter what the circumstances. All the people of our country now have good reason to rejoice at our acquisition of a Bill of Rights and the Human Rights culture it engenders.

Our post-apartheid structures are contributing to the development of a new character for South Africa, and her multi-cultural composition is beginning to develop a new phase of tolerance and acceptance that transcends the ugly blemishes of prejudice that once formed so much of our social setting. Our greatest task is to learn to appreciate that religion in its essential nature is trans-social and individual in its appeal and function; it has a secondary yet significant role in the important sphere of social relations. Religion as practiced has been very parochial in outlook and, given our unfortunate history, also racially tinged to the detriment of the universal characteristics they sometimes engender. So precisely how the universal elements of religion can be made to predominate is a crucial question for our social regeneration.

One of our great difficulties is that religions have yet to become more appreciative of the fact that our common humanity must be the basis of our belief that a Supreme Almighty Being is ultimately responsible for much that will happen when the real task of concern with Ultimacy is faced. Eschatological concerns are not the exclusive preserve of any one religion, especially not to the total exclusion of all others. So the religions practiced in South Africa have the crucial task to recognize themselves as members of a family of approaches to God and also as members with an inalienable duty to recognize their place in South African society as citizens of a single political unit.

It is the restrictions that religions have placed upon their own perceptions that have in some ways restricted communities from assuming combined responsibilities for social actions. One of the more obvious features of life in South Africa is that the different races and religious communities have to live together. Our social, political and economic responsibilities make cross-cultural intercourse inevitable. But very little of any real and substantive religious goodness emerges at any level in our society as a result of this interaction. On the contrary, one often becomes aware of the competitive and unspoken suspicions that characterize relationships because some think that true religions speak with authentic voices while it is the false religions that lay undue claims to equality.

Individual Responsibility

Perhaps the most radical element of the entire religious enterprise is for people to understand how faith in humanity plays a crucial role in religious transformation. Religion will be an effective and positive force in society provided that we go about it the right way. The right way is for us to understand that we are human beings first and followers of any one of the religions second. The human element should remind us of our responsibilities as equal players in the game of life. The human element teaches us that belief in God can be brought to its ultimate fruition when we share with fellow human beings common elements.[8]

Hindu teachers have emphasized for several thousand years that enquiry into religious Truth must result in human emancipation at the level of spiritual insight.[9] Hinduism, or more correctly Vedanta, approaches life with a view to a holistic solution to the agonies of everyday life. Vedanta teaches the oneness of all life, before which the fictitious difference between religion and life in the world must vanish. The ideal of religion, according to Vedanta, must cover the whole field of life, center all our thoughts, and find expression in all our actions.[10]

Our greatest responsibility lies in understanding religion in the most practical way. It is at once a high ideal which is to be put into practice without compromise. Unfortunately, however, there are those of us who do compromise our positions, diluting the ideals we live by. Much of Hindu thought declares that if we set our sights on the Ultimate Ideal to which we aspire, the present life should be made to conform and coincide with those ideals.

The task of remaking the individual, the human person, is the task of religion.[11] We should look within ourselves, for the purpose of transformation. We should cleanse ourselves of destructive habits and weaknesses. The fallen side of human nature needs constantly to be re-examined. We need to raise ourselves to levels of discipline that accord with the religious and cultural ideals our scriptures have delineated for us.

Religious communities should not become too involved in politics. It is crucial for religious comunities to stand above politics and to ensure that politicians are doing their work under the moral codes that our religions have prescribed.[12] Our task is purely to ensure that our national life is not jeopardized and that our moral standards are never compromised. Thus, serious consideration should be given to the ways government upholds principles of morality, democracy and justice. Virtually everthing the government has been entrusted with is a matter of serious concern to our various religious communities. Religions are not expected to interfere as busybodies but ensure from a safe distance that the principles we uphold are never compromised for any reason whatever.

Certainly no narrow, dogmatic or prejudiced opinion must ever be allowed to dictate the rules. Religions have the real task of coping with the more important problems of human life such as the problems of poverty, greed, selfishness, anger and violence.

The future lies in education; in character-building education;[13] in a system of education that ensures that we have instilled in ourselves the ideals of the highest values of moral and spiritual discipline. Our present system seems to ensure that the religions do nothing more than instil in us suspicions of one kind or another, more especially religious suspicions that do nothing more than enhance prejudices of every kind. When the decision was taken to bring about a new political dispensation in the country, it was common sense more than anything else that called for a transformation of our society.[14]

So the transformation of our society will mean facing up to such demands as the eradication of poverty and the disparities in wealth. No religion can ensure the attainment of these objectives. Rather it is market forces that will bring about the mixed economy to which we are committed. The greatest challenge for the present is economic growth, not how badly we need to respond to God's dubious revelations. Our important objective is the improvement of the quality of life for all our people. Only when that is achieved will the African National Congress, the Communist Party and the Congress of South African Trade Unions step aside so that God's words in their many forms will take on a meaning appropriate to the twenty-first century.

NOTES

1. A. Radhakrishnan, *Towards a New World*, Orient Paper, New World, 1980, p. 9.
2. Ernie Regehr, *Perceptions of Apartheid 1979* (Pennsylvania: Herald Press), p. 161.
3. Hitopadesa, Vasudeiva Kutumbakam.
4. *Krishnamurti Foundation Trust Bulletin 70*, 1996, p. 4.
5. Swami Vivekananda, *Complete Works Vol. 1* (Calcutta: Advaita Ashrama, 1986), p. 133.
6. Swami Ranganathananda, *Eternal Values for a Changing Society* (Bombay: Bharatiya Vidya Bhavan, 1971).
7. Fast Facts, May 1995, South African Institute of Race Relations.
8. M.K. Gandhi, *The Basic Works Vol. IV* (Ahmedabad: Navjivan Publishing House, 1968), p. 213.
9. Swami Tapasyananda, *Bhagavad Gita II*, 59 (Ramakrishna Math Madras, 1986).
10. Swami Nikhilananda (Tr.), *The Gospel of Sri Ramakrishna* (New York: Ramakrishna-Vivekananda Centre, 1973).
11. J. Krishnamurti, *The Future of Humanity* (India: Krishnamurti Foundation, 1987).
12. J. Krishnamurti, *Commentaries on Living* (London: Victor Gollancz, 1969), p. 30.
13. Swami Vivekananda, *Complete Works Vol. III* (Calcutta: Advaita Ashrama, 1986), p. 224.
14. Wally Mbhele and Rehana Rossouw, ANC Report, *Mail and Guardian* Vol. 13, no. 31, August 8-14, 1997.

Issues in Shona Religion:

A Metaphysical Statement and Dialogical Analysis

Jameson Kurasha

Department of Religious Studies
University of Zimbabwe
Mt. Pleasant, Harare, Zimbabwe

The Shona religion is a product of the Shona worldview. In that worldview, the world is a composition of physical entities like the Great Zimbabwe, Nyanga mountains, the mighty Zambezi river, elephants, crickets, living people and the living timeless or ancestors all living together in one environment. The ancestors continue to participate in family life and their living family members and descendants are consistently conscious of their presence. In fact, a ceremony called *Kurovaguva* (beating the grave) is held a year after a member of the family dies to invite him or her to rejoin the family. The Shona religion, when all is said and done, is a religion that centers primarily on the nature, function and activities of ancestors, their relationship with the living and their relationship with the environment. The issues that Christianity might contend with Shona religion have to do with:

1. The nature, the ranks, and the roles of ancestors.
2. The status of God or of gods.
3. The doctrines of revelation, faith, worship and salvation.

I. The Nature and Domain of Ancestors

In the Shona religion ancestors are forbearers who have died and are now living in a spiritual mode of existence with one another and with us, the living, in time. The closer the deceased is in terms of biological connection and time of death, the more influential he/she is in terms of directing and protecting the family members as an ancestor. Such influence is due to dual components of the ancestors in the sense that ancestors are both human and spiritual, once living in time and now living timeless, related to the living yet existing in spirit, products of humans in the spiritual realm, of ritual significance yet sacred. The ancestors whose voices and expectations are often heard are very "junior" ancestors, usually one or three generations back, recently dead, hierarchically very "junior" but presumably more energetic. Most of the ancestors families interact with have a narrow domain in that they interact roughly with approximately four or five extended families. At the family level ancestors are referred to as *midzimu* (pl.) and *mudzimu* (sing.). However, as families extend into clans, the common ancestors assume greater power and rank. A clan or national ancestor whose domain is wider than the family is called a *Mhondoro*, while an ordinary family ancestor is a *mudzimu*. A *mhondoro* or a *mudzimu* could be either male or female of great spiritual and social consequences; gender is not an issue.

Since Shona people have common totems, common clans and common ancestors which are intricately intertwined, all Shona people are, hence, related to each other. For example, the Maphosa people or vaera Ngara are in-laws of vaRozvi, and the vaera Shoko are the same as Phiri people. I am not related to Mr. Robert Mugabe, the president of Zimbabwe, in the formal sense of the family tree, yet through the clan tree he and the I are "related" through cross-clan marriages. Hence, we share the same ancestors, and those ancestors (*mhondoro*) guide us and protect us all at the national level. Thus ancestors are the unifying force and a source of patriotism.

II. Ethics in the World of the Living and the Living Timeless

If ancestors are offended, say by an injustice, violation, omission, insult and/or negligence, they may unleash their anger, wrath (*ngozi*) or spirit of vengeance on the individual, family or the entire nation. For example, if you beat your mother or father, the ancestors of either side may express their displeasure by inflicting sickness, disease, misfortune or death on you or someone you love.

At this stage, a point has been made and demonstrated that there is indeed a Shona religion; for religion is about supernatural expectations of the living persons and their response to the expectations. The ancestors have expectations and the living Shonas invariably respond.

III. The Nature of the Ethical Relationship

The nature of the relationship between the ancestors and the living is best characterized as "participation."[1] The ancestors are involved in the lives and activities of the living. They are constantly consulted, formally and informally, when a major event takes place in the home, e.g., when the family or a member of the family relocates, or if a water well is being prospected and dug. The living are ever conscious that the trees, rivers and mountains are associated with ancestors. During the wars of African liberation, ancestors were part of the liberating teams, both during the first war of 1896 and the second war of liberation of 1972-79.[2] My point here is that the ancestors participate in the spiritual, social, political, moral, health and environmental affairs of the family. Ancestors are not far away. They are always present.

IV. Disputation with Christianity

Even though the roles and ranks of the ancestors are hardly contentious among African religionists and theologians, the nature and place of the ultimate ancestor, Mudzimumukuru, is disputable. It is argued here that the idea of one ultimate ancestor is a product of early African Christians who had "pride," during the heyday of the Western colonial missions, to stand up and say: "The idea of God is foreign to Africans. Religion yes but, God no." Their pride or desire to identify with the master led them to the "we had it too" syndrome. During those days, for a "native" to claim that an African had a form of religion was radical enough. "We had religion too." "And in our traditional religion we had a conception of God too whom we called several names, e.g., Mwari, mudzimu mukuru, Musiki, Samatenga—something akin to the inscription seen by St. Paul on one of the monuments in Athens."

Many feel these African Christian fathers had to come up with this sort of theory so they could secure coveted teaching jobs in the Westernized mission schools. It may have been considered imperative to identify with the theological structure of the master. Teaching was the best profession for Africans and before they were hired they would have had to sign a statement of faith. By signing such a statement it meant that they would abandon even intellectual engagement with traditional ideas. To explore such ideas, according to the missionaries, was a sign that "Satan was controlling their minds." Anyway, the point being made here is that in the Shona religion the interaction is between *midzimu* (ancestors) and the rest of *the environment*. The idea of a single supreme spirit is a western import. In the African tradition, the living are responding to the expectations of the community and specific ancestors. Not only would I argue that *this is not a monotheistic religion*, but might boldly go so far as to say that this is not a theistic religion at all.

V. The Premises of the Argument

The conclusion that the Shona traditional religion is "person centric" (i.e., a communication of the environment, the living in time and the living timeless) is *behavioristic*. There is nothing in the behavior of a Shona traditionalist to suggest that the ultimate reality or point of reference is a single being called God. For instance, if my problem is the sickness of a child, the *n'anga* might advise me to put matters right with my Living Timeless, probably an aunt whom I might have offended somehow. Another example is that if there is a serious drought, a *svikiro* (spirit medium) might suggest that the community brew beer for the *varipasi* (buried ones) *because they are "thirsty."* By calling the ancestors *varipasi* or "buried ones," the medium (*svikiro*) cannot even identify them individually and the reference is to many and certainly not just to a single ancestor. The point of all the parties involved is to bring the community or family together.

VI. Linguistic and Historical Fallacies[3]

In any event, calling God "Musiki" does not necessarily imply the One God of the Judeo-Christian tradition. "Kusika" is a verb. "Musiki" is the noun. "Musiki," in the traditional context, basically means the originator, especially of a fire. In traditional Africa fire was generated by rubbing pointed mutsubvu tree[4] sticks on big mutsubvu tree blocks; and such fire makers were referred to as "vasiki." In reality, fires in Africa had many originators. Could it be that the universe then is like one of the fires? Also, the creation of fires uses materials; it does not resemble the Christian notion of creation ex nihilo.

In addition, the idea of "mudzimu mukuru" cannot properly be compared to God. In Shona tradition every family has its own mudzimu mukuru, i.e., the ancestor who is the center of a number of extended families or clans. The oldest of the brothers in that extended group of families usually bears the name of the mudzimu mukuru besides being the custodian of the family animal (mombe yedanga). Again like the vasiki, midzimu mikuru are as multiple as the extended families themselves. Certainly it was a mistake to call God mudzimu mukuru. And if those titles were metaphors then that is all they were. It is argued here that at best most of such terms were poor, if not misleading translations.

Three classes of Shona words are usually prefixed with "mu." The first group of the categories usually refer to humans. In Shona, a person could regularly be referred to by what he or she does; such a title is a combination of a verb and the prefix "mu." Hence a teacher is referred to as "mu-dzidzisi." The verb kudzidzisa refers to the task of teaching and mudzidzisi is one who teaches—the noun. "Mu" is a polite and respectful way of referring to a person who does what he or she does. For example, one who fishes is a muredzi (kuredza is "to fish"). One who sings is a muyimbi (kuyimba is "to sing"). To exist is kuva or kuri, the verb being ari or wari (Chinyika dialect). One who exists is mu ari (ari is one who is). This only means that the Shona could provide a translation.

But Shona grammar forbids, if it can be avoided, joining words with two vowels. The rule (or vowel coalescence) is to drop "u" from the prefix mu besides dropping "a" from the verb "ari" and then substitute both vowels with a "w," so when you refer to the one who claims to be or the one who claims that "I am," i.e., "ari," that rule requires that the person be called "Mwari."

There is also a rule which allows one to drop the "u" from the prefix mu. In the Chinyika dialect where the verb "to be" or "to exist" could be translated as "wari," the rule of dropping "u" from the prefix mu leaves them with the noun mwari, meaning "One Who Is."

So on the face of it, what the Shona have is a language that accommodates the Old Testament declaration by the Judeo-Christian God when he claimed to be the "One Who Is." However, it is argued here that having a translational facility is not tantamount to having an ontological being, namely: God.

It is also worth noting that the Shonas who claimed that we had God in our tradition do not seem to come up with a corresponding claim that "we had Satan or Lucifer too."

I reiterate my view that the Shona religion is not a "theistic," single-God centered religion. There is no need to be apologetic about that. When theological emancipation arrives eventually, the African will state without fear the character of the African worldview that produced such a family-centered religion.

VII. Worldviews: Fundamental Source of the Problem

It is argued here that other religions, especially western and eastern Christianity and other monotheistic religions, had to have one God because they are a product of such worldviews. The Greek worldview argued that the Form or the Idea was the source of material product which is merely a copy. So the Great Zimbabwe monument is in fact a copy of the ultimate reality, The Idea, of the Great Zimbabwe which is the form of the monument. In the same spirit, the universe is a product of the "Idea" or of the Form which is eternal, absolute and independent. When all is said and done, God is the Idea. So all the 747 planes are from one—the Idea or the Form of the 747. All persons are therefore from the Idea of a person—God. The Hebrews had a personal living God—Yahweh —and the synthesized conclusion between the Greek and Hebrew worldview was the Western and Eastern Judeo-Christian statement that the Idea or Form (Word), became flesh and lived. This is why we find scholarly work which suggests that their religions are products of Greek, Roman and Semitic traditions. The idea of one (monotheistic) ultimate being might not be helpful as a dominant hermeneutic when looking into other traditions.

In this section it is argued that the Judeo-Christian worldview is based on Greek and Hebrew worldviews, and that it is fantastic.[6] The same Idea, which had earlier become the universe in which we participate, now becomes flesh and dwells on earth. Then the Nicene Creed says that God is the same as or identical to Christ who was nailed on the cross. The point here is that such a scenario requires imaginative powers, and faith to prescribe to it. It takes an extraordinary step to understand the whole notion of the idea as Plato and Augustine understood it, likewise to see how the "logos" or Idea reified itself into a human. If the Judeo-Christian theology is correct, then the place for faith, for glorification of God, is necessary. Glory involves worship, adoration and praise.

It is my view that the tasks or steps required by Judeo-Christian religion are basically imaginative, hence it is, when all is said and done, a logo-centric undertaking. As a game of ideas, it was loved by our Greek brothers. The major Idea, theos, is brought to them by our Hebrew brother, Paul. Theology is the key to Judeo-Christianity. Yet how many of us qualify to deserve the title "Theologian"?

Some have argued that the Judeo-Christian worldview leads either to "fantastic theologizing," to the gospel of material prosperity or to the theology of fear. In other words, the more philosophical observers become "theological," while the second group can become materialistic. Observers who are not interested in such studies as Epistemology can become fascinated by an idea becoming material. The third group worships God, not for the fantastic scenario of word turning into materiality, but rather because God can punish.

Shona religion does not single out any Metaphysical Idea or person as a source of creation. This is a participatory religion, and that religion is a product of a culture whose wisdom is expressed in proverbs like "Chara-chimwe hachitswanye inda" ("Production requires organic cooperation") and "Kuwanda kunorambwa navaroyi" ("multiplicity of families is objectionable to wizards"). Creation involves everyone, the living and living timeless, and all the times. Hence creation is not an event but a process; you do not start a new endeavor without consulting and announcing.

VIII. Salvation Impossibilities and Chimhundu's Social Snob[6]

Chimhundu is an African languages lexicographer at the University of Zimbabwe. When all is said and done, he is an Africanist in the sense that he is very familiar with many aspects of African life, including social mannerisms and thinking.

Chimhundu reported some of his social observations at a workshop of university administrators held at Club Mazvikadei in Mashonaland West province of Zimbabwe during the weekend of January 29, 1995. He observed that the new Shona upper class is constantly confounded by the thought of how the poor manage to live. A case is told by Chimhundu of two women who had watched the TV drama "Santa Barbara." The rich woman from the suburb of Mount Pleasant told the story with much detail and excitement. The "not so well-to-do" friend from Mufakose high density suburb indicated that she did not notice the other details because her television set was black and white. To which the Mount Pleasant socialite replied "munogara seiko musina color TV" "How do you manage without a color TV"? It is now a characteristic remark of the "haves" over the "have nots": e.g., "Munogara seiko musina microwave?" "How do you manage life without a microwave?" The spirit is not just confined to social classes in Zimbabwe alone. In the age of the Information Superhighway, those with Windows are now wondering how those using old 86XTs manage life!

However, contrary to the Snobs' rhetorical question, people are happily surviving with black and white television sets and without color ones. Others are eating warm healthy food without the microwave. Great scholars and theologians wrote memorable works without Windows.

Theological snobs who wonder how life is possible for a Shona religious practitioner might be pleased to know that the ancestors take care of things. "Munorarama seiko?" "How do you live (without God)?" The Shona might see that as a form of Chimhundu's snob paradigm—albeit a theological or religious snob. Each time one flies over Northern Canada one often wonders how life is possible under such cold conditions. I am sure that when Northern Canadians fly over African deserts or humid tropics they probably wonder how we Africans live under such conditions. Both sides manage happily. North Canadian wintery conditions can never be imposed on equatorial conditions; neither can the desert or equatorial conditions be imposed on northern Canada. Both parties can only hold a dialogue and learn through each other about the beauty of diversity even in religion. That is the strength of Heinrich Beck's Bamberg School with its "creative peace though cultural encounter."

IX. Creative Encounter of Religions

Was it a necessary condition for salvation to Hellenize Christianity? Was it a necessary condition for salvation to synthesize the Greek "Idea" and the Hebrew personal God? Was it a necessary condition for salvation for an African to give up his ancestors? Is it necessary to contextualize Christianity? While the theological snob might answer "yes" to all the above questions, the God of Abraham, Isaac and Jacob Himself might say "not at all." Jesus of Nazareth had no room for snobs. The ancestors in their multiplicity might just remind the snob that "Kuwanda kunorambwa nomuroyi." "Multiplicity is only objectionable to the wizard."

Nobody is calling born again Christians "wizards." Shona religion will not. But the time of theological imposition might be over. It is a new day for creative encounter of cultures and religions.

Even the idea of a supreme devil and the originator of sin is not of Shona religion. This is not a religion about a single Satan and a single Fall. Again just as number one is not so significant in regards to God, it is equally insignificant in regards to sin. There are many evil spirits "mashavi" (plural) "shavi" (singular) and they are all responsible, in their own ways, for the human plight.

NOTES

1.

Ancestors	Humans

- Guardians of land & people
  positive   - wealth
                     - health
                     - prosperity
                     - fertility
 	
- Negative   - illness
                     - drought
                     - misfortune
                     - death
                     - pestilence
 	
- Mediators - vehicle of
                     communication
                     between sacred
                     & human
 	
"REVELATION" - In nature
	- Ritual - impromptu: danger/
	                           crisis/fortune
	- situational: rites of
	  passage (birth, initiation,
	  marriage, death)
	 - periodical: harvest, sowing,
	  agricultural
	
	- Sacrifice - gifts
	- tobacco
	- beer
	- meat
	
	- Action "CONCILIATION"

Fig. by Dr. Tabona Shoko

2. David Lan, *Guns and Rain: Guerrillas and Spirit Mediums in Zimbabwe* (Harare: Zimbabwe Publishing House, 1985).

3. This section might seem escetoric and obscure to non-African readers but the opposite is the case among African philosophers and theologians. To ignore it for the sake of the "market" is to bypass a vital part off the dialogue. The targeted proponents here are post-independence Shona/ Ndebele theologians such as Ambrose Moyo, Canaan Banana, and followers. However, their line of thinking, criticized here, is popular in Sub-Saharan Africa among theologians and philosophers. John Mbiti is the champion.

4. An indigenous tree species common in Central Africa.

5. The word "fantastic" is ambiguous but deliberately chosen. To a believer it implies that the hellenized Judeo-Christian world view and the monotheisms which germinate from it are *wonderful, awesome, marvelous, tremendous,* i.e., the typical ordinary language testimony of a born-again Christian. To a sceptic or an atheist the word "fantastic" is used as dismissive for a theory that is just hard to believe.

6. The word "snob" is used in its most neutral sense. A snob is a man or woman who is always pretending to be something—especially richer or more fashionable—than they are. (*Webster's New Universal Unabridged Dictionary* [New York: Dorset and Barber, 1979], page 1719.)

Swazi Royal Ceremonies and Religious Tolerance in the Kingdom of Swaziland

Hebron L. Ndlovu
Head, Department of Theology and Religious Studies
University of Swaziland

This essay highlights the contributions made by two main royal ceremonies towards the promotion of a culture of religious tolerance and interreligious dialogue in Swaziland. The two ceremonies are (a) the *Incwala* and (b) the Good Friday Ceremony. The *Incwala* is an indigenous Swazi ritual which dramatizes the centrality of the King as the key symbol of Swazi culture and society.[1] The Good Friday Ceremony, on the other hand, is a new Swazi royal ceremony which defines the Swazi dual monarchs—the King and the Queen Mother—as the patrons of the Christian religion in Swaziland.[2]

My contention is that these two royal ceremonies have promoted a process of informal dialogue between adherents of Swazi Religion and Christians. I maintain and demonstrate that the two royal ceremonies—which are deeply rooted in Swazi traditional culture and religion—have played a pioneering role in cultivating the spirit of tolerance and fraternal relations among Swazi belonging to different religious traditions in the country.

Conceptual Framework

There are two main assumptions undergirding this paper. First, Swazi Religion and Christianity represent two different religions with varying conceptions of salvation. By "Swazi Religion" I mean the indigenous religion of the Swazi which has been transmitted from one generation to another through oral tradition. Notwithstanding the difficulty of ascertaining the percentage of adherents of Swazi religion, this indigenous faith is alive, vibrant and respected in Swazi society. In fact, Swazi Religion is a cultural fact and its formal representatives are the King, the Queen Mother, diviners and herbalists.[3]

Swazi Christianity, on the other hand, may be divided into two main streams, namely: the Mission Churches and African Indigenous Churches. African Indigenous Churches refer to an eclectic group of African Independent Churches which were founded and run by Africans themselves, as opposed to Mission Churches which were under the control and supervision of European or American missionaries. Most of the Indigenous Churches commonly include the word "Zionist" in the official titles of their denominations. The salient feature of the "Zionist" churches is their advocacy of faith healing through the power of the Spirit.[4] In comparison with Mission Churches, "Zionist" Churches tend to be more tolerant of traditional religious beliefs and ethics. In statistical terms, Zionist Churches boast the highest number of Christian followers in Swaziland.[5]

The second assumption of this paper is that the object of inter-religious dialogue is not to speak past one another, but to learn from the other so that together we can grow in our perception of ultimate reality.[6] As the case studies of the *Incwala* and the Good Friday ceremonies will show, many Swazi Zionist Christians draw a clear distinction between the Christian faith and Swazi indigenous religion. We shall also observe that the Zionist clergy do not make a formal attempt to displace Swazi Religion. Instead, there is mutual borrowing of concepts and reciprocal support of one religion by the other.

Before I describe this informal dialogue between Traditionalists and Christians in Swaziland, it is essential to outline the historical and cultural background of the relations between the monarchy, Swazi religion and Christian Churches in Swaziland.

Swazi Monarchy and Divine Kingship

The Kingdom of Swaziland is a sovereign state which regained its independence from British colonial rule in 1968. With a population of about one million persons, Swaziland is one of the smallest countries in the world. It is a landlocked country in South Eastern Africa. It is adjoined to the Republic of South Africa on the north, west and south, and to the Republic of Mozambique on its eastern borders.

The Kingdom was established in the nineteenth century by the Dlamini royal clan led by Sobhuza I, also known as Somhlolo (1818-1836). The Dlamini, a Nguni clan, migrated from the present day Republic of Mozambique to Swaziland, conquering and incorporating some of the hitherto autonomous clans, many of whom were of Zulu and Sotho ancestry. However, it was not until the reign of Mswati II (1839-1865)—after whom the Swazi state was named—that the formerly autonomous clans were decisively brought under the political and economic control of the Dlamini clan.

The kingdom that was consolidated by King Mswati II was a dual monarchy in which the King—*Ingwenyama* ("the Lion")—and the Queen Mother—Indlovukazi "the She Elephant"—shared administrative duties. The King, on one hand, was the chief administrator and by tradition, he was expected to be modest, benevolent and impartial. The Queen Mother, on the other hand, was the chief patron of national ceremonial rituals and her residence constituted the capital of the Swazi nation. In addition, the Queen Mother's residence served as a place of refuge and an appeal court for persons with particular grievances, including complaints about a King's decision.

Thus, during the reign of King Mswati II the monarchy was constituted as the focal point of the Swazi culture and society.

Divine Kingship

In addition to the consolidation of the dual monarchy, King Mswati II institutionalized the *Incwala* ritual. The *Incwala* ceremony was initially a harvest festival in which the Swazi, like the Zulu, celebrated the first fruits of the summer harvest in December. But beginning with the reign of King Mswati, this agricultural ceremony was modified to express the doctrine of divine kingship which defined the king as the symbol and an embodiment of the Swazi nation.[7] During the *Incwala*, the King communicated with the royal ancestors on behalf of the Swazi nation. Significantly, it was during the *Incwala* that the king—as an embodiment of the nation—was ritually cleansed, purified and strengthened. A strong and fortified King symbolized a powerful, secure and prosperous nation.[8]

Participation at the *Incwala* ceremony was made obligatory on the part of all Swazi males. As a result, the *Incwala* attracted an inclusive assembly of able-bodied Swazi who were classified according to age-regiments that cut across clan, rank and regional loyalties—thus promoting and fostering national unity through the monarchy. This important national ritual took place at the royal residence of the Queen Mother, who was regarded as "the Mother of the nation."

Therefore, by tradition, both the King and the Queen Mother performed religious and political roles. These social structures have persisted up to this day, albeit in modified forms due to the impact of colonial rule and modernization. Today, the dual monarchs are the custodians and outspoken representatives of Swazi religion.

Swazi Religion

Swazi religion revolves around the belief in the power of the ancestors (dead relatives) over the living. The ancestor can communicate with the living relatives through dreams, omens and diviners. In addition, the ancestor can communicate with the supreme being, Mvelincanti ("the First to Appear"). However, Mvelincanti is a remote being, and no rituals are specifically directed to him.

The power of the ancestors emanates from their ability to protect and regulate the lives of the living. For example, through the services of the *sangoma* ("diviner"), the family ancestors can give forewarnings, protect their kin from witchcraft, heal the sick, reward good behavior and punish social delinquents. At the family level, it is the head of the homestead or the clan who can communicate the concerns and wishes of his people to the ancestors. Likewise, the royal ancestors are regarded as the national ancestors and the King is the mediator between the Swazi people and the national ancestors. As the chief priest of the nation, the King receives and transmits important messages from the national ancestors to the people.

For an example, King Somhlolo (1818-1836) dreamt that "white-skinned people with hair like tassels of tails of cattle" would arrive in the country carrying two objects: the *indlilinga* or a round metal, and the *Umculu* or a scroll. The following morning the king summoned his councillors to inform them of this important dream. He interpreted the dream to mean that white people would be coming to the country with money and the Bible. The Swazi were to accept the Bible and try to avoid money. More importantly, the Swazi were enjoined to refrain from fighting the white people for fear that, by spilling the white man's blood, the nation would be cursed.

In keeping with this insight from Swazi religion, the Swazi monarchy adopted a tolerant attitude towards colonialists, traders and missionaries. In particular, the Swazi monarchy took the initiative to invite missionaries to Swaziland.

Mission Churches

The first Christian Mission was established in 1885 at the invitation of King Mswati II. By 1920 Swaziland was inundated with several missions, each establishing its own set of mission stations with its own following. These included the Anglican mission (1860), the Lutheran Church (1887), the South Africa General Mission (1890), the Scandinavian Evangelical Alliance (1894), the Church of the Nazarene (1910), and the Roman Catholic Church (1914).

But the missionaries, together with their converts condemned and described indigenous Swazi religion as pagan and demonic. Hence many Christian converts stopped participating in traditional royal ceremonies such as the *Incwala*. Yet the Swazi rulers remained strongly committed to Swazi religion. In fact, for the Swazi rulers, conversion to Christianity would have implied the renunciation of their priestly—and hence political—functions in Swazi society. In addition, conversion for the rulers implied the renunciation of basic social practices such as polygyny, which was used, among other things, to foster alliances between the king and a wide range of Swazi including influential commoners and chiefs.

Thus the relationship between the Swazi rulers and the Mission Churches has always been complex. On one hand the Swazi monarchy appreciated and acknowledged the contributions of the Mission Churches to social progress. On the other hand, the Swazi monarchy has always been resented the attitude of many Mission Churches towards Swazi culture and religion. Indeed many Mission Churches are covertly charged with fomenting social division in Swazi society.

In contrast to the uneasy relationship between the Swazi monarchy and the Mission Churches, the relations between the monarchy and the Zionist Churches have been very cordial. Most Zionist Christians have been ardent supporters of the Swazi monarchy. This relationship has been cemented by the active participation of the leaders of the Swazi Zionist Churches in the two main national ceremonies, namely: the *Incwala* and the Good Friday Ceremony.

The *Incwala*

The main activities of the *Incwala* take place at the Ludzidzini royal residence, a site that is rich with secular and sacred symbolism. The royal residence is the *Umphakatsi* or "the centre of the Swazi nation" in the sense that it is the ritual and administrative capital of the kingdom of Swaziland. First, Ludzidzini is the residence of the *Indlovukati* (the Queen Mother). The *Indlovukati* is the "mother of the nation," as her homestead constitutes the ultimate venue for the holding of crucial family meetings. Second, the Queen Mother is the custodian of the *Indlunkhulu* or the sacred shrine dedicated to the spirits of the former Swazi kings. As the guardian of national rituals, the *Indlovukati* officiates in all national ceremonies, including the *Umhlanga* (Reed dance ceremony for girls) and the Royal Easter Ceremony.

Third, the Queen Mother's Residence boasts the *Sibaya* (Cattle Byre), The *Sibaya* is the arena for secular and sacred activities. Its sacred allusion concerns the link between every cattle byre and family ancestors, Like every conservative Swazi who normally addresses his own ancestors at his respective cattle byre, the Swazi nation remembers and honors royal ancestors in the *Sibaya*. As a result, the *Incwala* is danced at the *Sibaya*. More importantly, inside the *Sibaya* there is the *Inhlambelo*, a temporary sacred enclosure that is constructed during the *Incwala* to serve as the site for the ritual purification and strengthening of the King by the national priests.

a. The Sequence of Events

The time frame of the *Incwala* spans a period of about two lunar months (November and December), and the performances are subdivided into five sections. First, the *Incwala* begins when the National Priests set out to fetch sea water and river water to be used at the ceremony. Second, the National Priests return with the sacred waters and other medicines to the royal capital at Ludzidzini. The return of the National Priests marks the beginning of the Small *Incwala*. The third section is called the Big *Incwala*, and is characterized by more nationwide participation. The Fourth phase is the weeding of the King's field by the national regiments. This practice highlights the significance of tribute labor as a sign of one's loyalty to the Swazi State. The final phase is the dismissal of the national regiments by the King. This event normally takes place in January and the marks the end of the *Incwala* season. Significantly, the King normally makes a policy statement on this occasion.

b. National Significance

The *Incwala* can be described as the main indigenous Swazi ceremony that affirms and embodies the distinctive features of

Swazi culture, which include: the dual monarchy, sacred kingship, and the affirmation of indigenous cultural beliefs and values.

The basic aim of the *Incwala* is to affirm the King as the primary symbol of Swazi culture and society. Every *Incwala* ceremony is intimately linked to a particular king, and there can be no *Incwala* during the minority or the death of the king. Thus, the *Incwala* of 1991-92, which I observed and participated in, was the fifth *Incwala* of King Mswati II since his coronation in 1986.

Since the King is the primary symbol and embodiment of the Swazi nation, the *Incwala* requires the active participation of all Swazi. As a rule, every Swazi has to dance the *Incwala*, and he or she is expected to wear the *Incwala* costume. The popular exclamation during the *Incwala* ceremony is: "*Incwala* Ayibukelwa," meaning, "You do not watch other people dancing the *Incwala*." Everyone ought to dance the *Incwala*!

By tradition, every Swazi male is a member of the *Emabutfo* (age regiments), and during the *Incwala* the regiments represent a cross section of the Swazi adult population since the social composition of the age regiments cuts across clan, regional and ethnic loyalties. Thus, in theory, the thousands of the *Emabutfo* who dance the *Incwala* represent all Swazi.

Significantly, the *Emabutfo* dance the *Incwala* dressed in colorful traditional attire which is as follows: white and black feathers pinned into the hair; a cloak made of cattle-tails hanging from the shoulders to the waist; loin covering made from the pelt of an antelope or leopard; a selected *Mahiya* (woven cloth tied around the waist); and a war shield made of ox-hides and plain sticks. Considering the different colors of the cattle-hides, bird feathers, wild animals, and cattle tails, the costumes for the *Emabutfo* make an impressive sight.

The *Bemanti* (National Priests) are the key religious specialists of the *Incwala*. The *Incwala* formally begins when the *Bemanti* leave the Ludzidzini royal residence for the Indian Ocean in neighboring Mozambique and for the main rivers of Swaziland to fetch sea and river water and other medicines for the ritual strengthening and protection of the King. The main task of the National Priests, then, is to treat the King with fortifying and ancient medicines. As the leading ritual specialists, the National Priests also enforce the observation of taboos during the sacred period of the *Incwala*. Even the King has to observe certain taboos, one of which is that he is in seclusion and cannot handle administrative issues until the entire ceremony is over.

Different social groups participate in the *Incwala*, and these include the aristocrats, commoners, Christians, boys and un-married young men, married men, and *Lutsango* (the married women's regiment). Women, however, do not play a significant role in the *Incwala*. in fact, with the notable exception of the main day of the ceremony where the ordinary woman is represented by the *Lutsango* women's regiment, the rest of the *Incwala* includes only a few women from the royal house, such as the Queen Mother, the Queens and the princesses.

c. *The Participation of Christians at the* Incwala

The Swazi monarchy takes the symbolism of participating in the *Incwala* very seriously. Thus a directive is made over the radio by the governor of the Queen Mother's residence calling upon all Swazi to participate in the ritual. This order renders non-participation a form of defiance or civil disobedience. Theor-etically, participation in the *Incwala* is optional, but in practice many rural Swazi are coerced to participate lest they pay a fine for failing to honor the ceremony.

Many Swazi belonging to Mission Churches and African Indig-enous Churches do participate during the main day of the *Incwala* ceremony. On the main day, more people converge on the *Sibaya* (the Cattle Byre). Every Swazi who enters the kraal dressed in western clothing is given a stick by the ushers so that he too can dance the *Incwala*. Those Swazi wearing western clothes include church leaders from Mission Churches, and this group of Christians normally forms its own regimental group which is dubbed the *Libutfo Labokhololo* (the regiment of those who wear the white collar). Significantly, these church leaders dance the *Incwala*, although they are pushed towards the back and the "real regiments" in traditional costume occupy the first two rows of the troupe.

Another significant performance on the main day is the conspicuous presence of church leaders belonging to the African

Indigenous Churches who also dance the *Incwala* wearing their clerical gowns. These church leaders are given a prominent place in the ceremony in that they are placed next to the *Inhlambelo*, the sacred enclosure in which the king is ritually strengthened and rejuvenated with special medicines.

That the Church leaders from African Indigenous Churches play an important part in the *Incwala* ceremony was affirmed by the fact that prior to the beginning of the *Incwala* ceremony, leaders of the indigenous Churches are called upon to pray for the success of the *Incwala* ceremony. In particular, the leaders are asked to "prophesy" or look into the future and forestall through prayer, where possible, any anomalies that might disrupt the normal proceeding of the *Incwala*.

The Good Friday Ceremony

Popularly known in Swazi society as "I Gudi," the Good Friday Ceremony is a five-day Easter convention in which about forty thousand Swazi Christians—primarily those belonging to Swazi Indigenous Churches—gather at the capital royal village of Lobammba and Lozitha to commemorate the death of and resurrection of Jesus Christ together with the *Indlovukati* (Queen Mother) and the *Ingwenyama* (the King). This ceremony was formally established in 1937 by Swazi Indigenous Churches in consultation with King Sobhuza II (1899-1982). For all intents and purposes, the Good Friday festival is a royal ceremony. The ritual defines the Swazi rulers as divinely appointed politico-religious leaders whose guidance has led, and will continue to lead, the Swazi nation to peace and prosperity.[9]

Indeed to many "Zionist" leaders the Easter festival is a royal ceremony. Without the royalty the ritual may not be performed. Significantly, the Queen Mother, who is the traditional custodian of all major national ceremonies, is the chief hostess of the Good Friday convention. Further, the King, who is the patron of the Zionist Churches, plays an active role in the ceremony. Since each day of the ritual is graced by the active presence and participation of either the King or the Queen Mother, the Good Friday festival has effectively become an official, national ritual requiring the presence of leading royal figures and the political elites.

a. Sequence of Events

The Good Friday Ceremony begins on Friday and ends on Tuesday. On Good Friday—the first day of the ritual—the Queen Mother is the hostess, and this session takes place at the Swazi national Church. On this day the Queen Mother is accompanied by the Queens, senior princesses, senior royal councillors, the prime minister and several cabinet ministers. More importantly, the Queen Mother addresses the nation, and the queens normally entertain the Christian congregation with music.

On the subsequent days of the ritual such as Saturday, Sunday and Tuesday, the King becomes the host, and he is expected to make a speech on each occasion. On Saturday, the church leaders representing different denominations meet with the King at Lozitha Palace, the King's Residence. This day is devoted to the discussion of moral or doctrinal problems affecting the Christian Church in general. Invariably, the King makes a definitive ruling or recommendation on the particular issues discussed.

On Easter Sunday—the main day of the ceremony—the King meets with the Christians at the Somhlolo National Stadium. On this day, the multitude of Zionist Christians is supplemented by a conspicuous group of church leaders belonging to Mission Churches. The clergy belonging to Mission Churches are regarded as "visitors," and they are usually given the opportunity to preach to the congregation. Again, on this day, the King makes the final address following several sermons preached mainly by Zionist clergy.

The following day, on Monday, the Zionist clergy hold a short prayer session with the Queen Mother at her residence at Ludzidzini. Normally the church leaders give presents to "the Mother of the Swazi Nation." The session ends with a short speech made by the Queen Mother.

The last day of the ceremony, on Tuesday, the Zionist clergy meet with the King at Lozitha Palace. Here the leaders report to the King about general administrative issues in the various Zionist denominations. This session, like all the other sessions involving the King, ends with an address by the King.

Thus the Swazi monarchy takes the Easter ritual very seriously, and royal representatives are always involved in the preparation and organization of the entire ceremony.

b. Discontinuity between Swazi Religion and Christianity

Despite their active involvement in the Good Friday festival, the Swazi royalty makes a clear distinction between the *Incwala* and the new Christian ritual. To the monarchy, the Easter festival does not displace the *Incwala*. In fact, by Swazi royal standards, the King and the Queen Mother cannot become Christians in the confessional sense since by so doing they would compromise their sacred responsibilities as religious leaders in the Swazi Religion.

Thus the King and the Queen Mother always meet the Christians in their traditional roles as religious leaders in the traditional sense. The King, for example, always appears in his casual indigenous attire, and he never meets the Christians in the Cattle Byre on these occasions. His attire normally includes the traditional *Emahiya* (woven cloth), leopard skins and sandals.

Given the fact that the dual monarchs represent the Swazi Religion, their mere presence coupled with the addresses they make on each day of the Good Friday Ceremony can be seen as form of informal dialogue between Christians and adherents of the Swazi Religion. For example, when the Queen Mother addresses the Christians on Good Friday, she frequently reminds them that the Christian religion came to Swaziland largely through the agency of the Swazi royalty. She gives credit to Swazi royalty taking the initiative to invite missionaries to Swaziland. Indeed, the Swazi royalty also claims that it was God who sent a vision to King Somhlolo advising him to accept the Bible and reject money.

Likewise the King, when he addresses the Christians at the National Stadium and at the Lozitha Palace, reminds the Christians that he, as King, was divinely appointed by God to serve as the *Indvuna* or headman of the Swazi Nation. In one instance, for example, King Mswati III poked fun at those Christian leaders who insisted that the King should be baptized lest he be cast out of the Kingdom of Heaven. To this charge, King Mswati III said:

> We [the monarchs] are God's headmen here on earth. When the headman is left behind, who will represent you in heaven. We have to inform the nation tomorrow [Easter Sunday] that it has been resolved by this assembly that your King will go to Heaven by virtue of his status as God's Headman.[10]

Although this principle was presented in a jovial manner, it underscores one of the basic themes of the royal Easter ritual, namely that the Swazi rulers are "Christian leaders" only in a nominal sense and that the monarchy holds firmly onto Swazi Religion and culture as the basis upon which the stability of the nation rests.

This point becomes clearer when one observes the Saturday Session of the Easter Ritual, called *Lunyawo LwaJesu* or (Following Jesus' Footprint).

Lunyawo LwaJesu: The Debating Session

Although the stated purpose of the *Lunyawo LwaJesu* is "to search for the Footprint of Jesus," the dominant theme of the session is that Swazi tradition has primacy over the various Western customs introduced by Mission Churches. At this session, Swazi church leaders from different denominations discuss (and frequently engage in heated debates) selected moral issues arising from the tensions between biblical ethics and Swazi culture, and conflicts among the different Christian doctrines over specific Swazi customs.

Topics for discussion, for instance, in the 1980s and 1990s have included mourning rituals for widows, the Sabbath day versus Sunday, and the need to baptize the Swazi rulers. More recently (1994-97), moral problems which have been debated include: the ordination of women, new religions such as Islam, and homosexuality. As mentioned before, the dominant theme of this session is that the behavior of the Swazi ought to be grounded in Swazi tradition.

However, this position is often challenged at the *Lunyawo LwaJesu* by other church leaders belonging to Mission Churches who assert the supremacy of the Bible or God's law over Swazi traditions. Nonetheless, these "non-conformists," who include members of some Evangelical Churches, the Seventh Day Adventists and Jehovah's Witnesses, are always in the minority and they are often ridiculed as misguided Christians.

The *Lunyawo LwaJesu*, then, is the only forum in Swaziland in which Swazi belonging to different Churches can exchange ideas on matters pertaining to moral and religious differences.

Invariably, the session turns into a lively debating period in which Zionist clergy normally affirm the primacy of Swazi tradition while Mission Christians emphasize the supremacy of biblical values.

For example, Mission Christians tend to use this forum to challenge specific aspects of Swazi culture such as the sacralization of Swazi rulers, ancestral beliefs and the alliance between Zionist Churches and the monarchy. In addition, Mission Christians tend to highlight individual morality and the equality of all Swazi, including the monarchs, before God.

Nonetheless, the dominant rhetoric of this session is unequivocal, namely that the Swazi royalty, which is the ultimate symbol and custodian of tradition, are God's special appointed leaders. Indeed Swaziland is described by many Zionist pastors as "a beloved blessed nation," and outstanding royal ancestors like King Somhlolo (1816-1836) and King Sobhuza (1921-1982) are "beatified" and presented as God's messengers to Swaziland and the world at large.

Conclusion

The overall meaning of the two royal ceremonies described above can be fully appreciated if one takes cognizance of the fact that these rituals are annual cultural performances which affirm, dramatize and embody the fundamental beliefs, values and social philosophy of the Swazi. As current students of public rituals observe, the basic aim of national rituals is to define dominant social values.[11]

In the light of the above considerations, I contend that the values of religious tolerance and interfaith dialogue which are dramatized at the two royal ceremonies should be seen as representations of actual informal dialogue that prevails at grassroots levels in various Southern African communities. Additional research is required to ascertain the extent of dialogue at regional levels.

But religious tolerance should not be confused with political tolerance. As my latest study indicates, the beauty of Swazi royal ceremonies is compromised by political conservatism in which the monarchy is now perceived by many urban Swazi as intolerant of political dissent.[12]

Nonetheless, my prediction is that as soon as the political ground is cleared, and many urban Swazi feel that the Swazi political structure is democratic enough, the royal rituals will continue to serve as models of religious tolerance and peaceful co-existence between Swazi belonging to different faiths.

NOTES

1. Hilda Kuper, *An African Aristocracy: Rank among the Swazi* (London: Oxford University Press, 1947).
2. Hebron L Ndlovu, "The Royal Easter Ritual and Political Actions in Swaziland" (Ph.D Thesis, McMaster University, 1993).
3. Hilda Kuper, *The Swazi: A South African Kingdom* (New York: Holt, 1986), pp. 60-68.
4. Bengt G.M. Sundkler, *Zulu Zion and Some Swazi Zionists* (London: Oxford University Press, 1976).
5. Roger J. Cazziol, "The Swazi Zionists: An Indigenous Religious Movement in Southern Africa" (Unpublished paper, 1987), p. 1; Marjorie Froise, ed., *Swaziland Christian Handbook* (Welkom and Johannesburg: Cristian INFO., 1994).
6. Leornard Swiddler, "The Dialogue Decalogue: Ground Rules for Dialogue," *Journal of Ecumenical Studies* 20 (1), pp. 1-4.
7. Philip Bonner, *Kings, Commoners, and Concessionaires: The Evolution and Dissolution of the Nineteenth Century State* (Cambridge: Cambridge University Press, 1983).
8. Hilda Kuper, *Sobhuza II, Ngwenyama and King of Swaziland* (New York: African Publishing Company, 1978), p. 65.
9. Ndlovu, *op. cit.*
10. March 30, 1991: Archives of Swaziland Broadcasting and Information Services.
11. Christine Lane, *The Rites of Rulers* (Cambridge: Cambridge University Press, 1981); David I. Kertzer, *Ritual, Politics, and Power* (New York and London: Yale University Press, 1988); Sherry Ortner, *Sherpas Through Their Rituals* (Cambridge: Cambridge University Press, 1978).
12. Ndlovu, *op. cit.*

The Role of Religion in the Transformation of Southern African Societies:

The Botswana Case

Obed Ndeya Kealotswe
University of Botswana

To discuss the role of religion in the transformation of Southern African Societies we must first ask if southern African societies have been transformed by religion or by Western culture which followed religious missions.

This essay outlines the major events that have been experienced by the Southern African societies that have to a large extent transformed them.

Religion in Traditional African Societies

There is a lot of literature defining African Traditional Religion (ATR) which explains the beliefs, practices and social impact of ATRs. Such works include those of John Mbiti, Idowu, Edwin Smith, Callaway, Geoffrey Parrinder and Willoughby, to mention a few. Together these works and others give a clear picture of the religious beliefs and practices of the African peoples. The most important point to note is that, according to all these authors, ATR is a way of life. It is very difficult to separate any aspect of African life from religion. All life activities are governed by religious beliefs, rituals, taboos and prohibitions. In this manner it is difficult to distinguish between religion and life. ATR is also dynamic and adapts itself to social change. It is in this context that it becomes difficult to determine whether religion in the form of Christianity and Western culture have actually transformed the Southern African societies. Below, I argue that ATR has adapted itself to western culture and Christianity. This adaptation takes the form of using vernacular concepts to express Christian beliefs. Christianity came with ethical principles and prohibitions which to some extent resembled those of the African peoples. Such ethical rules included several taboos, respect for parents and elders in society, faithfulness to God and so forth. The emphasis on the sovereignty of God resembled that of the Africans because in the African worldview God is central. Although this God is approached through the ancestors who are guardians of the living, the whole life of the African is controlled by God. Jesus Christ, preached by Christianity as the sole representative of the people before God, was not refused by the Africans; they accepted him as the highest of the ancestors. Myamiti's argument of Jesus as our ancestor finds support in the minds and beliefs of ordinary Africans. In this sense it is difficult to see religion as a transforming power. But the Christian religion and other religions which came to Southern Africa also carried a certain culture. It is the combination of religion and Western culture which transformed the African societies.

The first transformation took place within the ATR itself. As stated above, the use of the vernacular made the Christian religion acceptable. It is important to note that missionaries used untrained evangelists. The evangelists were not Christian theologians, and in some cases the missionaries themselves were not trained theologians. Because of this, unexpected things occurred. For example, the translation of the Old Testament into the vernacular to a large extent endorsed some of the African taboos and customs such as polygamy. Although the New Testament tended to see people as

equals, both males and females, the Old Testament had more taboos and prohibitions for women rather than for men. Again, such
taboos were very similar to those of the Africans. Many African
customs, especially among the Batswana, were not acceptable to
Western culture, which was equated with Christianity. Robert
Moffat described the Batswana men as lazy, with all the hard work
being done by women.

The Batswana had no concept of God at all and believed in a
creature called *modimo*. Livingstone, who worked among the Bakwena, struggled very hard to make Sechele leave some of his wives.
It was impossible to convince Sechele to set aside his traditional
customs in spite of his acceptance of Christianity. Later missionaries to Botswana, such as Hepburn Mackenzie Willoughby and
Tom Brown, tried all possible ways to acquaint themselves with the
customs of the Batswana. Among the Bamangwato, Kgama was
converted to Christianity and used the ten commandments as the
sources of tribal law. This, however, did not convince all the people
in Ngwatoland. Among the Batswana, Christianity was accepted as
a means of bringing education, western commodities, trade and
prosperity. Christianity was not accepted as a religion as such but
because of the benefits going along with it. It is along this process
that social transformation took place.

The first form of transformation was cultural and in the area of
customs. The contact between Western culture and Botswana culture brought many changes in customs. The social structure with
the chief being the head of the tribe or nation and with subchiefs
and headmen was almost replaced by the rule of the missionaries,
magistrates and District Commissioners. The introduction of
Western forms of government disintegrated Botswana societies by
changing their social stratification and disrupting even household
life, where the head acted as the link with the ancestors and
modimo. This social change, on the other hand, gained recognition
for those who had been regarded as serfs. The new form of government also brought with it Western forms of education which
differed from the initiation (*bogwera, bojale*) of young men and
women, as was the old practice. Education and the ability to read
and write gave social status and recognition to whoever had access
to education. New Western clothes also came into vogue. The bar-
ter economy gave way to a monetary system which greatly affected

the lives of the Batswana. Having Western education, money and European goods became a status symbol.

The first Bakwena men who took Livingstone to the Kgalagadi ridiculed the trousers that he wore, but in a few years' time they came to consider wearing trousers to be a great privilege. The communal society was gradually transformed to an individualistic and capitalistic one. In the late 1920s and the early 1930s the sharing of commodities and wealth among the Batswana had almost disappeared. The extended family also began to suffer and collapse because the rich were more interested in accumulating wealth than in sharing. Customarily Western or Christian values took priority over traditional Botswana values. The integrity of the family was strongly challenged by new individualistic values. Also, the growth in migrant labor at the South African mines and growing industries contributed greatly to the transformation of society because many people no longer relied on arable land and pastoral farming but on earning money through jobs. This regular income was then used to buy Western goods, such as radios and gramophones, and bicycles and motor cars.

These phenomena brought great social transformation which also led to religious transformation. The dependency on money earned by labor led to the decline of dependence on *modimo* and the ancestors for survival. Some customs and taboos relating to pastoral and agricultural life were dismissed as superstition. Christian values became more and more accepted and ATR beliefs became suppressed and practiced secretly.

Revitalization of ATR Practices

From the late 1930s through to the early 1960s, enormous growth of the African Independent Churches (AICs) occurred. These movements started in South Africa in the late 1880s. Their main cause was dissatisfaction with Western Christianity and its impact on South African people. Sundkler pointed out a number of such causes which included the color bar system practiced by white people against the blacks in spite of the gospel message preached by Western Christianity. The most important impact of the AICs is that they provided a way for people to reconsider their traditional values against the rapid social changes that tended to destabilize rather than build up African societies. The AICs tended to base their form of Christianity on the Old Testament. The Old Testament appealed to them because it was written from a cultural perspective that more closely resembled that of the Batswana and the African peoples generally. Some customs of the Batswana—such as marriage and taboos relating to social life, environmental issues and family life, relationships between people and God—were contained in or strengthened by the Old Testament. In this manner many Batswana were attracted to the AICs. Members of missionary-founded churches such as the London Missionary Society still remained members of their churches but often turned to the AICs for help, such as in times of illness. The AICs combined traditional healing and Christianity. In this manner they attracted many people who could not get healed because hospitals lacked good psychological care of the patients. Some attitudes of Western doctors also led the patients to distrust the doctors.

The coming of the AICs had a great impact on social transformation. The first impact was religious. The Gospel message was indiginized so that people understood the Gospel within their cultural perspective. The prophet replaced the role of the *ngaka* or traditional healer. Prophecy replaced divination by traditional bones or stones. The power of the Holy Spirit guided the life of the church instead of the ordinances made in Europe and America.

Socially the AICs attracted many people, especially the poor and uneducated. The dissatisfied deacons from the missionary-founded churches joined the AICs and provided some form of guided leadership. Leaders of AICs became popular and recognized by society. The AICs in Botswana not only challenged the churches but also challenged the political systems. Those who were not satisfied with church polity also posed a challenge to local authorities who ruled with the missionaries. Status in society no longer centered on Western education and the acquisition of Western goods. Interestingly, however, the AIC leaders became rich and popular through fees charged for healing people. Members of AICs organized themselves as strong, coherent groups catering to each others' needs, both physically and materially. In this manner they brought significant social transformation. Workers who migrated from the villages to the towns joined new families in the form of AICs which had a more solid social cohesion than the missionary-founded churches. These social groups worked together and helped each other to make a better life in the midst of rapid social change. The 1930s saw great social changes with the rapid growth of towns and industries in Botswana. The chiefs in the villages also made some social reforms which changed traditional government to a more Western type of government. Some traditional tribal practices and customs and land tenure were changed, negatively affecting the majority for the benefit of the few.

Botswana became independent in 1966, when social transformation was gaining a strong impact. The Independent Government made social transformation faster by providing the basic infrastructure for easy communication, increasing the number of schools to spread education, and allowing freedom of worship, enabling religious bodies to spread themselves. The government also encouraged industrialization by allowing mining companies to explore for minerals, and allowing manufacturing companies to manufacture goods and provide employment to those who left school.

The period after Independence also witnessed a new religious movement in the form of Pentecostalism and charismatics with American ties. These groups tried to reform the society by spreading a "born again" Gospel which despised all other religions in Botswana. Their attitude to society was very negative. That movement, however, could not distract people from their economic interests and pursuits in the time of rapid development. Eventually, it had to turn its attention to some of the problems raised by urbanization and industrialization; especially premarital sex, teen-age pregnancy and the increase of unmarried mothers and single-parent families. These problems arose due to the decline in traditional social values which were destroyed or discouraged by Christianity and Western culture.

The present social situation in Botswana is very difficult to define in one word. Due to the nature of the country, which is very big and lightly populated, many people have retained some of their traditional values, but the impact of migration and urbanization is also felt in all parts of the country. In the urban areas the majority of the people are torn between modernity and tradition. People in the towns are still loyal to the villages where they have homes, lands and cattle posts. These connections with the rural realities make it very difficult for any person to claim to be completely Westernized or modernized. Social life in Botswana is currently guided by religion, semi-religious organizations, and social organizations. There are more than 300 different religious bodies in Botswana; altogether these have attracted more than 60 percent of the population. Semi-religious organizations include burial societies and other related bodies. These have attracted many people, especially migrant laborers to the towns. Social organizations include football clubs and other sporting activities. These organizations do attract many people who identify themselves with these different movements and organizations. The attachment to organizations becomes more pronounced during either times of unhappiness, like death, or times of celebration. People who have been uprooted from their biological families by migrant labor see these organizations and societies as substitutes for a wider extended family life.

The Future of Botswana Communities

At the present time there is a great cry in Botswana that the society is lost and suffering. Many people are negative about Botswana's future. The blame is put on Christianity and the many religious bodies which people claim are alienating people from their cultures. Secondly, blame is put on industrialization which increases the pace of urbanization. Urbanization brings with it unemployment, poverty, robbery, rape and other related evils such as prostitution. These problems create pessimism about any possibility of a better future. But other people and myself have realized that the more people become exposed to Western individualism, the more they are prone to reject it and resort back to some form of communal life. This is the reason why many people belong to organizations and societies. Funerals of friends and relatives attract people from all over the country, as do weddings. Urban people share their wealth with rural people who take care of their lands, cattle and homes. Religious societies preach brotherhood and familyhood. In this manner the seemingly disintegrating societies are in actual fact becoming ever more integrated.

Conclusion

In conclusion let me point out that the impact of Western Christianity on African societies in Southern Africa has tended to be viewed negatively. This is true of all the periods from the mid 1600s to the end of the 1880s. The 1900s saw great social transformation. This is transformation in the sense that two cultures with their religions, i.e., Western and African, came into contact and clashed. Eventually a working solution arose due to the impact of the AICs. Modern Southern African societies are an expansion of the transformation brought about by Western Christianity and its values, and ATR and its values. The future, especially for Botswana, is bright with hope in spite of the seemingly negative signs in contemporary society.

Eco-Stories and Transformation

Christina Landman
UNISA Research Institute of Theology
Pretoria, South Africa

1. Introduction

Through ecofeminism Christian, Buddhist, Hindu and Goddess[1] feminists share some common ideals. These are as follows:

- Social transformation needs to take place according to non-dualistic and nonhierarchical relations as taught by nature. In order for humanity to survive and be just, associations need to be nonviolent, noncompetitive, participatory, and mutual.[2]

- Science and religion need to be integrated into a value laden praxis. Social transformation presupposes an intellectual transformation, that is, a transformation of thought into non-dualistic and nonhierarchical forms. This eco way of thinking will give intrinsic value to nature and not assess it hierarchally according to its value to humanity. Also, human diversity will be viewed not according to a hierarchy of values but as valuable in its diversity, while the interdependence of humans is accentuated.[3]

- Ecofeminism acknowledges a spiritual dimension to her activism. An "internal" spirituality of "greening the self" is integrated with an "external" social engagement in order to educate consumers as to a new culture, one that is peace-loving and nonhierarchical.[4]

This essay wants to present an answer to the question: How can African women contribute to these ideals of global ecofeminism, namely the ideals of

(a) theology (or rather "divine talk") going public, that is, becoming activist,
(b) nature being integrated into human experience,
(c) spiritually being (privately and socially) liberative, and
(d) women, nature and spirituality forming an interrelationship for the empowerment of both women and nature?

There is no ecofeminist movement in the Third World parallel to ecofeminism in North America (and in Western Europe).[5] However, African women share a heritage of traditional stories which, if retold today as eco-stories, can put African ecofeminists on par with the global ecofeminist ideal of public conscientization by stressing the interdependence between nature, humanity and God/spirituality.

Mercy Amba Oduyoye has made a memorable attempt to retell folk-tales as a source for a Christian women's theology. In her book, *Daughters of Anowa: African women and patriarchy,*[6] she retrieves the traditional stories of the Adan (southern Ghana) and the Yoruba (southern Nigeria) as a basis for a Christian theology for African women. Although it is noteworthy to see how Oduyoye roots contextual theology in traditional stories, she does not explore the eco-dimension of the stories. This essay argues that a rereading of traditional stories as eco-stories should be on the priority list of African women theologians.

This essay, then, has a threefold aim:

In the first place, stories told by traditionalist Venda women will be analyzed as to

(a) their critique on the (hierarchical nature of) human relationships;

(b) the insights they offer on the relationship between nature and women's spirituality; and

(c) their liberative value, that is, their potential role in social transformation.

In the second place, suggestions will be made as to how these stories can form the basis for dialogue between African Traditionalist Religions and Christianity.[7] It will be indicated that African ecofeminists have a decisive role to play in this dialogue.

In the third instance I shall try to make a contribution to the question whether eco-stories can indeed lead to transformation. Again, African ecofeminists, it will be argued, can play a leading role in this transformation.

A note on the concept of *eco-stories* is relevant here.[8] This term presupposes that stories told about women in previous centuries, have indeed explored the empowering relationship between women, nature and spirituality, but that this interrelationship has been lost in subsequent retellings of the stories. This liberative relationship can now be retrieved by rereading/retelling the stories as eco-stories, that is, as stories in which nature (and her relationship to women and spirituality) plays a dominant part.

The Eco-stories of Venda Traditionalists

During the early 1990s Ina le Roux retrieved, translated[9] and interpreted several stories told by traditional Venda[10] women as part of her doctoral research.[11] Le Roux's interpretations are contextual and tested against the interpretations of other members of the tribe. However, she still leaves space for rereading these stories in the light of the aims of this essay, that is to interpret the stories as eco-stories, to establish their value for social transformation and to describe their role in the dialogue between Traditionalists and Christians.

In terms of their references to patriarchal (hierarchical) structures, the stories vary from depicting women as (a) fully powerless, (b) using covert power to get what they want/need, (c) using power against other women, to (d) fully able to empower themselves.

These categories of looking at women's position in hierarchical power games will now be used to analyze the relationship between nature and women's spirituality in the stories.[12] The first story points to woman's social powerlessness when she is not interrelated to the forces of nature:

Women Have No Power in Patriarchal/Hierarchical Systems

A poor man with no family and no wife carves a wife from a tree trunk. He adorns it with clothes and hair. Miraculously the trunk turns into a woman. The king commands the women of his tribe to come and work in his garden. The king holds the beautiful woman back. The man goes to the king's house and asks for his wife in a song. When she is not permitted to return, he pulls off her hair. She is changed back into a tree trunk.[13]

This story illustrates the power relations in a hierarchical system. The man has the power to make (create) a woman. The king has power to force the man to send his wife to work for the king. When the king does not return the man's possession, the man has the power to turn her back into his possession. In all this, the woman plays no active role; she has no voice. The spirits who effect witchcraft and turn the woman into a human being and later again into a trunk, are on the side of the man. The woman's relationship with nature is passive.

A spin-off of patriarchal power is women suppressing one another in order to gain qualitative attention from the dominant male culture. The next story represents an important theme in the stories of Venda traditionalists: Women using (evil) spiritual power to gain power in the female subculture.

Women Using Covert Power Within Patriarchal/Hierarchical Systems at the Expense of Other Women

A woman is angry with her husband. He has taken another wife. She curses her husband while she grinds grain. She has no power to address him. She therefore uses her magic power to turn the younger woman into a zombie to act on her command. She buries the younger woman's body under the grinding-stone. She calls the younger woman: "Why-are-you-sleeping-with-my-husband" and makes the life of the younger woman's ghost working for her, unbearable. Eventually the ghost of the younger woman manages to escape to her people. The older woman is happy because she now has her husband to herself. However, her iniquities are discovered and the body of the younger woman is retrieved and revived from underneath the grinding-stone. The older woman is punished: she and her parents have to pay five head of cattle.[14]

The older woman has no overt power in the hierarchical system. She uses her spirituality (witchcraft) to take control over the younger woman. She enters into a pact with nature to control the other woman's body and ghost. However, she is not permitted by society to use her spiritual power in this way. She is punished, not for using her power against another woman (as she herself intended) but for using it against her husband (as society sees it).

In the final two stories, women use the spiritual power of nature to liberate themselves not from other women, but from people using patriarchal privileges against them.

Women Can Empower Themselves Against Patriarchal/ Hierarchical Systems

A man has two wives. He loves the one and neglects the other. He gives a hoe to the beloved wife and none to the rejected one. The rejected wife steals an axe and makes her own hoe from a tree trunk. The man and his beloved wife ridicule the other wife while she is working on the lands with her wooden, hand-made hoe. Their hoes are made from iron. Eventually nature looks kindly upon the rejected woman. Her lands are full of sugar-cane, peas, mealies and water melons. The man then wants to regain the favour of the previously rejected wife. She tells him to "voertsek."[15] *She happily lives off her own produce.*[16]

A woman with no social power finds her hope in her connection with nature. She breaks with tradition and finds a future within her own empowerment.

An old mother lives with her cripple son and his family in a cave. Every now and then the cripple man steals some cattle to feed his family. The only way in which he can do this, is to escape into the cave through a passage which only his old mother knows to open. However, he and his wife do not treat the old woman well. They take the good meat for themselves and leave only the heart to the mother. One day the mother deliberately does not open the

passage to her son and his pursuers kill him. Her daughter-in-law
becomes extremely angry at the mother. He deserved it; I got
back at him, is all the old mother says.

The only power this old woman has is the secret and magic
knowledge of how nature works. She uses this against her son, who
previously has benefited from her magic powers but has, nevertheless, treated her badly.

The liberative dimension of these stories lies in the women using
their spiritual contact with nature to free them from the oppression of social situations, that is, from hierarchical systems where
they had little power.

Eco-stories as a Basis for Dialogue Between African Traditional Religions and Christianity

Dialogue between the African Traditional Religions (ATRs) and
Christianity is needed for (a) mutual appreciation, (b) cooperation
in social strategizing, and (c) the acknowledgment of differences.[17]
This essay claims that the empowerment of women through eco-
storytelling should be a priority point on the agenda of the ATRs-
Christianity dialogue since eco-storytelling serves all three of the
aims for dialogue just mentioned.

In the above ATR stories the liberation of socially oppressed
women through (a) inner strength and (b) an interconnectedness
with nature is emphasized. Since Christianity traditionally does not
acknowledge women's power in these areas, Christian women will
gain in insight by exposing themselves to dialogue with these eco-
stories.

Christianity falls short of a tradition of innerconnectedness and
interconnectedness because of two reasons:

(1) In the Christian tradition women have been constantly
identified with nature, and men with culture. However, this identification was negative and women's inferior nature was presup-
posed and even argued on the grounds of her solely physical
existence. Christian ecofeminists, in dialogue with the ATR-spirit-
uality retrieved above, can be empowered to reread the stories of
their Christian foremothers in order to reintroduce the interconnectedness of women and nature into the Christian tradition.

(2) "Christianity has traditionally maintained that God herself has established the distinction between divine reality and the world."[18] This tenet of Christianity has kept women from inner-connecting with the divine in themselves and has disempowered them with regard to their access to spirituality. Again, dialogue with the ATRs can empower Christian women to retrieve the tradition of female innerconnectedness as part of the original Christian tradition.

This can obviously be done by retelling the stories of Christian foremothers as eco-stories, that is, as stories of the interrelatedness of women, (activist) spirituality and nature, and the innerrelatedness of women to their inner selves. This may lead to a retelling of the Thecla-story, emphasising the scene in the arena where Thecla, a convert of Paul, is thrown to the beasts. However, the mad lioness who is supposed to devour Thecla as a sign of female against female, licks Thecla's feet and defends her against the male lions. This empowered the women spectators in the arena, having been taught by the example of nature, to side with Thecla and to embrace her form of spirituality. This may even lead to the retelling of the Jesus-stories, where his spiritual teachings are placed within the pastoral surroundings of hills, lakes and fishing people. This may lead to a rereading of the Gospel of Mary Magdalene and the Gospel of Thomas where Jesus emphasized the spirituality of God's presence in the inner-self as well as in the everyday activities of interconnected contexts.[19] This may even lead to the retelling of the history of the witch hunts of the later middle ages and a rediscovery of the interconnected and innerconnected powers of the convicted women and the threat they posed to established hierarchical power.

While women scholars like Luise Schottroff[20] and Anne Jensen[21] have brilliantly explained the social relationships and positioning of women in early Christianity, no studies are available of the relevant women's relationship to nature, that is, to their inner-relationship with themselves and their interrelationship with nature and the empowerment it offers.

Eco-Stories and Transformation

Finally, we have to ask ourselves: Can eco-stories heal the earth? In the above we have suggested an interconnectedness between women, spirituality and nature as if nature is as powerful as it was when "in the beginning God created heaven and earth." Knowing that this most certainly is not the case we, on the contrary, have to ask ourselves the following question: Are we not, through the empowerment of women, adding to consumerism and the eventual exploitation of nature?

In order to avoid the possibility of empowerment leading to exploitation, the values taught through eco-stories therefore have to be these:

(a) Nature and women heal and serve each other *mutually*.
(b) Having both been used as functions in hierarchical systems, women and nature acknowledge each other's *intrinsic value*.
(c) Women and nature need each other for the survival of both; they therefore acknowledge their *interdependence*.

If mutuality, the acknowledgement of intrinsic value and interdependence are the *values*, what are the *techniques* and *structures* for educating women through eco-stories?

Research on Faith and Earthkeeping

Conscientizing women through eco-stories should be done in three phases to ensure that the process is owned by the very women who are being conscientized. In the first phase the eco-experiences of the women are to be retrieved in order to establish their needs. In the second phase these experiences are being "theologically reflected upon," which means that the eco-stories of contemporary women are being placed in line and understood from the perspective of the eco-stories of their foremothers in the faith, whether they are Christian, Traditional, Buddhist, Hindu, etc. The role of ecofeminist theologians of different faiths—who are in dialogue with one another—is of obvious necessity in this regard. In the third phase the eco-stories of the women are being put to action. The liberative elements in the stories are actualized in development projects.

The Research Institute for Theology and Religion at Unisa is, at present, engaged in three projects which aim at educating people in ecological consciousness. The first is a research project called *Africa, women and environment* which is conducted under the auspices of the Gold Fields Faith and Earthkeeping Project.[22] This project has already engaged 58 women from a majority of African countries with post-graduate theological training to do and publish research within three fields, corresponding to the three phases of conscientization through eco-storytelling described above:

(1) case studies retrieving the religio-ecological experiences of African women
(2) religious ("theological") reflection on grass-roots experiences from the perspective of sacred scriptures and tradition/dogma
(3) descriptions of action plans in development and environmental care.[23]

The research from this first project forms the basis of a second project, which aims at educating religious people in ecological care. The rationale behind the process is that training programs should be based on and address the eco-stories of the women they are meant for.

Teaching Women Religious Skills in Ecological Caretaking

The activist and social nature of the ecofeminist vision of educating society in eco-consciousness prohibits her from subscribing to the traditional view of limiting tertiary religious education to training a few individuals for official religious ministry. Her vision is that people over a broader spectrum of society should be educated in religious skills. In this endeavour ecological conscientizing and skills in ecological caretaking play a major role.

In this regard the abovementioned Institute is developing a certificate program called "Human and environmental issues"[24] and another entitled "Women's religious skills," consisting in part of a module called "Skills in community development."[25] Throughout these courses eco-stories are used as the vehicle of instruction, both for student and lecturer. After having empowered the students to tell their own eco-stories, they are guided to reflect theologically on their experiences. Eventually they are exposed to possible plans of action to heal the earth. However, this is not a patronal exercise in which teacher and student stand in an hierarchical relation to one another. This is a process of participatory learning, a process facilitated through the telling of eco-stories, a process aiming at the transformation of society where everybody is a learner.

Within these initiatives, then, eco-stories are in the process of proving themselves to be effective vehicles for transforming societies into

(a) ecologically caretaking teams, as well as
(b) interreligiously sensitive milieux.

Conclusion

At the beginning of this paper the question was asked: How can African women contribute to the ideals of global feminism? African women, having entered into a process where they retrieve and analyze eco-stories both from the past and from the present, can make a meaningful contribution to a theology of ecology and a praxis of development and caretaking, precisely because their eco-stories testify to their "natural abilities" of integrating nature into human experience and of experiencing spiritually as liberative.

NOTES

1. Anne Primavesi, in "Ecofeminism," Lisa Sherwood and Dorothea McEwan (eds.), *An A to Z of Feminist Theology* (Sheffield Academic Press, 1996), p. 46, notes that readers often "assume that the term 'the Goddess' must mean a female equivalent of the traditional God of Judaism, Christianity and Islam. In fact, 'The Goddess' is a shorthand term for a more varied set of concepts coming from three major sources: the feminist movement, native and classical religions and forms related to Judaism and Christianity. From whatever source, the concept of 'the Goddess' within women, of the sacrality of female sexuality (not to be confined to fertility), and of freeing the female divine, is part of a contemporary movement to reconstruct the world."
2. Nancy R. Howell, "Ecofeminism: What One Needs to Know," in *Zygon, Journal of Religion and Science* 32.2, June 1997, pp. 231-241.

3. *Ibid.*

4. Primavesi, "Ecofeminism," pp. 45-48.

5. Rosemary Radford Ruether (ed.), *Women Healing the Earth: Third World Women on Ecology, Feminism, and Religion* (SCM Press, 1996), p. 2.

6. Orbis, 1995.

7. Here I would have liked to invite women from other faiths to join this dialogue by adding the eco-stories of their religious past. However, this calls for another paper.

8. In "The Cosmic Creation Story" in Mary Heather and Moni McIntyre, *Readings in Ecology and Feminist Theology* (Kansas City: Sheed and Ward, 1995), pp. 249-250, Brian Swimme makes a passionate plea for the telling of stories in modern society: "I am suggesting that this activity of cosmic storytelling is the central political and economic act of our time.... Why story? Why should 'story' be fundamental? Because without storytelling, we lose contact with our basic realities in this world. We lose contact because *only* through story can we fully recognize our existence in time. To be human is to be in a story. To forget one's story is to go insane. All the tribal peoples show an awareness of the connection between health and storytelling. The original humans will have their cosmic stories just as surely as they will have their food and drink. Our ancestors recognized that the universe, at its most basic level, is story. Each creature is story. Humans enter this world and awaken to a simple truth: 'We must find our story within this great epic of being.'"

9. into Afrikaans.

10. The Venda people is a black tribe living in the northeast of South Africa, south of the Zimbabwe border.

11. Net die woorde het oorgebly: 'n godsdienswetenskaplike interpretasie van Venda-volksverhale (*Ngano*). Unpublished D Litt et Phil dissertation, University of South Africa, June 1996.

12. Please note that one story in its oral form can last for several hours, even one full evening. What is represented here, is my own very short summary of a selection of these stories in English.

13. Le Roux, *op. cit.*, pp. 221 ff.

14. *Ibid*, pp. 634 ff.

15. to push off.

16. Le Roux, *op. cit*, pp. 233 ff.

17. The ATRs are complaining that Christianity is stealing ancestor worship from them, which is actually their main attraction on the market place.

18. Elizabeth Green, "The Transmutation of Theology: Ecofeminist Alchemy and the Christian Tradition," in *Ecofeminism and Theology: Yearbook of the European Society of Women in Theological Research"* (Kok Pharos, 1994), p. 54.

19. See Lieb Liebenberg, *The Language of the Kingdom and Jesus: Parable, Aphorism and Metaphor in the Sayings Material Common to the Synoptic*

Tradition and the Gospel of Thomas (Dissertation, Humboldt-Universität Berlin, 1997), p. 167.

20. *Lydia's Impatient Sisters: A Feminist Social History of Early Christianity* (SCM Press, tr. 1995).

21. *God's Self-confident Daughters: Early Christianity and the Liberation of Women* (Kok Pharos, tr. 1996).

22. run by Rev. David Olivier.

23. What is noteworthy about this project is that the women from mainline religions who responded to the invitation to participate in the project were not willing to incorporate mythology (folk-tales) in their theological reflection, as was recommended in the earlier part of this paper. This is an initial set-back for the dialogue between the ATRs and Christianity/ Islam/Hinduism Buddhism—and needs to be addressed by the coordinators of the project.

24. The modules offered are:

    Module 1: A dying world—a growing challenge
    Module 2: The quest for sustainable living
    Module 3: Religions—part of the problem or part of the solution?
    Module 4: Is Christianity "green"?
    Module 5: Congregations and environmental actions
    Module 6: The Gold Field Faith and Earthkeeping Project—
                a possible way?

25. The modules for this course in "Women's religious skills" are

    Module 1: Skills in developing mutual relationships
    Module 2: Skills in the spirituality of politics
    Module 3: Skills in health matters
    Module 4: Skills in dealing with violence
    Module 5: Skills in developing moral leadership
    Module 6: Skills in community development